Jews and Diaspora Nationalism

THE TAUBER INSTITUTE SERIES FOR
THE STUDY OF EUROPEAN JEWRY
Jehuda Reinharz, General Editor
Sylvia Fuks Fried, Associate Editor

THE BRANDEIS LIBRARY OF MODERN JEWISH THOUGHT
Eugene R. Sheppard and Samuel Moyn, Editors

This library aims to redefine the canon of modern Jewish thought by publishing
primary source readings from individual Jewish thinkers or groups of thinkers in reliable
English translations. Designed for courses in modern Jewish philosophy, thought, and
intellectual history, each volume features a general introduction and annotations to
each source with the instructor and student in mind.

FOR THE COMPLETE LIST OF BOOKS THAT ARE FORTHCOMING IN
THE SERIES, PLEASE SEE HTTP://WWW.BRANDEIS.EDU/TAUBER

Jews & Diaspora Nationalism

Edited by
Simon Rabinovitch

WRITINGS ON

JEWISH PEOPLEHOOD

IN EUROPE AND THE

UNITED STATES

Brandeis University Press

Waltham, Massachusetts

BRANDEIS UNIVERSITY PRESS

An imprint of University Press of New England

www.upne.com

© 2012 Brandeis University

Manufactured in the United States of America

Designed by Eric M. Brooks

Typeset in Albertina and Verlag by

Passumpsic Publishing

Israel Knox, "Is America Exile or Home? We Must Begin to Build for Permanence," is reprinted from COMMENTARY, November 1946, by permission; copyright © 1946 by Commentary, Inc.

For permission to reproduce any of the material in this book, contact Permissions, University Press of New England, One Court Street, Suite 250, Lebanon NH 03766; or visit www.upne.com

Library of Congress Cataloging-in-Publication Data
Jews and diaspora nationalism: writings on Jewish peoplehood
in Europe and the United States / edited by Simon Rabinovitch.
    p. cm. — (The Tauber institute series for the study of European
Jewry) (The Brandeis library of modern Jewish thought)
Includes index.
ISBN 978-1-58465-761-3 (cloth: alk. paper) —
ISBN 978-1-58465-762-0 (pbk.: alk. paper) —
ISBN 978-1-61168-362-2 (ebook)
1. Jewish nationalism—History. 2. Jews—Identity. 3. Jewish
nationalism—Europe—History. 4. Zionism. 5. Judaism and
politics. 6. Socialism and Judaism. 7. Jews—United States—
Identity. I. Rabinovitch, Simon.
DS 143.J485   2012
320.54095694—dc23   2012018561

For my parents,
Martin and Belinda

Contents

I | From Haskala to National Renaissance

II | Socialism and the Question of Jewish Peoplehood

III | Preservation and Reconstruction in the Republics

Epilogue

Foreword

Perhaps no other force has so permeated the thought of modern times as nationalism. But the practical implications of nationalism have never been clear, especially for peoples with so originally distant and continually vexed a relationship to a specific territory as the Jews have had. *Jews and Diaspora Nationalism: Writings on Jewish Peoplehood in Europe and the United States* addresses the centrality for much of modern history of the notion that Jewish nationalism may not need to revolve around full possession of a unique place. Self-evidently, this version of "nationalism" has come to seem counter-intuitive in the wake of the Holocaust and the establishment of the State of Israel, when Jewish nationalism and political Zionism appear as synonymous with each other. This volume offers readers an incisive introduction to how, before that equation occurred, Jewish thinkers mobilized, innovated, and adjusted notions of national belonging within the diaspora centers of Europe and the United States. Simon Rabinovitch's presentation of French, German, Russian, Yiddish, Hebrew, and English primary source materials bespeaks wide-ranging articulations of Jewish nationhood, which have all too often been forgotten with Zionist devaluations of Jewish existence outside of the land and state of Israel. Yet the sheer difference between diaspora nationalism and current views risks obscuring how contentious were the debates about how to define diaspora nationalism in the first place, a struggle for a plausible vision which this volume beautifully captures. And while diaspora nationalists and Zionists typically engaged in heated polemics, Rabinovitch argues that diaspora Jewish nationalism did not suddenly end but was eventually transformed into affiliation with and support for the State of Israel. For this reason, it is not easy to interpret the trajectory of Jewish collective politics as the aspiration to collective unity and self-protection made its way through the great age of nationalism that modernity brought to the world as a whole. Reviving lost alternatives and showing how Jewish nationalism both in Israel and for its many observers around the globe assumed its current form is the task of this volume's important exercise in recovery.

Eugene R. Sheppard and Samuel Moyn, Editors
The Brandeis Library of Modern Jewish Thought

Preface and Acknowledgments

A Note on the Texts, Translations, and Annotations

In putting together this volume, I attempted to select readings representative of the major trends and individuals who debated the nature of Jewish peoplehood in the diaspora. Few of the writers included were associated with diaspora nationalism as an ideology or a movement. Several considered themselves Zionists or were sympathetic to Zionism, and others were not nationalist at all. The only criterion I applied to each selection was whether it grappled with the question of the Jews' continued existence in the diaspora as a people, irrespective of Jewish territorial concentration or political sovereignty. My goal was to strike a balance between foundational texts by recognizable names and works by individuals (in one case, by an institution) who may be less well known now but who had a significant impact in their own day. My selective bias was toward translations of works previously inaccessible to the English reader and, to a lesser extent, important works originally written in English. In the case of Simon Dubnov, Nathan Birnbaum's "Jewish Autonomy," and I. L. Peretz, I considered the existing translations for the key texts selected to be incomplete or inadequate enough to require new translations. The other items translated here, with the exception of the piece by Simon Rawidowicz, have not previously been published in English. In addition to what is mentioned in the Suggestions for Further Reading, students looking for more English primary sources relating to diaspora nationalism will find some relevant materials in the anthologies edited by Lucy Dawidowicz (*The Golden Tradition: Jewish Life and Thought in Eastern Europe*), Joshua Fishman (*Never Say Die! A Thousand Years of Yiddish in Jewish Life and Letters*), Arthur Hertzberg (*The Zionist Idea: A Historical Analysis and Reader*), and Jehuda Reinharz and Paul Mendes-Flohr (*The Jew in the Modern World: A Documentary History*).

The question of how to preserve, reconstruct, or build a new Jewish peoplehood in the diaspora germinated in the late nineteenth century in the region of the world where most Jews lived at that time, the Austro-Hungarian and Russian Empires. The question also emerged in the areas of the most significant new Jewish immigration—in particular, the United States and to a lesser degree France (I discuss the specific reasons why diaspora nationalism emerged in these places and not elsewhere in the section of my introductory essay titled "The

Geography of Diaspora Nationalism"). I thus organized the volume's sections according to what I see as three overlapping phases in the debate about how to preserve Jewish nationality, or peoplehood, in the diaspora. The first, "From Haskala to National Renaissance," includes essays that deal with the question of how to preserve or build Jewish peoplehood in the context of multiethnic empires. The second, "Socialism and the Question of Jewish Peoplehood," deals primarily with the question of how to redefine Jewish peoplehood in the context of radical societal reconstruction (whether real or desired). The third and final section, "Preservation and Reconstruction in the Republics," deals with the question of how to maintain Jewish autonomy and national self-consciousness in the context of liberal democratic states. Although Jewish "diasporism" still exists today, this anthology focuses on diaspora nationalism before the creation of the State of Israel in 1948. The essay by Simon Rawidowicz appears as the volume's epilogue because it the only one in the volume written after that time.

Where possible, I have included whole texts or complete chapters. Where this is not the case, within the text "[. . .]" indicates where a section has been removed. My annotations, distinguished from the authors' by square brackets, aim primarily to fill in where possible details that the author presumed the reader already knows, but that may not be familiar to the modern reader. I tried to leave interpretation and editorializing to my introductory essay and headnotes. All of the sources I drew on to write the headnotes and annotations appear in the Suggestions for Further Reading and/or the footnotes in my introductory essay, with the important exceptions of the helpful online resources *Encyclopedia Judaica* and the YIVO *Encyclopedia of Jews in Eastern Europe*. Transliterations follow the style of the Library of Congress for Russian and German, the style of the YIVO Institute for Yiddish, and the Academy of the Hebrew Language 2006 guidelines for Hebrew. For proper names that have a conventional English spelling, such as I. L. Peretz and Chaim Zhitlowsky, I used that spelling instead.

Acknowledgments

An anthology is always a collaborative effort, and this book is no exception. First of all, the volume originated with Eugene Sheppard's inspiration as much as mine. I am tremendously grateful that Eugene, as well as Sylvia Fuks Fried, Samuel Moyn, and Phyllis Deutsch, gave me the opportunity to pursue such a gratifying project. At the proposal stage I received valuable advice about the prospective table of contents from James Loeffler, Kenneth Moss, Noam Pianko, Antony Polonsky, Eugene Sheppard, and Jeffrey Veidlinger. Kenneth Moss and

Joshua Karlip both kindly directed me to, and sent me, material that made its way into the volume. Alejandro Lorite Escorihuela, Shmuel Feiner, Kenneth Moss, Jess Olson, Robert Seltzer, Jeffrey Veidlinger, and Ruth Wisse all kindly read and substantially improved portions of the volume. Michael Steinlauf generously provided me with his own unpublished translation and an article that helped to improve the chapter on Peretz. I'm very thankful to my generous colleagues at Boston University—in particular, Brooke Blower, Charles Capper, Tom Glick, Pnina Lahav, Nahshon Perez, Michael Zank, and Jonathan Zatlin, who all gave up their own time to read and substantially strengthen my introductory essay. Others, such as Charles Dellheim, Louis Ferleger, and Bruce Schulman, assisted in the equally valuable task of mentoring and support. I began work on this volume while at the University of Florida and had helpful conversations with many wonderful colleagues there, but I would like to single out Nina Caputo, Mitchell Hart, Jack Kugelmass, and Ken Wald for thanks. I have also benefited from Adam Mendelsohn's wise advice on this project (and others) for many years. During the volume's final editing and production stage I was a research fellow at the Helsinki Collegium for Advanced Studies, and the supportive work environment and my freedom there helped me to bring the project to the finish line.

I would like to thank all of my translators, editorial assistants, and research assistants for their careful and assiduous work (more specific acknowledgments appear in the Translation Credits at the end of the volume). Two in particular require special mention: Anna Fishman Gonshor had a hand in translating all of the Yiddish texts in this volume (and more that ended up on the cutting-room floor) and always did so passionately and thoughtfully. Our conversations and her advice were valuable in their own right. Shaina Hammerman at several points in this project wore one or all of the hats of translator, editorial assistant, and research assistant, and her many hours of work helped me to complete the project in a timely manner. I also benefited from the diligent copy-editing of Jeanne Ferris. I owe a tremendous debt to Mr. Peter Paul, as his generosity and the professorship I hold in his name provided me with the crucial resources necessary to complete a project such as this at a time of new professional responsibilities. Finally, I would like to thank Jodi—my hero—and our two kids, Zoe and Jonah.

Simon Rabinovitch

Diaspora, Nation, and Messiah
An Introductory Essay
Simon Rabinovitch

When I teach survey classes on modern Jewish history, I often end the semester by discussing a public exchange of letters between Jack Wertheimer, at the time provost of the Jewish Theological Seminary in New York, and Joey Kurtzman, then an editor at the online journal Jewcy.com.[1] In their correspondence they debate whether American life has made the concept of Jewish peoplehood anachronistic. To Kurtzman, the openness of American society is a gift, and Judaism, if it is to remain relevant, must move beyond an identity based on "ethnocentrism" and "jettison the language and ideology of peoplehood." To Wertheimer, Jewish peoplehood is self-evidently based on the religious and communal ties in Judaism that bind Jews together as a people; the distaste for those things among the younger generation only reflects the hollowness of much of Jewish life in the United States. As Wertheimer points out, their conversation merely recapitulates an earlier debate that absorbed European Jews about universalism versus particularism in Judaism, and about whether, in adapting Jewish life to the modern world, Jews should refocus what it means to be Jewish based on Judaism's universal or particular traits (or both). In other words, if Jews are to be good citizens, how separate, if at all, should they remain from the dominant culture and body politic? Within the United States much of this debate took place roughly a century ago, during the most intense period of Jewish immigration from Eastern Europe, and it used two dominant metaphors representing America as a new nation. For some, the United States should be seen as a melting pot or crucible that would melt away the differences between Jews and other Americans. In opposition to this viewpoint, others saw the United States as an orchestra in which each instrument represented a different nationality, with all playing together harmoniously when combined in a symphony (see Horace Kallen's chapter, "Democracy Versus the Melting-Pot," in this volume).

Today, diaspora nationalism implies a sense of national affiliation to a place where one is not at the moment—in most cases, a distant homeland. In that sense, for Jews in the diaspora today, and indeed since the establishment of Israel in 1948 (at the very latest), Zionism has become the dominant form of Jewish diaspora nationalism. While not everyone between the two poles of America as melting-pot and America as symphony would describe himself or herself as a Zionist (a term that today has greater resonance in the diaspora than in Israel), from my teaching I can anecdotally surmise that when most think of Jewish politics or Jewish nationalism, it is Israel that comes to mind, and for perfectly comprehensible reasons. In order to fully understand the development of Jewish nationalism, Jews' new definitions of Jewish peoplehood, and indeed the Jewish experience in the modern world, however, it is important to see the full scope of the debate between Jewish universalism and particularism—especially during the late nineteenth and early twentieth centuries, when Jews became swept up in both European national movements and the question of civic equality. During this time, when the vast majority of Jews lived in the diaspora without political sovereignty, many of them sought to recast Jewish peoplehood in a largely secular way that would preserve, reconstruct, or fortify Jewish nationality for survival in the diaspora. The many different ways people attempted this can be seen in the diversity of ideas represented here.

The question of whether the Jews can or should constitute a secular nation in the diaspora was most acutely debated between the beginning of the twentieth century and the treaties following the end of World War I that recognized the dismemberment of the Austro-Hungarian and Russian Empires, as well as the rights of national minorities in the new states (however unenforced those treaties were). The two most significant centers in this debate were Eastern and Central Europe and the United States, in part because of the demographic concentration of Jews in those places, and even more because of the heterogeneous and multiethnic nature of these states, whose various groups had different, and often competing, conceptions of how the systems of government should be constituted.[2] Many who participated in Jewish radical or liberal politics in Eastern and Central Europe came to the United States with great faith in the tolerance of American liberalism and, equally important, the rule of law.[3] Jews who felt their future rights to be at stake took a particularly strong interest in seeking to shape the rule of law in Europe. It is for similar reasons that Jews in the United States joined the conversation about cultural pluralism or assimilation, and what the American nation should look like. Yet perhaps the most significant continuity that one sees between the Jewish experience in modern Europe and that in the United States is the extent to which Jews served as the archetypal minority during periods of transition. From the eighteenth to the twentieth century, how

European states determined Jewish rights and privileges, as well as their limits, tested principles of enlightened government and often reflected the way states would treat not only other minorities but indeed all of their citizens and subjects.

The Meaning of Diaspora

The debate about what kind of people the Jews constitute in the diaspora was born from the specific circumstances of modernizing Europe, but the idea of the Jews as a diasporic people is one that has continually evolved since the ancient period. To start at the very beginning, a Jewish—or, more accurately, Israelite—diaspora first appeared in the eighth century BCE at the very latest, when the Assyrians conquered the northern Israelite kingdom of Samaria and deported most of its inhabitants (one of the very few biblical events corroborated by other sources). Though the Samarian Israelites disappeared into the Assyrian population, later waves of émigrés from Judea, both voluntary and involuntary, clung more stubbornly to Jerusalem. The very idea of Jerusalem as the seat of temple worship, like the Greek word "metropolis" (mother city), meant that the Israelite God could be venerated from elsewhere. A substantial Israelite community existed continuously in the diaspora since the destruction of the First Temple in Jerusalem and the Babylonian exile in the sixth century BCE. With the Persian conquest of Babylonia, many Israelites returned to Jerusalem, but many also stayed in Babylonia, ushering in the duality of diaspora and Holy Land that exists in Jewish life to this day. The diaspora grew over the next thousand years, spreading to further and further reaches in the Hellenistic, Roman, Byzantine, and Muslim periods and throughout much of the Islamic and Christian realms.

The two failed revolts against Rome in 70 and 132–35 CE led first to the destruction of the Second Temple in Jerusalem and then, in most quarters, to the end of practical expectation for its restoration. The definitive end to Judean sovereignty and the physical center of Israelite religion might have created a cognitive dissonance for a people marked as divinely chosen in their own religious texts. Yet in the hands of the rabbis, the texts themselves provided a framework for understanding catastrophe: it was clear enough to most that Israel sinned, and God punished. The fact that God took special care to punish and disperse the Jews, and used all of the nations of the world as an instrument to do so, only reinforced the sense of Jewish chosenness. For millennia, a sin-punishment paradigm would remain the dominant lens through which Jews viewed their historical existence. It is in fact because of the use of "diaspora" in the Greek translation of the Bible, the Septuagint, that common usage of the term in

Western languages until very recently referred only to the Jews in dispersion.[4] Deuteronomy 28:64, where "diaspora" appears in the Septuagint, suggests that the Lord would scatter (in the original Hebrew, *vehafitsekha adonay*) the Jews to the earth's ends if they did not obey the law, establishing the link between diaspora and divine punishment.

Jews made their homes throughout the ancient and medieval Mesopotamian, Mediterranean, and European worlds. When their hosts uprooted them—from southern Italy and the Kingdom of Naples (1288–94), England (1290), France (1300s, especially 1306 and 1315), much of the Rhine valley (sporadically throughout the fourteenth and fifteenth centuries), Spain (1492), and Portugal (1497)—the expulsions, forced conversions, and murder that some experienced had an indelible effect on how Jews, especially European Jews, viewed their status in the diaspora. As Yosef Hayim Yerushalmi famously argued in *Zakhor*, Jews have a long tradition of merging their present circumstances with the memory of the past. This memory is not historical, in that it does not seek to know or understand the past. Instead, Jewish memory eliminates the distance between past and present by putting all events in the context of religious time.[5] Rather than merely record the violence or expulsion that befell them, Jews used liturgy and ritual to commemorate events such as the Crusades, forced conversions, and blood libels in a religious context. Many years before Yerushalmi, Avrom Golomb made this point explicitly: "Jewish Tradition never made a monument of the past but rather constantly endeavored to make it a partner in the present" (see the chapter "What Is Jewish Tradition?"). Even after the Jewish expulsion from Spain, when some Jews began to write historically about their exodus, historical knowledge lost out to mythology in the new Lurianic kabbalistic cosmology that saw Jewish exile as a result of God's own cosmic exile before history itself.[6]

In a theological sense, then, it never mattered to Jews why historically they came to be spread across a vast diaspora. What mattered was that just as God had chosen them as a people and led them to a promised land, so God chose to scatter them to the ends of the earth until redemption. This is not to say that Jews never felt secure and rooted enough to feel the permanence of their existence in a given place, but to observe that a genuine theological barrier prevented Jews from seeing an end to their exile apart from the messianic ingathering. Jews in the diaspora may have historically maintained the centrality of the land of Israel through prayer, pilgrimage, and ritual, while taking for granted the legitimacy of living at a distance, but "exile" as a mythological concept was rooted in the biblical texts. Recent scholarship has emphasized the hybrid nature of Jewish culture and even Jewish identity, and some centers of Jewish life were indeed secure enough to feel permanent. Ashkenazic life in Poland, for example, was fruitful for at least 600 years, so much so that Jews possessed their own mythological explanations for their presence there.[7] Nevertheless, the sin-punishment paradigm remained in place, and messianic hope for restoration alternated between passively praying for redemption and a return to Jerusalem, on the one hand, and occasional outbursts of active messianism, on the other hand. The messianic impulse in Judaism, impossible as it is to separate from the end of exile, has been present at least since the beginning of a Judahite diaspora, if not before. Just as God warned that Israel would be dispersed among the nations for breaking its covenant, God also held out the promise of protection, restoration, and redemption. Thus, according to Heinrich Graetz, the messianic idea that took shape even before the Babylonian exile could be perpetually applied and reinvented to fit different circumstances.[8] In fact, instead of a single messianic idea, one might say that "messiah" became a metaphor in Judaism that took on new and extended meanings as circumstances required.

The paradox of Jewish life in exile was built into the Jewish languages through the terms Jews used to describe their existence: the two Hebrew words for exile, *galut* and *gola*, and the word for redemption, *geula*. Furthermore, because the arguments between Jewish nationalists and other participants in the so-called new Jewish politics of the late nineteenth and early twentieth centuries came in no small part to center on the Land of Israel's role in national liberation, these terms inevitably took on new meanings. *Galut* attained a heightened political meaning in part due to the famous exchange of public letters in 1909 between the spiritual Zionist Ahad Ha'am and the diaspora nationalist Simon Dubnov over Ahad Ha'am's letter "Shelilat ha'galut" (usually translated as "The Negation of the Diaspora," or "The Negation of Exile").[9] The terms *tfutsot* and *pizur*, both meaning dispersion, commonly conveyed the same meaning as diaspora. However, by the time distinct Jewish political ideologies emerged, it was *galut*, or exile—*golus* in Yiddish, Russian, and German—that the new Jewish politics adopted universally as the term for both the geographical existence and the physical condition of the Jews in Europe. Gradually a distinction emerged between *galut*, which came to mean exile as a state of mind, and *gola*, indicating the place or places where Jews lived.

Such linguistic gymnastics reflects not only politics, but also the challenges inherent in developing Hebrew as a modern literary language and vernacular. Simon Rawidowicz, a scholar of philosophy and Hebrew, claimed that some

Zionists after Israel's creation became concerned about the danger of using the word *tfutsa* and even accused him of having invented the term *tfutsot*.[10] Though the accusation was certainly false, it stemmed from Rawidowicz's attempt to popularize the term *tfutsa*—dispersion in the singular—to describe what he called "Jewish existence outside the Land of Israel as a historic empirical fact, free of an attitude of cursing or blessing."[11] Needless to say, Rawidowicz's attempt to detach politics from language was itself a self-conscious political act, taken against those who sought to devalue or criticize Jewish life in the diaspora. Interestingly, though *tfutsa* fell largely (but not completely) out of usage, *tfutsot* completely supplanted *galut* and *gola* as the Israeli Hebrew word for the Jewish diaspora, exactly as Rawidowicz's opponents feared would be the case. Anita Shapira dates the change in colloquial Hebrew to 1958–59, when the Israeli Education Ministry, attempting to deepen Jewish consciousness in young Israelis and repair their image of diaspora Jewry (in particular, their view of Holocaust victims and the Jewish community in the United States), chose to use the term *Yehudei ha'tfutsot* rather than *Yehudei ha'gola* in its literature.[12] The multicultural reality of Israeli society served to further erode the compulsion to "negate," especially as the waves of those migrating to Israel since the 1960s arrived with far less sense of their previous existence as "exile."[13] If any argument can be made for the declining relevance of such ideological debates to Israelis today, and the realization of the exile's "negation," it is the fact that the language of exile—*galut* and *gola*—has become anachronistic and now sounds archaic in colloquial Hebrew. No better example of this can be seen than in the museum dedicated to the Jewish communities of the diaspora, opened in Tel Aviv in 1978, which took the name Beit Hatfutsot. The museum also calls itself the Museum of the Jewish People (*muzeyon ha'am ha'yehudi*) and, in doing so, breaks down the distinction between diaspora Jews and Israelis in a manner similar to the equation of Jewish peoplehood that Rawidowicz called "two that are one."[14]

Yet even if the perceived problem of *galut* mentality has more or less been resolved, at least as an issue for the Jews in Israel (with the exception perhaps of anti-Zionist Jews), the distinction between the historical experience of exile and Jewish life in the Land of Israel is built into the Hebrew language. The most frequently cited example is the continued use of *aliya* (ascent) and *yerida* (descent) as the words for immigration and emigration, respectively. Another would be the very name Eretz Yisrael, the Land of Israel, which refers to a geographic conception of Israel in all historical periods, regardless of who held or lived in the territory—a practice long predating Zionism but given greater meaning with the movement's ascendance.[15] If one needs a further reminder that a dichotomy still exists between Jewish existence inside and outside of the Jewish homeland, as does the understood difference between the Jewish diaspora and the parallel situation of other diaspora groups, it is necessary only to point out that Israeli Hebrew has adopted a different term to describe non-Jewish diasporic communities. When other diasporas are considered, the term used in Israeli Hebrew is *pezura* (like *pizur*, from the verb *lefazer*, to disperse). In other words, non-Jews can have a diaspora (*pezura*), but only the Jews have *the* Diaspora (*ha'tfutsot*).[16] This is a distinction preserved for a long time in common English because of the theological meaning that Christians attribute to Jewish dispersion. Finally, a new term developed in the Jewish settlement before the creation of the State of Israel: *huts la'arets* (outside the land), used to describe the universe beyond the Land of Israel. Although today *huts la'arets* (and its abbreviation, "*hul*") is equivalent to the English "abroad," when the term began to gain popularity in usage, it seemed obvious to some—such as Israel Knox—that Zionists intentionally sought to reinforce the difference between the redeemed Jews in the Land of Israel and those Jews still in the communities of exile (see the chapter "Is America Exile or Home?").

Modern Jewish nationalism is a product of the diaspora, however one might believe that Jews fared outside of the geographical bounds of contemporary Israel. In other words, whether one sees ending the diaspora as the only remedy to Jewish persecution and insecurity or sees positive and negative aspects of Jewish history and continued existence in the diaspora, modern Jewish national movements first arose outside the Jews' historic homeland. Introspection about the nature of Judaism increased in the seventeenth and eighteenth centuries, however, only the debates about the desirability and feasibility of Jewish integration into the political fabric of the various European states, and with it the attenuation of the Jews' corporate status, made the question of what it means to be a Jew relevant to all. Only the possibility of remaining Jewish while belonging to, and being governed by, something other than a community of coreligionists could propel the kind of debates that would extend the meaning of Jewish peoplehood into the secular realm of nations and states. At the moment Jews first began to consider such questions, they did so because of how they perceived the political realities of Jewish life in centers of the diaspora such as France, Germany, Austria, Russia, the United States, and even the Ottoman Empire (including, but not especially Southern Syria, where Palestine lay in the Ottoman governance structure). Resulting from Jewish engagement in a Hebrew idiom with European philosophy, theology, science, and literature—commonly known as the Haskala; from questions of Jewish social, economic, and political integration in the diaspora; from antisemitism; and, more broadly, from the Jewish experience with modernity was an array of visions of Jewish peoplehood and community that sought to preserve or create anew the meaning of *am Yisrael*, the people of Israel.

Diaspora Nationalism, Jewish Renaissance, and the Messianic Impulse in Judaism

From a theological perspective, Zionism and diaspora nationalism both challenge a fundamental tenet of a Judaism in exile. In essence, both negating the exile and affirming the diaspora are equally problematic to a religious tradition that continually yearned for the end of exile through redemption but affirmed the immediacy of exile and, with a number of notable exceptions, the distant future of that redemption. Nevertheless, both Zionism and diaspora nationalism emerged out of the challenge of creating a secular nationalism that channeled rather than violated this religious perception. In fact, among the figures we consider most responsible for reorienting the Haskala away from acculturation and toward Jewish nationalism, we can find the idea that Judaism's redemptive hope historically served a crucial role in preserving Jewish national self-consciousness in the diaspora, an idea predating the articulation of most Zionist ideologies. One could come to the conclusion—as Perets Smolenskin, the editor of the important Hebrew journal *Ha-Shahar*, did—that the Jews' attempts to negate their individual national self-consciousness would lead nowhere, but it was not necessary to further conclude that the Jews' self-determination must take place in a land of their own. As is well known, Smolenskin did later become a Zionist. But when in 1872 he wrote his landmark essay "The Eternal People" ("Am olam"; see the chapter "The Eternal People"), questioning efforts to reform away the national element in Judaism, it did not occur to him that a Jewish national renaissance could not take place in the diaspora. Ironically, perhaps, the key issue that led Smolenskin to write "The Eternal People" was the proposal by some German reformers to remove the hope for redemption and restoration to Zion from the prayer book. To counter those who believed this prayer undermined Jewish loyalty to Germany or Austria, Smolenskin argued that if Jews wanted physical restoration in their day, they would have achieved it, yet such was not the purpose of the messianic impulse in Judaism. The purpose of the hope for redemption—this passive messianism—is its universality among Jews and its function in providing the fraternal cement between Jews around the world who have little else in common. Perhaps most important, the hope for restoration to Zion preserved a national difference between Jews and non-Jews. According to Smolenskin, "this hope is what makes [the Jews] a nation *despite* not having a land and sovereignty" (my emphasis). To the reformers, in Smolenskin's view, the hope for redemption identified the Jews as "the other," whereas to Smolenskin, freedom and equality were impossible without preserving Jewish national difference. It is understandable that when Zionism emerged as a movement, it would fit Smolenskin's worldview perfectly. Nevertheless, "The Eternal People," an essay that became a symbol of national reawakening, was fundamentally about preserving and redefining Jewish nationalism in the diaspora. Its key principle was to foster Jewish national unity internationally, without acting on the redemptive impulse in Judaism.

Although Smolenskin was a *maskil* and someone who had left traditional Judaism, he favored some form of Jewish religious reform.[17] But, like the earliest Haskala thinkers, Smolenskin believed that reform was possible only if it remained rooted in Jewish sources.[18] Even in a place and time when Jews could make personal decisions about which religious practices to observe and which to ignore, to Smolenskin, Judaism's key doctrines should not be diluted to be made more acceptable to non-Jews. To do so would be to weaken the spiritual and national bond between Jews and would, in essence, be an attempt to deny Jewish national difference. It is precisely because of the challenges posed by secularization that Smolenskin took such exception to attempts to neuter the hope for redemption to Zion. No matter how a Jew fell away from practice, this fundamental hope is something held in his heart, uniting him with other Jews and preserving his nationality. Furthermore, this messianic hope's disconnection from the political reality of statehood ensured its eternality. As Smolenskin put it, "the hope for Israel's future redemption is stronger than other beliefs, because also it provides us with national life while asking of us neither tax nor any royal burden, nor will it require our sons to defend it. Therefore, we are obligated even more so to hold onto this hope."

It is helpful to think about the development of Jewish nationalism in the late nineteenth and early twentieth centuries in the framework developed by Israel Bartal, as "territorialist" and "autonomist" movements.[19] For "territorialists," or Zionists, Jewish exile is the cause of Jewish helplessness, and the problem that must be rectified through mass immigration, territorial concentration, and some form of self-determination or sovereignty. In contrast, the "autonomists," or diaspora nationalists, viewed the Jewish diaspora as a natural historical condition and believed Jewish nationalism could thrive there, provided there was sufficient internal Jewish autonomy. When Zionism became organized as a political movement, certain divisions became immediately obvious. Namely, a major division existed between those who sought to create something completely and radically new and different from what existed in the diaspora, and those who sought to end the condition of exile by creating a national movement based on continuity with Jewish religious traditions. It is important to emphasize here that all efforts toward territorialism—to separate a defined territory for Jewish government that would end the experience of exile—whether in the Jews' ancestral homeland or elsewhere, equally sought to end the condition of exile.[20]

A similar dichotomy existed within streams of diaspora nationalist thought, between those seeking to harness the Jewish desire for national self-determination to socialism (the true cause), and therefore to radically reconfigure Jewish society, and those primarily concerned with creating a Jewish national identity in the diaspora equipped to weather the eroding powers of religious compulsion in the modern state. As in Zionism, these two broad trends—the political and the spiritual—were not mutually exclusive. What one might call the spiritual wing of diaspora nationalism took a page from Smolenskin's belief that in order to remain at home in Europe, the Jews needed also to remain conscious of their exile. The famed Yiddish literary figure I. L. Peretz similarly credited the messianic hope in Judaism with allowing Jews to suffer persecution, endure, and quickly forget: "Only to move on, only to survive, only to live to see the Messiah . . . at least the pre-Messianic pangs!" (see the chapter "Paths That Lead Away from *Yidishkayt*"). Yet a critique of such passivity was also part and parcel of Peretz's meditation on how to preserve Jewishness (*Yidishkayt*) in the modern world. Thus Peretz endowed the mission to build Jewish cultural life in the diaspora, to create a Jewish renaissance, with messianic meaning:

> The flag of *Jewish* renaissance, of *Messiah and world-judgment*, of *world-liberation*—of a future free humanity must be raised again!
>
> This is the mission of the eternal people, the world-people. This is what Jewish life must be, the Jewish home, Jewish school, Jewish theater, Jewish books and everything that is Jewish must be.

Others, like the French rabbi and communal figure René Hirschler, in search of the essence of "Jewish consciousness" in the past and for the future, pointed to the people of Israel's eternality (see the chapter "A Basis for Jewish Consciousness"). Mordecai Kaplan similarly suggested: "As a collective consciousness, Judaism has a passion for immortality which it must satisfy" (see the chapter "The Future of Judaism"). Kaplan, who founded Reconstructionist Judaism, considered himself a Zionist but was equally concerned with preserving Judaism, and Jewish nationality, in the United States. He made virtually no distinction between the hope for redemption's purpose and the purpose of contemporary Zionism. Writing in 1916, Kaplan defined Zionism as "the pledge that Judaism is eternal: The real Zionist platform is not the one formulated in the Basle program, but the prayer in our ritual which reads, 'Let our eyes behold Thy return to Zion.'" Thus Kaplan holds that for diaspora Jews, the simple longing for redemption through restoration to Zion, whether or not one acts on it, has always prevented, and will continue to prevent, the assimilation of Jews into other nations. It is precisely for this reason that Rawidowicz so vehemently opposed the Zionists' "negation of the exile." Ending the exile was, in essence, leaving those outside of Zion unredeemed. With Judaism's eternality, or endlessness, resolved, why remain Jewish? With the end of history, what is left to build of national culture in either the diaspora or the Land of Israel?

In fact, if a single theme can be identified in diaspora nationalist writing, it is the persistent search for what was known as a Jewish Renaissance, or rebirth. Smolenskin, Dubnov, Peretz, and many others who came after them believed that the essence of Jewish nationality was embodied and preserved in the Jewish religion, and any Jewish renaissance, however secular, therefore needed to draw on religious texts, traditions, and historical understanding. These ideas emerged in an area where nationality and religion were intimately bound together. Dubnov, for example, stated over and over again that religious life created a fortress protecting Jewish national self-consciousness throughout history in the diaspora, and he argued that not merely the laws but the spiritual content of Judaism created a particularly unique form of European nationalism. Since the idea was to construct a form of Jewish nationalism inclusive of secular and religious Jews alike, Dubnov equated the ethical ideal in Judaism to spiritual nationalism, framing the latter as a force of historical preservation in the diaspora (see the chapter "Jews as a Spiritual [Cultural-Historical] Nation among Political Nations").

The language of renaissance and rebirth pervaded the Jewish national debates of the late nineteenth and early twentieth centuries.[21] Whether they sought to empty the diaspora or preserve it by maintaining the redemptive hope in

Judaism, the purveyors of renaissance all sought a transformation of Jewish life that responded to the realities of the modern world. Integration and exclusion, secularism and antisemitism, freedom and insecurity—the new possibilities and the perils Jews faced in the nineteenth and twentieth centuries produced a broadly shared desire to create something new from the old. In the eyes of diaspora nationalists, renaissance could come about only through preserving the ultimate promise of a final messianic redemption. As Rawidowicz wrote, "The eternal union of Babylon-and-Jerusalem [diaspora and Israel] shuns the deception that the redemption has come; it proclaims not: 'Yours is the task of completion'" (see the chapter "Jerusalem and Babylon").

Jewish Renaissance, National Suicide, and Jewish Socialism

No less than Zionists, Jewish socialists could also promise an end to *galut*, the mentality of exile. At exactly the time when Jews began to debate the parameters of Jewish nationhood, socialism took powerful hold of many Jewish intellectuals. Various different kinds of European socialisms developed in the late nineteenth century, some of which were tied to European national movements, while others were hostile to nationalism of any kind. Those Jews drawn to socialism were at first overwhelmingly also attracted to the idea that Jews would assimilate into the working classes among whom they lived. While some sympathized with Jewish laborers, many Jewish socialists also accepted the socialist critique of the Jews as exploiters and agreed that true emancipation would render any kind of distinct Jewish life anachronistic. And Jewish socialists, like Zionists, promised a kind of messianic utopia and end of exile—only instead of an ingathering to the Promised Land, exile would be made irrelevant as the differences between fellow men disappeared.

Syntheses of Jewish nationalism and socialism eventually and inevitably took Zionist and diaspora nationalist forms.[22] In one sense, both Zionism and communism were prefigured in a single individual, Moses Hess, who as a Young Hegelian helped craft the principles of communism and, later, wrote the first tract of political Zionism, *Rome and Jerusalem*. Published in 1862, *Rome and Jerusalem* combined utopian socialism and liberal nationalism, proposing that Jews create a state and Jewish Renaissance in Palestine based on their return to the soil and productive labor. Hess also saw the Jews' biblical past as the source of their natural inclination to social justice, an idea also present in the philosophy of Hermann Cohen (albeit not in a Zionist form) and one that proved very popular among later labor Zionists.[23] Like Hess, Chaim Zhitlowsky, in the words of Jonathan Frankel, was "anxious to build a bridge between the Prophetic past of the Jewish people and the messianic future promised by socialism."[24] Zhitlowsky, however, saw this messianic future occurring in the diaspora—in particular, in a Russian Empire transformed by socialist revolution. When Zhitlowsky published *A Jew to Jews* in 1892 (see the selection included here), he constructed a socialist argument for Jewish nationalism and a Jewish argument for socialism. To Zhitlowsky, capitalism meant an end to Jewish peoplehood, and the Jews' experience in the West (equated as it was with assimilation) provided the best evidence of that effect. Looking at the Russian Empire, Zhitlowsky argued that if the Jews achieved equality in a constitutional democracy, they would swamp the middle classes, adopting Russian and Polish culture, and in doing so would exacerbate antisemitism. Therefore, the only path forward to national salvation lay in radical social and political revolution. After a socialist revolution in Russia, the Jews could settle the land and demand the same rights over language, culture, and political representation as other nations in the new revolutionary state. Zhitlowsky employed language that one sees repeatedly among Jewish intellectuals who had left the confines of their religion but continued to search for the meaning of their national existence. Especially to Eastern European Jewish critics of Western European Jews, emancipation in the West caused Jews to commit "national suicide" and become the most enthusiastic proponents of their new nations' culture.[25] To Zhitlowsky, Jewish socialists had fallen into the same trap, and he wondered why, when it came to assimilation, Jewish socialists had adopted and even taken to extremes the position of the Western European Jewish bourgeoisie.

For some, such as Nahman Syrkin, Zhitlowsky's contemporary and one of the founding ideologues of socialist Zionism, the complete social reconstruction of the Jewish people could take place only if the prophetic past and utopian future came physically together, in Palestine.[26] In contrast, for Zhitlowsky and many subsequent socialist diaspora nationalists, Yiddish became a natural place to turn for the means to create a new secular Jewish national culture (see the chapter "Why Only Yiddish?"). In fact, socialist movements among other nationalities at the time were also attempting to navigate the waters between cosmopolitanism and nationalism—the universal and the particular—and in doing so, they too focused on oppressed or suppressed languages. Even so, for those Jewish socialists fighting to counter assimilation, their Yiddishism and diaspora nationalism always had to be balanced against an inherent internationalism that distrusted nationalism of any kind, an uncomfortable balance made even worse by the religious nature of Jewish peoplehood and a clear agenda of solving social problems before any other kind. The Bundist theorist Vladimir Medem provides the best example of a socialist attempt to tiptoe between demanding Jewish national rights and insisting on Jewish nationalism. Although he argued against viewing the Jews as a "worldwide Jewish nation," he nonetheless acknowledged the existence of many Jewish nations with local national needs (see the chapter "The Worldwide Jewish Nation"). Medem was instrumental in steering the Jewish Labor Bund toward a national policy that embraced secular Jewish culture (in particular Yiddish) and national and cultural autonomy, while preserving the internationalism at the core of the Bund's ideology.[27] And while he failed to appreciate (or, more accurately, intentionally minimized) the degree to which the unity of Israel and its shared hope for redemption lay at the core of Jewish national self-consciousness, Medem correctly observed the rapidity with which Jewish culture and identity evolve in different geographic and political circumstances.

Jewish socialists, especially in Eastern Europe, had very practical reasons for shifting toward recognizing particular Jewish national needs, if not full-fledged nationalism. How could socialists attract Jewish adherents when most Jews in the Russian Empire and Austrian Galicia had no desire to shed their Jewish identity? Even given a degree of pragmatism, Jewish socialists genuinely came to empathize with the plight of the Jewish "folk" and believe in the revolutionary promise of the Jewish people. As such, Jewish socialists were forever anxious about the need to bridge the gap between the "folk-masses" and themselves, the intellectuals. Yiddish proved an effective means to do so, both as a language and as material for constructing a new socialist Jewish culture. The socialist autonomists and others took a maximalist position on Jewish sociopolitical autonomy, demanding the highest possible degree of Jewish self-government through a national parliament (this movement's foundational texts were published in a short-lived journal called *Vozrozhdenie*—meaning renaissance, or rebirth—and in a volume of essays by the same name).[28] Others, such as the Bundists, were more concerned that Jews control their own educational system and cultural organizations and receive recognition as a separate socialist movement, though a wide range of opinions on the Jewish national question coexisted within the Bund.[29]

The February Revolution of 1917 in Russia gave all of the Jewish parties the opportunity to turn thought into action, and the institutions of Jewish autonomy were quickly constructed on an edifice already built during the chaos of World War I. After the Bolsheviks took power, the Jewish sections of the Communist Party took down this edifice even more quickly than it had been raised. Yet for a brief moment, especially in independent Ukraine (1918–20), many Jewish socialists threw themselves into the task of creating the institutions of Jewish autonomy and a new revolutionary Jewish national culture appropriate to the new era (see the chapter on the Kultur-Lige and its programmatic statements). No doubt everyone sensed that the revolution had brought with it a new era, but given the dramatic ideological shift leftward in Russian, Polish, and Ukrainian society even well before the Bolsheviks' October Revolution, socialists believed that a long-awaited period of radical social transformation had arrived. A new era required a reinvention of Jewish culture, and some among the "Jewish culturalists," as Kenneth Moss calls the Yiddishist and Hebraist purveyors of a revolutionary new Jewish culture, "shared the modernist convictions of the pan-European avant-garde, which saw wholesale cultural and psychic reinvention as essential to the creation of a new world."[30]

As Jewish socialists sought to participate in the construction of a new society and build Jewish autonomy within it, they also sought to cast the attainment of Jewish autonomy as a product of the historical forces of class struggle. For example, the Marxist sociologist Jacob Lestschinsky—who moved from Warsaw to Kiev in 1917 to help found the United Jewish Socialist Workers' Party, known as the Fareynikte, and to build socialist Jewish autonomy—recast Jewish history as a struggle for Jewish autonomy, in the vein of Dubnov, yet with a socialist twist (see the chapter "Jewish Autonomy Yesterday and Today").[31] Lestschinsky portrayed the poor working masses, the folk, as the keepers of Jewish nationality and autonomy, even while the wealthy and upwardly mobile Jews in the nineteenth century sought to dismantle Jewish autonomy and join the Russian and Polish nationalities. In the twentieth century, to Lestschinsky, the middle classes' attraction to Zionism seemed insincere: "On the one hand they hopelessly climb assimilation's ladder, while on the other hand the prayer for Messianic redemption still hangs on their lips." For Jewish socialists who saw themselves as *Jewish* socialists, assimilation and national suicide became the foils against which they directed their efforts at national reconstruction and Jewish renaissance. The same Jewish socialists would have to adapt to the new realities imposed, for example, by the victory of Bolshevism in the revolutionary process or, more commonly, leave their country and try again elsewhere.[32]

The Geography of Diaspora Nationalism

The national framework of politics in the multiethnic empires of Austria and Russia clearly created fertile ground for diaspora nationalism in Eastern

Europe. The Russian Empire in particular contained millions of Jews dissatisfied with the pace of their political emancipation and living in areas of dense Jewish population, side by side with other dissatisfied national groups. Most important, political struggle in the Russian Empire was conducted along national and religious lines—a key reason why the government feared democratization. The end of these multinational empires did not, in fact, mean the end of diaspora nationalism in Eastern Europe, but the Holocaust and westward extension of Soviet power did. As for Central and Western Europe, although diaspora nationalism can be found in institutions and individuals devoted to building Jewish self-consciousness and national difference, it seems unrealistic to expect that diaspora nationalism as a political platform could take root anywhere except in a multinational context, where other national groups were making similar claims to a distinct way of life, language, and politics.[33]

To return for a moment to Smolenskin, it is no coincidence that he spent his entire life in Europe's two largest multinational states, the Russian and Austrian Empires. During his lifetime, national tension and movements for self-determination threatened the viability of these empires. At the same time, technological advances, greater freedom of movement, and steady urbanization had eroded the religious community's powers of compulsion. Smolenskin's own biography is a case in point. Born in the small town of Mosticzena in Mogilev, he spent much of his teenage years first in Shklov and then wandering the Pale of Settlement. After five years in Odessa (1862–67), he lived the remainder of his life in Vienna. Smolenskin left a Jewish universe—one that ordered most aspects of his everyday life—but in neither Odessa nor Vienna did he enter a new universe that required his complete acculturation. Neither city lacked Jews who were seeking to transform themselves into Germans or Russians, and both of these imperial identities left plenty of room for Jews to maintain a sense of separate nationality. While the accusation of Jews' dual loyalty that resonated in France and Germany was also prevalent in Austrian and Russian antisemitism, in the latter two states, dual loyalties were presumed to exist among national groups. In fact, in both the Russian and Austrian Empires, Jews found themselves accused variously by Poles and Ukrainians of identifying too strongly with the imperial culture, and Jewish advocacy for equality as a separate nationality provided the Jews with some flexible neutrality.

Furthermore, in the Russian and Austrian Empires before World War I, when the debate about how and where Jewish national aspirations might best be achieved was conducted almost entirely on theoretical grounds, the distinction between the territorial and diaspora-centered nationalisms was less acute and tended to be phrased as that between Zionists and Nationalists. We can see the close proximity of early Zionism and diaspora nationalism in the efforts to create united national parties in these empires, and it appears even more clearly in the efforts to create a national movement that transcended party and ideological lines. Such was the context of Nathan Birnbaum's essay "The Jewish Renaissance Movement" (see the first essay in the Birnbaum chapter). Although Birnbaum coined the term *Zionismus*, he soon came to see this kind of nationalism as "too weak and too narrow." He migrated intellectually to the idea of Jewish Renaissance because it affirmed that Jews anywhere could participate in national revival, and they could do so through a host of ideological lenses. Jewish poetry, theater, publishing, labor unions, and colonization all reinforced Jewish national self-consciousness in the modern era and therefore were integrally tied to the new Jewish renaissance. In the years before World War I, diaspora- and Zion-centered Jewish nationalisms waxed and waned depending on circumstance. Birnbaum suggested in "Jewish Autonomy" (see the second essay in the Birnbaum chapter)—his proposal for Jewish national autonomy in the Austrian Empire—that the political aims of the national renaissance were first oriented toward "the rebirth of a state" because it took some time for Jews (or, at least, his like-minded peers) to realize that a legal framework existed for Jewish national demands in Europe. When Jewish people's parties emerged—first in Austria, in 1902, and then in the Russian Empire, revolutionary Russia and Ukraine, and interwar Lithuania, Poland, and Germany—they did so with the explicit purpose of blurring political differences between Zionists and diaspora nationalists in favor of, simply, nationalism.

Zionism within the Ottoman Empire and post-1908 Turkey followed a similar model to many of the European Jewish people's parties, employing Zionist discourse to make claims for Jewish autonomy in a reconstituted multinational empire.[34] Diaspora nationalism, especially Dubnovian ideas about autonomy and self-rule, could be adapted even to Ottoman Palestine. As Bartal has shown, several Zionists in late-Ottoman Palestine, especially David Ben-Gurion, essentially advocated Jewish autonomy for all Jews in the Ottoman Empire.[35] Following the Young Turk Revolution, Ben-Gurion even moved to Salonika and then Constantinople (after Salonika fell to the Greeks), and he pressed Jewish community leaders to advocate Jewish autonomy throughout a federative Ottoman Empire, including an autonomous Palestine. As Bartal argues, the adaptation of diaspora nationalist ideas of autonomism to the Yishuv in the form of "the autonomism of the Land of Israel," allowed "autonomist" Zionists to approach the old Jewish community there as an integral part of diaspora Jewry, and vice versa, and in doing so to build a spiritual foundation for economic, political, and demographic development in Israel. In Bartal's words, "the Zionists' 'negation of the diaspora' was therefore not absolute, just as the historical image of the Jews held by the last generations was not clear-cut Zionist consciousness."[36]

Without accepting a bipolar historiography of Jewish nationalism—in which the West represents the politics of accommodation, integration, and oligarchy and the East represents Jewish nationalism, revolutionary socialism, and democracy—one still must address the question of why the political forms of diaspora nationalism failed to migrate westward, even when its advocates did. The European countries with the numerically most significant Jewish communities—for instance, England, France, and Germany—all produced Zionist thinkers and Zionist movements. Yet Zionism was possible for some in these countries, and only some, because it directed national aspirations elsewhere. In a civic sense, the Jews in Western Europe, including the religiously observant, believed in their integration into the body politic and consequently avoided any nationalism that might challenge their civic status at home. While in the Russian and Austrian Empires and the states that succeeded them diaspora nationalism had political meaning, in France and the United States, two countries with decidedly republican self-perceptions, one generally sees an emphasis on the religious significance of the Jews as a people in the diaspora. Thus for Hirschler, the national consciousness in the diaspora he speaks of must necessarily be phrased in religious terms. In some cases, the turn to an understanding of Jewish peoplehood as rooted in religious texts stemmed directly from the political failures of diaspora nationalism in the East. We can see this retreat to religion in *Oyfn Sheydveg* (At the crossroads), the journal created in Paris in 1939 by disappointed and disillusioned diaspora nationalist émigrés. In that journal, Avrom Golomb talks about the Jewish way of life, literature, and tradition as sustaining Judaism "more than kingdoms, dynasties, political heroes, holy books and so on" (see the chapter "What Is Jewish Tradition?"). By 1939, the political conversation among diaspora nationalists still in Europe had shifted its focus from a Jewish Renaissance to a spiritual separation represented by the metaphor of a return to the ghetto.

Both Kaplan and Rawidowicz also articulated a Jewish nationalism based in "religion rooted in everyday life," to use Kaplan's terms; a Jewish nationalism that was fundamentally beyond politics.[37] Idealized by Jews as a promised land (*di goldene medine*), the United States presented a unique set of opportunities and challenges to Jewish nationalism. The idea that exile ends when a Jew sets foot in the United States, as we see in Israel Knox, could be reconciled to a self-consciously Dubnovian outlook that viewed America as the Jewish diaspora's next great center. Jews placed a messianic emphasis on their own settlement in the New World, and in doing so crafted their own version of the Puritan narrative of America as a New Jerusalem.[38] Perhaps most important, in the United States more than any other place, Jews integrated into the dominant society by helping to shape its contours. In the late nineteenth and twentieth centuries, what it meant to be American, in a national sense, was an open question (as it still is), and Jews could and did participate in this debate. Much of the very terminology of "cultural pluralism" originated with the American Jewish thinker and educator Horace Kallen and the non-Jews, like Randolph Bourne and John Dewey, he influenced.[39] While democracy proved no antidote to assimilation (as Kallen, for example, believed it would), cultural pluralism did create an openness to multiple identities that, when combined with the success of Zionism, effectively made the debate about how best to construct a national renaissance less pressing and decreasingly relevant to people's lives. During World War I, as the European empires in the east were being torn apart into new (multiethnic) nation-states, new thinking on federalism, autonomy, and self-determination circulated in the United States in the midst of a heated discussion about race and immigration (both the Kallen and Kaplan texts in this volume were originally published during the war). Though President Woodrow Wilson may have approved of national minority rights in Europe, he railed against them in America. Even in the period following World War I, when momentum from minorities treaties led to widespread support for Jewish autonomy in the newly independent states in Eastern Europe, its advocates in the United States simultaneously emphasized the inapplicability of such ideas in an American context.[40]

By 1948, with a few important exceptions, the spaces of Jewish national culture in Europe existed only under communism (where it was not a graveyard). In the United States, diaspora nationalism was rooted more in resistance to assimilation and in confidence in the acceptance there of Jews as Jews than in the history and traditions of the Jews in the country. Furthermore, the United States is a place where ethnic long-distance nationalism can comfortably coexist with domestic civic nationalism. As a small illustration, the majority of the recent private donors who contributed to the massive renovation of the Israel Museum in Jerusalem live in New York City.[41] Meanwhile, at the National Museum of

American Jewish History, the word "national" in the museum's title refers very clearly to the United States.

Zionism and Diaspora Nationalism after 1948

It is difficult to measure the popularity of ideas, but it is safe to observe that no diaspora nationalist ideology, except Zionism in the diaspora, ever held the loyalty of the majority of diaspora Jews. Still, the key threads of diaspora nationalism were crucial in the development of modern Jewish nationalism, broadly speaking. For example, the idea that the diaspora played a positive role in Jewish national development provided the spine of early critiques of the Haskala's supposedly denationalizing tendencies. The very fact that the Jews preserved their sense of peoplehood through millennia of existence in the diaspora seemed to require explanation, and varied attempts at such an explanation led to several modern Jewish national identities. Jews soon demanded equal rights while affirming a separate national identity, and from there they argued that they could build a secular and autonomous culture in the countries in which they lived. Jewish political parties with large memberships, such as the Bund, incorporated aspects of diaspora nationalism in their ideologies. Zionists, though oriented toward a geographical and redemptive Zion, in many places demanded Jewish national rights. From a practical standpoint, in the multinational states of imperial Austria and Russia, as well as the Ottoman Empire, political Zionism normally included the demand for Jewish diaspora national rights as well. But, as Anthony Smith points out, "nationalism is a doctrine of authenticity," and in its connection to the land and messianic promise of redemption, Zionism held a natural advantage over competing diaspora Jewish nationalisms. This theologically rooted advantage was made only starker by the trends of nineteenth- and twentieth-century political development: "In a world of compact, exclusive and competing national states, minority autonomy was ultimately a matter of sufferance, not right."[42]

From the time when Zionism became a full-fledged movement until today, it has served as a political outlet for Jews seeking to affirm their national sense of Jewishness by devoting themselves to the cause of Jewish nationalism, while remaining in the diaspora. This was, if anything, one of the founding ideas of Zionism. Nevertheless, it is important to remember that most of those who immigrated to Israel did so in search of a better life, free from antisemitism, rather than for any purpose of identity reconstruction. With the creation of the State of Israel in 1948—only a few years after countless Europeans intentionally destroyed thousands of Jewish communities, large and small—the dynamic of Jewish nationalism in the diaspora changed permanently. Not only did Jewish life in Europe prove more fragile than even cautious diaspora nationalists imagined, but the national project in Israel, whatever its problems, was an evident success. Zionists and non-Zionists of different stripes—liberals and socialists, religious and secular—may not have put aside their differences in 1948, but they had for the most part come to see value in, and an urgent need for, the refuge provided by Jewish territorial self-determination. There are no doubt exceptions to this rule. In France in the 1970s, for example, Richard Marienstras questioned the very process through which Zionism became the sole expression of Jewish nationalism. He depicted Zionism as the triumph of statism among Jewish ideologies, and as an antistatist leftist, he saw Jewish diaspora nationalism as potentially not only an alternative to Zionism, but also as a model for minorities resisting state nationalism in Europe. Marienstras claimed not to oppose either Zionism or the State of Israel, but he objected to the centrality of Zionism in Jewish national identification.[43] This is an argument that has many recent echoes in the United States.[44]

Clearly not all Jews after 1948 viewed themselves as Israeli or Zionist, or even identified personally with the state (Zionism, of course, also produced and sustained Jewish anti-Zionism, both secular and religious). Nevertheless, for Jews who did, and do, feel a sense of national consciousness, Israel became the logical outlet for all national needs. There was a certain inevitability to the fact that Israeli symbols would become Jewish national symbols, an inevitability that only a small number of Jews resisted. The flag, the anthem, and the Hebrew language, to name just a few important examples, superseded all other national symbols for Jews in the diaspora. When Jews could take a ship or airplane to their ancestral homeland and arrive in a secular Jewish state, with Jewish national symbols and language rooted in religious consciousness, Dubnov's exhortations about the misuse of Jewish history by Zionists became irrelevant. Whether the Jewish condition in the diaspora was natural or unnatural, the Zionists proved the Jews could become a political and territorial nation. To some, the Jewish renaissance, or the creation of a new national culture, became solidly rooted in Tel Aviv and Jerusalem, and in Degania and Ein Hashofet. Yet in the global centers of great Jewish concentration, in Paris, London, and Moscow, and in New York and Toronto, to say nothing of the many smaller communities elsewhere, Jews also continue to create distinctly Jewish culture, construct evolving Jewish identities, and preserve Jewish communal structures.

Israel declared independence in May 1948; in September the first secular Jewish university in the United States opened to educate its first class of students, taking the name of the country's most prominent Zionist, Supreme Court Justice Louis Brandeis. Building a secular Jewish university—a "national" university to liberals, a "people's" university to socialists—had been a central aim of diaspora nationalists in Eastern Europe. In the United States, the founders of Brandeis University took on the more modest task of creating a Jewish-sponsored university that would be open to all, in the typically American tradition of privately sponsored colleges.[45] Simon Rawidowicz joined the Brandeis faculty in 1951, and in 1953 he became the first chair of its program in Near Eastern and Judaic Studies. Around the time he moved to Brandeis, Rawidowicz began work on his magnum opus, *Bavel ve'Yerushalayim (Babylon and Jerusalem)*; he had almost completed its two volumes when he passed away, in 1957. The central premise underlying the work is that the religious and cultural creativity that began in Babylon during the first exile continued even after Israel reconstituted the Temple in Jerusalem, and it became the source of a national identity that could sustain the loss of political sovereignty. Rawidowicz had long advocated both Zionism and diaspora nationalism, the construction of Jewish national culture in both "Jerusalem" and "Babylon." Although he had also long opposed the "negation of the *galut*," after 1948 he became particularly concerned with articulating why eternal Babylon should continue to be woven into the threads of the New Jerusalem being built in Israel. He wrote: "As long as Babylon remains open, neither she nor Israel shall perish . . . She must be characterized by a perpetual motion, the motion of Israel in the world. This is the way of Israel in her wholeness, of man in his wholeness, of the world in its wholeness." While the negation of the *galut* is no longer a pressing issue to most Jews, inside or outside of Israel, the question of Babylon and Jerusalem's wholeness—the unity of the people of Israel—has by no means been resolved.

Notes

1. "The End of the Jewish People," a dialogue between Joey Kurtzman and Jack Wertheimer, June 11–20, 2007, www.jewcy.com/religion-and-beliefs/joey1.

2. For a different view, see Moshe Behar and Zvi Ben-Dor Benite's anthology, *Modern Middle Eastern Jewish Thought*, forthcoming in the Brandeis Library of Modern Jewish Thought.

3. See Rebecca Kobrin, "The 1905 Revolution Abroad: Mass Migration, Russian Jewish Liberalism, and American Jewry, 1903–1914," and Eli Lederhendler, "Democracy and Assimilation: The Jews, America, and the Russian Crisis from Kishinev to the End of World

War I," in *The Revolution of 1905 and Russia's Jews*, ed. Stefani Hoffman and Ezra Mendelsohn (Philadelphia: University of Pennsylvania Press, 2008), 227–54.

4. The Greek origin of "diaspora" is "to sow" or "to scatter," and Robin Cohen suggests that the Greeks used the term to describe colonization and expansion and therefore saw it positively (*Global Diasporas: An Introduction* [Seattle: University of Washington Press, 1997], 2). On the evolution of the word's meaning in English with an eye to recent "theories of 'diaspora,'" see Rogers Brubaker, "The 'Diaspora' Diaspora," *Ethnic and Racial Studies* 28, no. 1 (2005): 1–19.

5. Yosef Hayim Yerushalmi, *Zakhor: Jewish History and Jewish Memory* (Seattle: University of Washington Press, 1996).

6. Ibid., 57–75. See also Gershom Scholem, *Major Trends in Jewish Mysticism* (New York: Schocken, 1995), 244–86. The Lurianic precept of God's exile following creation expands on the idea developed in the Babylonian Talmud (BT) that the Second Temple's destruction resulted in God's exile (and therefore the end of prophecy). See David Biale, *Power and Powerlessness in Jewish History* (New York: Schocken, 1986), 36, citing BT, Megillah 29b and Yoma 69b.

7. See Haya Bar-Itzhak, *Jewish Poland—Legends of Origin: Ethnopoetics and Legendary Chronicles* (Detroit, MI: Wayne State University Press, 2001).

8. Heinrich Graetz, "The Stages in the Evolution of Messianic Belief," in Heinrich Graetz, *The Structure of Jewish History and Other Essays*, trans. and ed. Ismar Schorsch (New York: Jewish Theological Seminary of America, 1975), 151–71. See also Biale, *Power and Powerlessness in Jewish History*, 27–43. For a thoughtful exposition on the relevance of exile to biblical, rabbinic, and modern Jewish thought, see Arnold Eisen, *Galut: Modern Jewish Reflection on Homelessness and Homecoming* (Bloomington: Indiana University Press, 1986). For the classic study on the concept of exile from antiquity until the early modern period, see Yitzhak Baer, *Galut*, trans. Robert Warshow (New York: Schocken, 1947).

9. In English, see Ahad Ha 'Am, "The Negation of the Diaspora," in *The Zionist Idea: A Historical Analyis and Reader*, ed. Arthur Hertzberg (Garden City, NY: Doubleday, 1959), 270–77; Simon Dubnow, "The Affirmation of the Diaspora," in *Nationalism and History: Essays on Old and New Judaism*, ed. Koppel S. Pinson (Philadelphia: Jewish Publication Society of America, 1958), 182–91.

10. Simon Rawidowicz, "Jewish Existence: The End and the Endless," in Simon Rawidowicz, *State of Israel, Diaspora, and Jewish Continuity: Essays on the "Ever-Dying People*," ed. Benjamin Ravid, foreword by Michael A. Meyer (Waltham, MA: Brandeis University Press, 1998), 80.

11. Ibid.

12. Anita Shapira, "Whatever Became of 'Negating Exile?,'" in *Israeli Identity in Transition*, ed. Anita Shapira (Westport, CT: Praeger, 2004), 87.

13. Ibid., 100.

14. Simon Rawidowicz, "Two That Are One," in Rawidowicz, *State of Israel, Diaspora, and Jewish Continuity*, 147–61.

15. For example, Eretz Yisrael "in the Byzantine period," or "in the Ottoman period" (Baruch Kimmerling, "Academic History Caught in the Cross-Fire," *History & Memory* 7, no. 1 [1995]: 48). Pnina Lahav points out that the very use of Eretz Yisrael in Israel's Proclamation of Independence as the geographic term to describe the place preceding the state served to

"implicitly banish the term Palestine" ("'A Jewish State . . . to Be Known as the State of Israel': Notes on Israeli Legal Historiography," *Law and History Review* 19, no. 2 (2001): 402.

16. There is a certain unintentional irony here, given that in the original context in Deuteronomy, as previously mentioned, the Lord warns the Israelites that dispersion will be their punishment for failing to observe the laws. On the other hand, in a Zionist reading of the Tower of Babel story, Daniel Gordis argues that "to scatter" (the verb root n-f-tz) is used three times in just nine verses to emphasize "God's objective, the 'branching out' of mankind into distinct peoples" ("The Tower of Babel and the Birth of Nationhood," *Azure*, Spring 2010, 27). Today, *pezura*, the modern descendent of this usage, describes others, most commonly the Palestinians (the Israeli Hebrew term for the Palestinian diaspora is *ha'pezura ha'palestinit*), but only rarely the Jews. Interestingly, the distinction between *tfutsot* and *pezura* existed in 1948 but evolved further thereafter. The second line of the Proclamation of Independence reads: "After being forcibly exiled from their land, the people kept faith with it throughout their Dispersion" (in Hebrew, *pezurav*)." Yet later in the document the term *ha'tfutsot* is used to describe "the Jewish people throughout the Diaspora" (in Hebrew, *ha'am ha'yehudi be'kol ha'tfutsot*). See http://www.knesset.gov.il/docs/heb/megilat.htm for the Hebrew text of the proclamation, and http://www.knesset.gov.il/docs/eng/megilat_eng.htm for the English text. By casting exile as a political rather than a divine condition, Pnina Lahav argues that the words "forcibly exiled from their land" represents victory for the secular Zionists. Lahav also notes several significant discrepancies between the original Hebrew text of the proclamation and its official English translation ("'A Jewish State . . . to Be Known as the State of Israel,'" 421, 430–32).

17. "The Road to True Reforms," Smolenskin's chapter following the two excerpted as a selection in this volume, recommends in rather vague terms a reform conducted from the ground up, to teach the people the Torah and see what they would create from it.

18. See Israel Bartal, *The Jews of Eastern Europe, 1772–1881*, trans. Chaya Naor (Philadelphia: University of Pennsylvania Press, 2005), 91–92. The literature on the early Haskala is vast and growing. Although there are considerable differences of emphasis on the Haskala's origins (for example, where Shmuel Feiner sees secularization, David Sorkin sees religious reform) and its transformative impact, all scholars stress its focus on Jewish sources. See, for example, Shmuel Feiner, *The Jewish Enlightenment*, trans. Chaya Naor (Philadelphia: University of Pennsylvania Press, 2004); David Sorkin, *Moses Mendelssohn and the Religious Enlightenment* (Berkeley: University of California Press, 1996); Shmuel Feiner and David Sorkin, eds., *New Perspectives on the Haskalah* (London: Littman Library of Jewish Civilization, 2001). With particular attention to Eastern Europe, see Immanuel Etkes, "Le'she'elat mevasrei ha'haskala be-mizrah eropa," in *Ha'Dat veha'hayim: tenu'at ha'Haskala ha'Yehudit be'Mizrah Eropa*, ed. Immanuel Etkes (Jerusalem: Zalman Shazar Center, 1993), 25–44; Nancy Sinkoff, *Out of the Shtetl: Making Jews Modern in the Polish Borderlands* (Providence, RI: Brown Judaic Studies, 2004); David E. Fishman, *Russia's First Modern Jews: The Jews of Shklov* (New York: New York University Press, 1995); Marcin Wodziński, *Haskalah and Hasidism in the Kingdom of Poland: A History of Conflict*, trans. Sarah Cozens (Oxford: Littman Library of Jewish Civilization, 2005).

19. Israel Bartal, "Autonomie, autonomisme, diasporisme," in *Les juifs et le XXe siècle: dictionnaire critique*, ed. Élie Barnavi and Saul Friedländer (Paris: Calmann-Lévy, 2000), 40.

20. For example, in an article about the meaning of the Uganda controversy, David Vital suggests that in the early debates over where, geographically, Zionism should focus its energy, the major division between various versions of Zionism came down to the question of whether the goals of Zionism should be to create a fundamentally "New Society" (in Herzl's words) or to reshape Jewish society in a way that preserved as many historic continuities as possible. Nonetheless, Vital suggests several points in which all Zionists were in full agreement: "that the Emancipation had failed to liberate the Jews; that, accordingly, the course of Jewish history must be reversed; that the *rule* of Exile must be ended and the Diaspora—all or most of it—wound up; and that, finally, by the setting apart of a defined territory into which the Jews would gather as a majority people, they would begin to govern themselves" ("The Afflictions of the Jews and the Afflictions of Zionism: The Meaning and Consequences of the 'Uganda' Controversy," in *Essential Papers on Zionism*, ed. Jehuda Reinharz and Anita Shapira [New York: New York University Press, 1996], 123).

21. In one of the better known works from the period, Martin Buber framed the Jewish Renaissance as a messianic reawakening of the Jewish soul that would do away with the mentality, though not the physical reality, of exile, and argued that Hasidism and Haskala were the two extant modern manifestations of Jewish renaissance, both having emerged due to the erosion of Jewish autonomy ("On the [Jewish] Renaissance," in *The Martin Buber Reader: Essential Writings*, ed. Asher Biemann [New York: Palgrave MacMillan, 2002], 139–44). See also Asher Biemann, "The Problem of Tradition and Reform in Jewish Renaissance and Renaissancism," *Jewish Social Studies* 8, no. 1 (2001): 58–87, and *Inventing New Beginnings: On the Idea of Renaissance in Modern Judaism* (Stanford: Stanford University Press, 2009).

22. See the classic work on this synthesis (focusing on Russian Jewry), Jonathan Frankel's *Prophecy and Politics: Socialism, Nationalism, and the Russian Jews, 1862–1917* (Cambridge: Cambridge University Press, 1981).

23. Hess's philosemitism represented a complete reversal from the 1840s, when he associated with Marx, Engels, and the other Young Hegelians. Hess's "On Capital," which Marx read before composing "On the Jewish Question," claimed Judaism originated with a cult of blood sacrifice (transformed into money sacrifice). On Hess, see Frankel, *Prophecy and Politics*, 6–28; Isaiah Berlin, "The Life and Opinions of Moses Hess," in *Essential Papers on Jews and the Left*, ed. Ezra Mendelsohn (New York: New York University Press, 1997), 21–57; Shlomo Avineri, *Moses Hess: Prophet of Communism and Zionism* (New York: New York University Press, 1985); Ken Koltun-Fromm, *Moses Hess and Modern Jewish Identity* (Bloomington: Indiana University Press, 2001).

24. Frankel, *Prophecy and Politics*, 266.

25. Dubnov also uses exactly this expression in the essay included here, "Jews as a Spiritual (Cultural-Historical) Nation among Political Nations," but the term "national suicide" in place of "assimilation" was ubiquitous in the late nineteenth century and can be seen in the writing of Dubnov's and Zhitlowsky's contemporaries, such as Moshe Leib Lilienblum and Nahman Syrkin.

26. See Frankel, *Prophecy and Politics*, 288–328.

27. See David E. Fishman, *The Rise of Modern Yiddish Culture* (Pittsburgh: University of Pittsburgh Press, 2005), 53–55; and "Tehiyat ha-kehila: ha-kehila be-mahashava ha-leumit

ba-gola," in *Kehal Yisrael: ha'shilton ha'atsmi ha'Yehudi le'dorotav*, ed. Israel Bartal (Jerusalem: Merkaz Zalman Shazar), 3:241-45.

28. The journal *Vozrozhdenie* was published in 1904. See also *Vozrozhdenie. (Evreiskii proletariat i natsional'naia problema). Sbornik statei* (London, 1905).

29. See Joshua D. Zimmerman, *Poles, Jews, and the Politics of Nationality: The Bund and the Polish Socialist Party in Late Tsarist Russia, 1892–1914* (Madison: University of Wisconsin Press, 2004).

30. Kenneth B. Moss, *Jewish Renaissance in the Russian Revolution* (Cambridge: Harvard University Press, 2009), 4.

31. Lestschinsky also published *Undzere natsyonale foderungen* (our national demands) in Warsaw in 1918.

32. On Jews, socialism, and the early years of the Soviet Union, see Moss, *Jewish Renaissance in the Russian Revolution*; Zvi Y. Gitelman, *Jewish Nationality and Soviet Politics: The Jewish Sections of the CPSU, 1917–1930* (Princeton: Princeton University Press, 1972); David Shneer, *Yiddish and the Creation of Soviet Jewish Culture* (Cambridge: Cambridge University Press, 2004); Yuri Slezkine, *The Jewish Century* (Princeton: Princeton University Press, 2004); Mikhail Beizer, *Evrei Leningrada, 1917–1939: natsional'naia zhizn i sovietizatsiia* (Moscow: Mosty kul'tury/Gesharim, 1999).

33. See Paula Hyman, "Was There a 'Jewish Politics' in Western and Central Europe?" in *The Quest for Utopia: Jewish Political Ideas and Institutions through the Ages*, ed. Zvi Gitelman (Armonk, NY: M. E. Sharpe, 1992), 109, 114.

34. Jewish nationalism in Turkey, while ostensibly Zionist, in Aron Rodrigue's terms, "appears in fact much closer to the diaspora nationalism of Dubnov. It constituted a modern reformulation of the traditional Ottoman paradigm within which the Jewish *millet*, restored to its corporate autonomy, would coexist with other groups within a multi-ethnic and multireligious empire" ("From *Millet* to Minority: Turkish Jewry," in *Paths of Emancipation: Jews, States, and Citizenship*, ed. Pierre Birnbaum and Ira Katznelson [Princeton: Princeton University Press, 1995], 255).

35. Israel Bartal, *Kozak ve-Bedvi: "am" ve-"erets" ba-le'umiyut ha-Yehudit* (Tel Aviv: Am Oved, 2007), 152–66.

36. Ibid., 169.

37. See Noam Pianko, *Zionism and the Roads Not Taken: Rawidowicz, Kaplan, Kohn* (Bloomington: Indiana University Press, 2010).

38. Biale, *Power and Powerlessness in Jewish History*, 192. See also David Biale, "The Melting Pot and Beyond: Jews and the Politics of American Identity," in *Insider/Outsider: American Jews and Multiculturalism*, ed. David Biale, Michael Galchinsky, and Susannah Heschel (Berkeley: University of California Press, 1998), 18.

39. Though neither Bourne nor Dewey was Jewish, both developed their ideas on cultural pluralism in *Menorah Journal*. Bourne called his famous term "trans-nationalism" a "Jewish idea," and he acknowledged Kallen as its inspiration. On Kallen, Dewey, and Bourne's relationship, see Mitchell Cohen, "In Defense of Shaatnez: A Politics for Jews in a Multicultural America," in *Insider/Outsider*, 37–42; David A. Hollinger, *Postethnic America: Beyond Multiculturalism*, 10th anniversary ed. (New York: Basic, 2005), 92–101.

40. See James Loeffler, "Between Zionism and Liberalism: Oscar Janowsky and Diaspora Nationalism in America," *AJS Review* 34, no. 2 (2010): 289–308.

41. Matthew Fishbane, "Elevated," *Tablet*, August 12, 2010 (http://www.tabletmag.com).

42. Anthony Smith, "Zionism and Diaspora Nationalism," *Israel Affairs* 2, no. 2 (1995): 15.

43. Marienstras was also responding to the practical question of Zionist control of French Jewish communal institutions. See Richard Marienstras, *Être un peuple en diaspora* (Paris: F. Maspero, 1975).

44. See, for example, Pianko's epilogue in *Zionism and the Roads Not Taken*; Caryn Aviv and David Shneer, *New Jews: The End of the Jewish Diaspora* (New York: New York University Press, 2005). A Palestinian antistatism with certain similarities can also be seen in Sari Nusseibeh, *What Is a Palestinian State Worth?* (Cambridge: Harvard University Press, 2011).

45. See Abram Sachar, *Brandeis University: A Host at Last* (Waltham, MA: Brandeis University Press, 1995).

From Haskala to National Renaissance

1

The Eternal People
Perets Smolenskin

"Am olam," in *Ma'amarim* (Jerusalem: Hotsa'at Keren Smolenskin, 1925), 1:1–162.

By the time Perets Smolenskin (1842–85) penned his essay "The Eternal People" in 1872, he had already played a central role in changing the direction of the Haskala, or Jewish Enlightenment. Although Smolenskin was born and raised in the Russian Empire and first became seriously engaged with the intellectual questions of his day while living in Odessa (1862–67), he then settled in Vienna, where he published a monthly periodical, *Ha-Shahar* (The dawn). *Ha-Shahar*, which Smolenskin founded in 1868 and published until his death, featured prose and poetry, literary and cultural criticism, and political essays, all in Hebrew. Smolenskin was motivated by what he saw as a move away from the use of Hebrew as a Jewish cultural language by proponents of the Haskala. Through *Ha-Shahar*, Smolenskin sought nothing less than to save the Haskala from itself. As he saw it, the universalism and antinationalism of many Jewish intellectuals represented an even greater danger to Jews than did those who were devoutly religious and antimodern (by their own definition).

Like many following him, Smolenskin saw Judaism as having historically served the primary purpose of preserving Jewish national self-consciousness in the diaspora. As such, he believed that those trying to reform Judaism to make it more acceptable to non-Jews would inevitably erode the essence of what preserved the Jews as a nation. Smolenskin later became a leading Lover of Zion and made some of the earliest arguments for Jews settling Palestine to serve nationally regenerative ends. But his proto-Zionism flowed naturally from the earlier arguments that he formulated in "The Eternal People" and other essays about how Jews historically preserved their nationality in the diaspora; why they could not and should not attempt to erase their nationality; and how the road to emancipation would come through Jewish nationalism in the diaspora, rather than through assimilation. Though these ideas would later become tethered to Zionism (mostly by others), when Smolenskin formulated them he did so without any intention of tying Jewish nationalism to geography. He spoke about Judaism as spiritual nationalism and quite explicitly argued that what made the Jews unique was that their nationalism was *not* dependent on either geography or politics.

Smolenskin's principal argument in "The Eternal People," and the one that would make the greatest impact in Jewish intellectual circles, was for a secular understanding of Jewish peoplehood, or nation, in the diaspora. In "The Eternal People," we find Smolenskin grappling with the question of what to do if one is personally secular but sees the essence of Jewish nationhood preserved in Judaism. What is the route to enlightenment for the secular Jew who sees the Jews as a Jewish nation? At this stage, much of the answer for Smolenskin lay in language and culture. He believed that earlier attempts by *maskilim* to turn Hebrew into a modern Jewish literary language were at the heart of the true Haskala. Yet he also talked more abstractly about the continued role of the laws and prayer as a link to the past and as a way of uniting the Jews as a people. As Shmuel Feiner has pointed out, when Smolenskin talks about Torah in "The Eternal People" and elsewhere, he means a spiritual system bonding all Jews together through the collective historical memory recorded in it. The parallels that Smolenskin draws to radical reform gone awry in the German Reformation and French Revolution are meant as a warning to all who seek a dramatic break with the past.

Smolenskin wrote "The Eternal People" not long after anti-Jewish violence shook Odessa in 1871. The fact that Jews could be violently victimized in this cosmopolitan city, where they played such a prominent role in public life, confirmed his doubts about the future of religious tolerance. He felt that it was time to reject all understandings of the Jewish people as a religious creed rather than a nation. In the essay, he reserves his greatest ire for the German Jewish reformers who sought actively to change the meaning of Judaism. His long discourse about religious changes in German-speaking lands focuses on attempts to change what it means to be Jewish in order to suit others. In particular, Smolenskin argues against any attempt to neuter the Jewish hope for collective redemption, a religious precept with a national and religious meaning unique to Judaism and a hope uniting all Jews. Smolenskin sees German reform not merely in the costume, but in the spirit, of Protestantism. The intended result, denationalization, would only weaken the Jewish position vis-à-vis non-Jews. In doing so, Smolenskin may have been the first intellectual to demand publicly that Jews be emancipated on their own terms. Foremost in Smolenskin's mind were the Jews of the Russian Empire, and he desired them not to forsake their Jewish spiritual nationalism for an ephemeral civil equality (there is a certain irony in Smolenskin's claim of Jews steadfastly holding to religion in the East, given that such a path certainly did not reflect his own reality). *Ha-Shahar* was widely read in Jewish intellectual circles throughout Europe, and "The Eternal People" in particular became both a formative text and a rallying cry for disillusioned *maskilim*, new nationalists, Jewish socialists, and many others who sought to counter assimilation with a Jewish Renaissance. Below are selections from chapters 14 and 15 of "The Eternal People."

How Is This Time Different from All Other Times?

It is apparent that the cornerstone that has supported the entire House of Israel throughout time was the Torah. She was the breath of life that revived his collapsing body, and in her he found salvation and consolation for all his sorrows.[1] The more he was denied life's pleasures and the more the light of freedom and justice dimmed, the more he found in the Torah delight and contentment, light and freedom, and she became his refuge and stronghold. And she united his heart and his spirit as a country to its kingdom. Therefore, he was not lost among the nations, even during times of terrible distress, because he found in it all that a nation would find in its land and kingdom. If not for the prophets and sages who rose to offer him the Torah as a safe haven in place of the land and the Temple, and if not for the sages who during the Second Temple wars infused the people's hearts with love for the Torah to replace their love of the land, and if not for the *Tannaim* and *Amoraim* and the rest of the sages who continue raising up the banner of Torah to this day, there is no doubt that any remnant or memory of this people would have been lost by now.[2] Not even the hope alone for future salvation could have sustained his heart had not the Torah been his delight. No doubt after hundreds of years of shameful crises the power of faith would have diminished had not the Torah kept it alive. If not for their beloved Torah, the misfortunes they endured would have depressed and pressured them to renounce their origins. Guarding the Torah provided them with capacity to suffer for her sake, and the misfortune also helped strengthen them in this terrible struggle. Because the Torah has been his breath of life, keeping his spirit and body alive up to this day, this can also solve the great puzzle, "How has Israel

1. [Throughout the essay, Smolenskin allegorically represents the people or House of Israel (*Bet Yisrael*) as a husband and wife. Because in Hebrew the gender of Israel is masculine and that of the Torah feminine, "he" and "she" can be read simply as "it" (Hebrew has no neutral gender). However, the anthropomorphized context here suggests the allegorical rendering.]

2. [*Tannaim* and *Amoraim* are names for several generations of rabbinic sages from the first centuries CE who were responsible for what would become one of the central texts of Judaism, the Talmud.]

dwelt among the nations at times of distress and succeeded in holding onto his faith in spite of all his enemies and expulsions?" The Torah has surrounded him with fences and forts, keeping his enemies away at times of mortal danger and infusing him with a spirit of life and liberty at calmer times, at moments of relief; thus it has been since then till now.

And if we judge by this we will surely conclude that no reforms or innovations were necessary since the people would choose this way of life according to their time. When given some rest would not they on their own, with no stimulant or inducement, take the yoke off their shoulders, as we can see happening these days? The many laws, not only those added by the later generations but also the original ones written in the Torah, would not bridle many, since many follow the desires in their hearts either covertly or openly and do whatever they wish with no reference to religious law. This has taken place not only in this generation but in previous generations as well, the moment their surrounding adversaries relented. At the time when life was calm for Israel in Spain, they threw the Torah's yoke off their necks and vied to emulate the people in whose midst they dwelt. Reliable evidence to that effect can be found in the Musar literature directed at those who strayed from the path of their religion by the sages of Israel from that time.[3] Just as they did, so many do in our generation. For the Musar literature sometimes sounds as if this generation had spoken it.

It is true that even if the ways of this generation resemble the ways of past generations during peaceful times, there is still a big difference between them. In the past, when plenty and comfort made people choose a new life, they chose it of their own will with no intention of changing their religion or faith or eliminating the statutes from the sacred texts, in order to have one law permitting for all people that which had been forbidden until then. The wealthy and the great did what their hearts desired, but we can confidently assert that had any rabbi intended to publicly lift one of the prohibitions, even the most insignificant, those great and wealthy who themselves threw the yoke of religious law off their necks would have surely risen against him to frustrate his counsel, as happens today in most Russian and Polish towns. Those wealthy who cast off all restrictions and do as they please with no fear are the ones who like zealots would always rise in defense of religion so not a pebble falls to the ground. They threw off their

3. [Musar literature, often called "ethical literature," is a genre of instructional Jewish texts covering all aspects of everyday life. The tradition of composing Musar texts began in the medieval period and continued to be popular through the modern period, as some maskilim adopted the genre in the nineteenth century.]

yoke because they were rich and therefore exempt from this burden. However, if a rabbi or a school teacher or one of those who depends on others' opinions would allow himself even a minute digression, then they would holler and displace him and cut off his livelihood, because by their might they have captured Karnaim, believing that the universe has been created just for them.[4] And since only they are entitled to enjoy life, how could the poor dare claim their share? And not only in the land of Russia and Poland, but also in Ashkenaz there are many who refer to themselves as "the strong ones" (Orthodox) shouting at the top of their voices all day long: thwart any free thinking, thwart inquiry and understanding, while in their own way of life they go along with the reformers and pay no mind to law or faith.[5] And they all do it out of malice, for as they are miserly about giving their poor brethren any of their wealth, so too they will not give them any freedom either. And this is how they had been in previous generations as well, except that at that time the rich and other pursuers of liberty kept liberty to themselves. Whereas now, when the spirit of freedom has taken over the whole world, when nations and individuals strive together to break off their bondage, supporting one another because ideas of love and brotherhood have penetrated their hearts, so too do many people of Israel who seek freedom and liberation. They do so not only for themselves, but rather for all people, small and large, rich and poor. The fact that reformers forcefully seek, unlike ever before, to do away with many of the rules is what makes this time different from the rest. Furthermore, since whether he wanted to or not Jacob has been small and weak, separated and spread among the nations, he has emulated the nations among whom he has dwelt.[6] Because his numbers were small he leaned

4. [See Amos 6.13. Karnaim is a biblical place in the land of Bashan; it was conquered by Israel at various points in biblical history. The name literally means "horns," a symbol of strength in the Hebrew Bible. The Amos quotation "—Did we not capture Karnaim/horns by our own strength/might?"—is often interpreted as an assertion of arrogance. Smolenskin adopts this biblical allusion to criticize what he sees as the arrogance of certain wealthy and powerful Jews who, while not observant themselves, insist that others follow Jewish law with rabbinic rigidity.]

5. [Smolenskin uses the term Ashkenaz here—the Hebrew term for the Jewish communities of the Rhine Valley. Since he occasionally uses the term Germania elsewhere in the essay, he most probably uses Ashkenaz to denote German-speaking Jewry in Central Europe broadly.]

6. [This section is a prime example of Smolenskin's approach to biblical literature. The language used here does not reflect any particular biblical text but rather is a patchwork of references and imitative style.]

toward the majority. In previous generations, therefore, when nations held fast to their faith and no one dared to question their lawmakers and priests lest he burn at the stake, making changes to the religion did not occur to anyone among Israel. Each did what his heart desired, ignoring the religious laws, but never attempting to openly change them and pronounce the forbidden to be permitted. Not so in recent times. Ever since reformers began to rise time and again among the nations, and began to break up into associations and groups according to their beliefs, they have been changing the face of religion from day to day.[7] The children of Israel observed this and decided (as usual) to do the same, and since religious reforms are held in high esteem these days, they decided that they too would like to share in this great honor lest they be looked down upon as falling behind their time. So this is the correct answer to the question we posed: "How is this time different from all other times?" And this answer will also solve the second question: "Why is it that only the land of Ashkenaz has produced seekers of reform and not other countries?" For most of the reformers originated in Ashkenaz and so too, up to this day, have most rebels against the Father in Rome and his decrees. So it follows that the Jews rose there to do the same. However there is one more correct answer to this question.

About a hundred years have passed since new ideas about freedom and liberty began to find a way into the hearts of all nations. The Middle Ages, the days of slavery, those bad days in which all people were considered mere slaves of the rulers, created for doing slave labor for kings, priests and noblemen, with no law or justice known in the land, those bad days have vanished and passed away ever since nations started making changes in their beliefs and throwing off the yoke of their priests who arrogantly trod them underfoot. From then on, the love of freedom started taking root in nations' hearts and they aimed at throwing off the burden of all noblemen and rulers, just as they had done with the priests.

The land of Britain was the first to fight for freedom and liberty. These ideas expanded and strengthened during the war of independence in America, and from America they came also to France, which had been suppressed under the feet of brazen rulers obeying the Father in Rome. And a new declaration became a light unto the nations: "liberty, brotherhood and one justice for all," they called

---

7. [Smolenskin argues that Jewish reform mimics Christian reform. He refers here both to the sixteenth-century Reformation initiated by Martin Luther and the gradual process of Christian secularization spurred by the seventeenth-century Christian Enlightenment.]

out publicly.[8] And during this struggle many compassionate people observed that dwelling among them was the remnant of a plundered nation, which had been oppressed and tormented more than any other was oppressed, slaves to the slaves. And while breaking their own chains off their feet, they rose to rescue [this remnant] from their distress as well. Furthermore, understanding the severity of the struggle ahead, as the clerics and noblemen had intended to fight with all their might not to let their prey out of their jaws, the freedom lovers realized that they needed allies and supporters in their struggle, and that the Jews had the power to help them, as they did not revere the clerics and nobles who had trod upon them like dust. And there is no doubt that now, at an auspicious time, they would fight them with all their might in order to free themselves, and they will not favor the clerics as many of the other nations would. Many of the nations, even when fighting for freedom with all their hearts, will nevertheless sometimes back away from restraining the clerics for fear of infuriating their fathers and mothers or their wives whose hearts are drawn to the priests. But not so the children of Israel, their hearts will not weaken in this struggle knowing that if they succeed they will have peace and security, and if they fail they will become the slaves of slaves again, plundered and looted as they have been for over a millennium.

This has become the children of Israel's deliverance in many countries, and they have been promoted like all the rest of the residents to be considered faithful sons of their land. And indeed they were loyal sons to their country; they never ceased wholeheartedly serving their liberty-respecting countries ever since. And they became soldiers in war, teachers in institutions of scholarship, law experts, administrators in governments, just like their fellow citizens. Their faith did not get in the way and they did all that the times and their situation asked of them. Therefore, their many religious laws were not considered an obstruction for them and they felt no need to change them, since they had posed no obstacle for them either at home or in public. Each would do at home as he wishes, he who accepts these laws would hold fast to them and he who does not find them pleasing will discard them since no one would impose this burden on him. In public, nothing will weigh them down, since the people among whom they dwell care mainly about love and liberty rather than faith. And the

8. [Smolenskin takes the phrase "light unto the nations" from the biblical book of Isaiah, in which the people of Israel is selected to serve as a source of moral guidance for the rest of the world. The biblical context also includes the promise to restore Israel to Zion.]

laws of love and liberty mean letting each one choose his way according to his wish. This is what came to pass in the countries where they reached the status of citizens, equal to the rest of the inhabitants. However, in those countries that had not as yet awakened from their deep sleep and still slumber calmly, in those prison-like countries, they remained unaware as their eyelids had been covered by the shadow of death, and had not yet seen the light of freedom. Over there it never occurred to the children of Israel to touch even one of their religious laws, since this was their only heritage, having no other legacy in their lives. And as they have always clung traditionally to their faith with all their might at times of misfortune, so have they done these days, since they continue to experience great hardship.

However, this was not the fate of those dwelling in the parts of Ashkenaz situated at the midpoint between both extremes: between the nations who bravely obtained freedom and those who still moan under the scepter of their rulers and will not dare raise their voices. Here, wars have erupted every so often between the rulers and the population, but the people are usually defeated and their rulers have laid even heavier burdens upon them. Therefore, the wars never ceased and the people never realized their will, and there was no deliverance for Israel either.

Furthermore, most countries that fought for freedom obeyed the Father in Rome and the clerics appointed by him, and at first the struggle was aimed against them. So the fighters rushed to liberate Israel so that they could help. Not so in the land of Ashkenaz, in which Luther had freed the people from the chains of the Father in Rome and their fight was aimed at the regime and not the Church and its teachers. Here, Israel was considered useless to the struggle and they were not allowed to participate in it lest they be rewarded afterward and claim a share in the liberty, and also because they greatly resented Israel.

And even though sincere and kind people like Lessing and Dohm and their like were inclined to warm up to Israel, they were a drop in the bucket compared to all the adversaries who wanted all memory of Israel forgotten.[9] It became a common expression used by the enemies of Israel to say as their haters have always said until today: "The Jews do not deserve freedom, let them first learn

9. [Gotthold Ephraim Lessing (1729–81) was a noted German Enlightenment philosopher famous in Jewish history for his close friendship with the Jewish philosopher Moses Mendelssohn (1729–86), often considered the father of the Berlin Haskala. Christian Wilhelm von Dohm (1751–1820) was a German historian who advocated Jewish emancipation, notably in a two-volume treatise called On the Amelioration of the Civil Status of the Jews.]

to become like us before we accept them." This caused a great turmoil within the House of Israel as their religious commandments weighed down upon them at home and in public—at home, because they have already seen some light of freedom even if not theirs, and wished to relieve the burden of their own faith as well—and in public, because they believed the words of their adversaries that becoming like them would bring them closer. So many of the rich rushed to emulate them and gave little thought to the fact that this was a ploy to ensnare them, as it was not enlightenment and understanding that was expected, but religious conversion. Once [the Jews] extended their hand to their foes, they were drawn to them, and little by little distanced themselves from their own religion and abandoned the very faith for which they spilled their blood like water until now. And the straight-hearted[10] see and agonize over them but are unable to help, even though they have tried many times to step into the breach.[11] This is what produced the new desire for religious reforms; first, because lovers of their people and faith believed that this might cure their distressed religion: if some of the religious burden were alleviated, and if it accommodated to modern times, then Israel would not be ashamed of its faith and would keep holding onto it. Second, the sages could find no other path to recognition than becoming religious reformers. In the lands of France, Britain, Holland, and the like, there is hope for a great man of learning from among the Children of Israel to achieve high esteem, since the gates of the court would open for him as a lawyer, or he could become head teacher in the houses of learning, or could distinguish himself in war and become an army officer, or demonstrate his skills in government and become a judge or emissary for the government, and other honorable positions that can be attained by an educated man. However, what could a learned man do in the land of Ashkenaz? He is not suited for any respectable position in the kingdom, nor is he good for teaching in public because he is a Jew, so what can he do with his learning but research his own religion and tradition?[12] And as he researches, he finds many things that are incompatible with modern times,

10. ["Straight-hearted" is a biblical idiom found in Psalms. It means good-hearted or well-meaning.]

11. See *History of Israel*, by the scholar Graetz part 11. [Heinrich Graetz's history was originally published in eleven volumes, concluding in 1870 with Jewish emancipation. An abridged English edition (from 1895) appeared in six volumes.]

12. [Prohibited from holding university professorships, some German Jews instead sought higher education and academic employment at the new modern rabbinical and teaching seminaries.]

and therefore raises his hand against these things, to change and reform them in order to make a name for himself as one of the great [sages]. This is why only in the land of Ashkenaz are there so many research books on the Jewish faith and wisdom and history, since in other countries the young have been brought up to choose professions and serve their country, while in Ashkenaz they were trained only in religious studies and there was no other way for them to distinguish themselves but to become rabbis and preachers for the congregation. And since in the other countries not much research had been done, it did not occur to them to make changes. While in the land of Ashkenaz, where much research in religion had been done, the desire for changes was born.[13]

In this discussion we find the answer to the third question: "Why do the reformers focus mainly on matters of congregation and houses of worship?" Because they believe that they do not deserve to be accepted by the nations, and therefore they make every effort to transform them beyond recognition. And since the ways of worship in the house of God were scorned and ridiculed by the excluders of Israel who always look for a pretext to vilify them, the reformers told themselves that if their houses of prayer would change and become like those of the nations, with organ music playing there in the manner of the nations, then they would be accepted as brothers. And so they made every effort to uproot the deeply planted hope of future deliverance from their hearts, because this hope might identify them as the other, a people that aspires to become a nation on its own land again. Therefore the reformers fear lest the nations say: How can we give them citizenship while they lift their eyes up to their land?[14] So indeed we have heard the haters of Israel say daily. So they conspired to remove all hope from the prayers and entreaties so it will not be mentioned nor remembered anymore, forgotten with time, never to be recalled, only then their slanderers will be silenced, and a relief will come for Israel. This is what should be done according to them. Indeed, whether they have done the right thing and succeeded,

13. [Smolenskin alludes here to the nineteenth-century movement begun in Germany to study Judaism and Jewish history academically, the *Wissenschaft des Judentums* (the science of Judaism). *Wissenschaft des Judentums* aimed to normalize both the academic study of Judaism and the notion of Jews as legitimate academicians, but was criticized by many, including Smolenskin, for being detrimental to Judaism.]

14. [Here Smolenskin again uses biblical language that recalls Psalm 121 ("I lift my eyes up to the hills"), which appears regularly in the Jewish liturgy. He makes this subtle reference as he chastises efforts made by reformers in Germany and elsewhere that sought to remove all references to Zion and messianic redemption from the traditional liturgy.]

or whether they have overpaid for the freedom they seek, having paid in advance before they received their wish, this is what we will discuss now.

A JUDGMENT OF REFORM

[. . .] The Germans' love for all of humanity resembles Don Quixote's love for Dulcinea—it exists only in the realm of fantasy, while the French love of humanity is as one loves gold and silver, for which one would toil to store in his treasuries. The Germans, while talking about humanism, forget that they as well as the rest of the nations are mere human beings who crave honors and status and wealth, and that it would take more than a brief moment to transform all nations into higher beings who would willingly decline it all. Preaching love for all people, they were obligated to include the elimination of all wars from the face of the land in order to make peace between all nations. However, they failed to realize that the rest of the nations were not yet inclined to embrace this idea and would take any opportunity to wage war on them and subjugate them. Only in a land that is ruled by law can one adhere to the straight path. But we cannot do so while lost in a wasteland or in a den of thieves, because then we must fight for our lives even by deceit or by scam, the same way we could preach love of humanity only when it is justly and honestly achievable, when we are being listened to. However, the Germans were not aware of this, and thus only weakened their nation's ability to succeed in war. They tore their country to pieces, into several nation-states, the most disgraceful nation-states of all, and in their time of need they did not help each other. When Napoleon swept over their land they fell into his hands like a fig ripe for the picking.

In contrast, the French, loudly proclaiming love and fraternity, proceeded to wage war against any ruler who oppressed his people—not in order to free that moaning people, but rather to enslave them and their rulers, and to expand their own borders to the ends of the earth. And while waging war they forgot their own teachings, raising taxes and oppressing the conquered people even further.

Both of these nations have long paid for their sins; the Germans for proclaiming an idea but not knowing how to carry it out—for had they known, they would have first strengthened their country against enemies and only then they would have been able to talk about peace. But since they did this from a position of weakness, they enabled their attackers to do as they pleased. And the French have also paid for their deeds—for while forgetting their teachings of love and fraternity and embarking on conquering lands, they followed a leader who succeeded in oppressing nations under his feet, and upon returning from war as a victorious hero he did not rest his sword, but rather swung it over his own people, subjugating them just as he had done to other nations. This was France's reward for robbing other nations of their freedom, as their own liberty was taken away from them.

Only one nation has internalized the lofty idea and was able to act on it as well; this is the nation of Britain, this nation of theory and action combined, who contemplated before taking action. This nation has risen to enhance this noble idea, and to surpass all other nations. This people did not consider hugging and kissing all human beings like the Germans, neither wished to bring them under their wings to subjugate them, as did the French. The British understood that man's first concern is for his own well-being, and after that for his nation, and only then for all human beings, as this is the only way to reach the noble aspiration of benefiting all human beings. The British, while caring for themselves and their people, pursued their liberty within their own land, unburdened the yoke of taxation when they could, and made every effort to improve trade and increase wealth (the greatest guardian of land, people and nation, as wisely argued by the great scholar, Buckle).[15] They refrained from war when they could; they desired neither conquests nor being conquered. When attacked, however, they were quick to demonstrate that no attacker will go unpunished—perhaps Napoleon I will recount the story of their might even in the netherworld. Had all nations acted like they did, surely all wars would have ceased and peace would have reigned on earth. The British, while loving their own people, were able to benefit all people, while the Germans and the French who declared their love of all human beings benefited no one, but harmed their own people instead. Only lately have the Germans begun to understand their ailment and tried to cure it, aspiring to unify their whole kingdom in order to increase their might and thus live fearlessly in peace.

And if we observe the Jews in those countries, we would find that they do just as the nations among whom they dwell, as far as faith and love for their people are concerned.

However, one might ask what do the politics of kingdoms have to do with

15. [Henry Thomas Buckle (1821–62) was an English historian who promoted the application of scientific method to the study of history, including examining a nation's character systematically. His ideas influenced many Jewish nationalist thinkers, notably Simon Dubnov.]

faith? These other nations are divided on matters of land and regime while the Jews are divided only in their faith. Even among their host nations it seems that religion and politics go hand in hand and support each other. All the more so for Israel, whose faith is like a land and a kingdom and a way of life, and whose religious laws and national customs and Torah are one and the same and cannot be separated. Ever since they came and went among the local populations and have learned their languages and observed their ways, they have tried to be like them. So it seems that some of the Children of Israel who dwell [in these lands] are the same as others found among the nations.

The Jews of Britain hold fast to their religious law, they do not overthink, nor ponder, nor examine laws and religion. Not only that, but they embrace all that is theirs and respect the laws of their faith in public, and are not embarrassed. Instead, they take pride in themselves just like the [British] people who would not even think of violating their own sacred laws. Not so the Jews of Germany who, following in the ways of their land's population, exceed in deliberating and investigating the ways of past generations, putting the Torah on trial. When the German critics began criticizing the Holy Scriptures, muddling the writings as they did not understand them, so the Jewish critics rushed to compete with them and did the same. The task of confusing the scriptures became a source of pride and honor and the more one entangles the more praise one deserves, since this is the common way among scholars of the nations. Any person of understanding will laugh seeing the annotations and suppositions made daily by these critics who do not know the rules of the language and do not comprehend what is in front of their own eyes. But why should they care about knowledge? They muddle because muddling is highly regarded. Since they have chosen to follow the locals, they too became attracted to humanism, proclaiming the idea of loving all human beings so that no attention would be paid to nationality and religion, as all people would be of one nation and one religion. And they too have harmed their own people just as the local thinkers had harmed theirs. They too forgot that other strong nations and religions still inhabit the earth, and they are not interested in submitting to this new faith that is being offered to them—the one faith for all. And while the humanists rise up against their own religious faiths and national aspirations, those of the other faiths get encouraged and squander money like dust sending their missionaries to remote corners of the earth in order to lead the children of Israel astray from their faith; not to create one faith on the earth, but rather to bring them under the shadow of their religion.

All this has not been noticed by [the German Jews] and as they degrade their faith, they also continue assisting the instigators in leading the children of Israel astray from their faith to take refuge under the wings of the ruling religion.

Had the religious leaders of every nation risen to instruct their people to abandon their faith in favor of one common faith for all, then it would have been justified to say: we do not want to stand apart. But all other nations remain sheltered by their faith and greatly exalt and promote it with all their might and resources in every way they can, so if the leaders of Israel endorse abandoning faith, they will find attentive ears. However, those heeding their call to abandon the faith will not replace it with a new common faith for everyone, but will rather go and hold on to the prevailing religion, due only to its dominance.

Surely not all people are strong minded and knowledgeable, letting reason alone guide their lives. The masses need a concrete icon rather than a state of mind, and if we take away from the crowd the folly it has held since youth, they would not forget it in favor of a newfound wisdom, but rather they will search for another folly to replace the old one. And just as with any other accepted convention, no man would listen to us if we were to say to him: why do you need to adorn yourself with precious jewels and dress up in fancy clothing, are you not satisfied with your competence to accomplish this and that? Surely he will not pay heed, because he is accustomed to flaunting his wealth by dressing well. The same applies in matters of faith. An educated man who has studied and sought understanding could say to himself: I know that it is not ritual but rather thought that matters most. However, if a common man who does not think deeply is also turned away from his practice, he will have nothing left but to look for another ritual.

This is all so much more the case with a faith that provides one with strength and courage in hard times; in good times he might find it easy to forget his faith, his God, and his people. But when in trouble, in sickness, when overwhelmed by cruelty, then, with no help found on earth, he will raise his eyes to heaven for help and believe in anything. And if he ceases believing in his faith, then he will look for comfort in another faith. This is what came to pass in Germany since the rise of Rabbi Moshe Ben Menachem [Moses Mendelssohn] who embraced the idea of humanism and his family and his followers concurred and agreed with him, but how did they end up? Almost all of them converted; all his family and followers who proclaimed the teachings of humanism did not wait until this idea was accepted by all of humanity.[16] Instead, while renouncing the ways of

16. [Four of Moses Mendelssohn's six children converted to Christianity. Although

their religion, they reached for the dominant religion, and this was the effect of the teachings of Ben Menachem. He and his friend Lessing both expounded upon the idea of humanism and still not one of Lessing's family and not one of his followers or friends converted to Judaism. Why is that? Simply because the supporters and defenders of the ruling religion will not allow anyone to treat it disrespectfully, and having wealth and honor to bestow upon all who seek it, they stand guard like a well-built fortress. Whereas the Jewish religion has no helper and no supporter, no one defends nor sustains it. All its strength originates from within, from its laws and aspirations. After all this had been damaged, after those who were in charge of supporting [Judaism] turned their backs on it and declared that it was time to seek a new faith, what did all the followers of these teachers do but hurry to leave it behind like something useless? And not only like a useless thing but also like a narrow well, because as long as [Judaism] was a dependable source for their way of life and their hopes, as long as they trusted it for support, it was not hard to bear the burden and suffer for it, since it was their ideal. So they did not envy the happiness and success of those of other religions, believing that a day would come when they would be rewarded for their sorrow, and that a pleasant light would shine upon them. But after this hope was shattered, after the Torah ceased being the source of pure spring water to them, why would they foolishly wear out their strength in vain? And therefore they did so—abandoning their faith on the spot and choosing its rival, the one that could provide them with a good life, peace, and respect.

Thus it has been in the land of Germany until this day, while the Jews in the land of France have contemplated unifying all Jews of various countries into one society, turning all of Israel into one alliance, just like the French ambition to unify all countries with theirs (only that the French have desired to subjugate other nations, thus what they did was wrong, but the Jews over there wanted to unite their scattered people, which is the right thing to do).[17]

---

only a few hundred German Jews (mostly from Berlin) converted out of Judaism at the end of the nineteenth century, the practice was most common among prominent society figures, which made such conversion a visible and controversial phenomenon.]

17. [The Alliance Israélite Universelle, an international organization based in France, had as its goal a "civilizing" mission for the Jews of North Africa, the Middle East, and Eastern Europe. They established a network of schools in these places emphasizing both French social ideals and Jewish education. Smolenskin believed the program had the potential to be a Jewish national organization (and not merely a French-Jewish one). He even conducted a mission to Rumania for the organization in 1874. However, Smolenskin

At the same time that the Jews of France aspire to unite their people, the new reformers in Germany proclaim their wish to separate into fragments and to dissolve the only bond connecting all of the Jewish people—its hope for future salvation. Why?[18] Because this hope is what makes them a nation despite not having a land and sovereignty. But according to the reformers, national loyalty contradicts the love of all human beings, and therefore they object to it.

Indeed, those who do object err and sin at the same time: they err as their effort is futile and has no chance to succeed, because no one is capable of ending hope. Only events may put it out of one's mind, but this hope has proven so strong and resilient that no event has ever been powerful enough to kill it. This hope that kept the spirit of Israel alive at all times, even when frustrated from two thousand years of waiting, this hope will never cease to exist in a Jew's heart. And even if [the reformers] succeed in removing it from the hearts of some, many of those would vanish from the House of Israel because with time they or their sons would abandon the faith and depart from the Jewish community. But the rest of the people will keep embracing their faith and their hope and will continue adding fences and fortifications, holding onto it with all their might, as is evident in most cities of southern Germany even today.[19] Also, Jews in the rest of the countries who do not follow in the ways [of the reformers], they too will oppose them and repeal their ideas about this hope.

If that is the case, they have been wrong thinking that they can remove the hope from Israel's heart. They are not only wrong but also guilty of a great sin, intending to kill this hope that has kept the spirit of the people alive at the time of their wanderings, and that still has the power to unify the people in all the countries of their dispersion.[20] If not for this, who knows if families will not depart from the Jewish community in the future? Because just as the life of a person would end after losing all hope and ceasing all activity, so is a nation in

---

criticizes the Alliance elsewhere in "The Eternal People" and even more so after becoming a Zionist.]

18. [For more on Jewish ideas about redemption and salvation, see my introductory essay to this volume.]

19. ["Fences and fortifications" alludes to the Mishnaic proverb (Pirkei Avot 1.1) that instructs the reader to "build a fence around the Torah," commonly interpreted as protecting Jewish law. Smolenskin here refers to the more rural southwestern German states like Württemberg and Alsace, whose Jews did not reform as rapidly as those in Prussia.]

20. [Smolenskin uses the Hebrew word *pizur* for dispersion; only later was *galut* (exile) politicized and used to refer to the diaspora. See my introductory essay to this volume.]

need of hope to keep it alive. And this hope in future redemption has been the source of comfort and salvation from the past until today, at times of calamity and peace. Because of this, it is still needed today and in future days, and now it is needed even more than in the past because until now the bonds of religion were strong. The study of Torah and Jewish tradition had enough authority and power to join their hearts together and keep them as one people. But now that many not only disregard the Torah's commandments but do not even care to study it anymore, and now that the Jewish way of life has been forgotten and each man follows in the ways of his land and its inhabitants, surely if the hope will also be uprooted from their hearts there would not be any bond left to tie them together. And how would they remain one people? Hope is not like laws mandated by religion, which burden us and obstruct our way, since hope stays only in our hearts and demands no action in order to keep it. It will not restrict our activity nor detract from our love of the land we reside in, because it is only a hope and stays only in our hearts. So what could happen if we kept it?

No sensible man of the land would blame or ridicule us for keeping it.[21] On the contrary, a man who forgets his own land and people is the one who is dishonored by everyone, so why forget our land? And even if we doubt that it would ever materialize we nevertheless ought not to remove it from our hearts, as many good ideas have not been realized, and yet we will not stop teaching them and pleading with the young to embrace them. A good idea is good even if not carried out, just as we will not tell a poor man to stop exalting the practice of charity and generosity because of his inability to practice it, so we cannot tell an oppressed nation: abandon your hope of becoming a sovereign people in your land because you are unable to realize your wish. And even if it were true that Israel's salvation and return to its land of old was unattainable, there are many cases in the world that are considered unfeasible today and become possible a few years later. If a hundred years ago someone would have predicted that the small nation, the remnants of the ancient Greeks, who too have been separated and dispersed throughout the world, that this small nation would reestablish its kingdom, or that the nation of Serbia, a despised nation of swineherds, would rise to establish a state, or that the Dark Mountain dwellers (Montenegro), a wild

21. Only those nations who deny citizenship to the Jews look for excuses saying that Jews do not deserve citizenship. Not so those who wholeheartedly favor it, they do not make arguments and excuses. The French granted this law before the Jews knew how to appreciate their good fortune, and similarly in Britain, Holland, and the like, and the hope for redemption did not stand in their way.

and unruly nation would become fit for sovereignty, and many more like them, if one would have predicted this a hundred years ago, all who would have heard it would have laughed at him and declared this prophet a fool.[22] Nevertheless it came to pass because the people wanted it with all their hearts. Had Israel wished to find its land, they would have found it by now, as they could afford to purchase it for full price and settle there all those pursued to their very necks in various countries. Also, the countries that have been persecuting them mercilessly would have ceased doing so had they known that they own a country and a state that is capable of saving them at times of need. For only the humble and weak are persecuted at all times as it is the nature of man to respect and appreciate only the mighty and successful. Therefore, the children of Israel have been persecuted because they have been foreigners, and had they a country and a state, they too would have been afforded respect just like all other nations.

But even if we assert that restoring sovereignty to Israel is unattainable, maintaining this hope is nevertheless our duty and commandment because it is considered to be our unifying link. Since this hope will not inspire us to act, to carry out our wish by force, but rather to wait for God's miraculous intervention, surely it should not pose any problem. And we should be able to dwell safely in all the lands where we have been dwelling, as it is nothing but part of our religion and not part of life—just like the faith in the Creator, or in resurrection, which no one would suggest to remove from the prayers, or like the Christian faith in the day of redemption when their savior will rise and the whole earth will speak one language and those will be the days of true peace. All these belong to faith and the believer does not care whether this will happen or is impossible, because how one perceives faith is a private matter just like the perception of one's God. The hope for Israel's future redemption is stronger than other beliefs, because it also provides us with national life while asking of us neither tax nor any royal burden, nor will it require our sons to defend it. Therefore, we are obligated even more so to hold onto this hope.

However I know that I will be told in response that Israel has ceased being a nation ever since sovereignty has ceased from its land and that a religion is the Jews' share. But this is a falsehood and a lie: Israel has never ceased being a

---

22. [In part due to conflict with Russia, the Ottoman Empire's reach in Europe waned throughout the nineteenth century, and various nationalist movements in the Balkans emerged. These included successful Serbian and Montenegrin efforts to win autonomy from the Ottomans.]

nation and never will, even if we wished it with all our hearts we could not have succeeded so long as we are considered a different religion. Even if such days of liberty do come, and if out of mercy they allow us residency in their lands, even then we will be guests and not citizens, as to the end of days religious resentment will never cease. And even if we say that religious fanaticism would disappear from the face of the earth envy between our people and the nations will not die, and since the nations consider us to be a different people they will not stop being envious when seeing us happy. And even if we say that religious and national zeal and personal jealousy all will fade away like a dissipating cloud, even then we ought not touch our hope to harm it, as it is still a long wait before those good days come. Let the future generations who might witness the goodness bestowed on them by the nations do as they desire. However, the good times have not arrived as yet, the cry of the children of Israel still sounds from near and far. Even in the places where they were given a rest, it has not been forgotten that they are Jews and letting them live as they wish is considered only an act of pity and patience. Evidence of this is found in periodicals everywhere, for Jews and for non-Jews, who instantly herald the news if a Jew is given respectable employment. This proves that a Jew is not yet considered an equal citizen, or else a Jew being promoted would not be news, and who can count the periodicals that daily write condescendingly about us?[23]

This is what I have been saying, that even if Jews renounce their peoplehood and their national hope, they still will be considered a foreign entity because the nations wish it so. And furthermore, even if all nations would have concurred on lovingly embracing all Jews and would grant them full citizenship, what identity would the remnant of Israel assume then? Will it be a common faith? Where is this faith then? Can a man from Vilna and a man from Berlin follow the same religious ways? Do all who dwell in these countries keep the fundamental religious laws? Shabbat, circumcision, forbidden foods, etc.? And if indeed it is true that Jews share only a religion, then they are certainly obligated to hold onto it more than to anything else, since only this can unite them. And if they choose faith why would they eliminate the hope for future redemption, which, too, is like a tenet of faith? Indeed, their ways are inconsistent and strange, undermining the religion's and nation's foundation for no good reason as they pursue

23. [This early and influential formulation of the notion that emancipation itself breeds antisemitism would later find a more complete articulation in the works of the Zionist thinkers Theodor Herzl and Max Nordau.]

vanity and tell themselves that this will benefit their people, that the nations will be kind to them once they see how deliberately they sacrifice their faith, their people, language and all that has been dear and sacred for generations.

This is a misleading vision! Being as firm as a rock is what has distinguished Israel so far. Even their enemies and haters have respected them at times, witnessing their courage and audacity while being humiliated or downtrodden, as this is human nature; just as we would not respect a monkey for mindlessly imitating us, and just as we would not honor a dog for being quick to obey any command, so the nations will not love nor respect us if we, like monkeys or loyal dogs, rush to do as they do. We would laugh and be amused for a short while watching a monkey's act, and would praise him, but he will be beaten the moment he disobeys our command, as a whip awaits the disobedient dog. This will be also the reward of the Jews who would foolishly copy all the ways of the nations, they will rejoice and praise them for a few days, and will raise a whipping stick if they dare refuse to do as they do.

As we ourselves have witnessed, the nations will not truly rejoice when Jews excel in ability and knowledge; on the contrary, they would greatly resent their success. And as soon as Jews lift up their heads, even their previous supporters would turn against them, fearful that with time the Jews would outshine them. And even if the Jews sacrificed their faith and religion and the memory of their ancestors, they would not be embraced as faithful brothers as long as their name remains Israel. If so, the only way to win the nations over is not only by giving up on faith and hope for redemption, but also by changing our name, so that the name of Israel would be forgotten. Only then if we assimilate into the nations, and no name or memory of our faith will be left, perhaps only then they will not treat us as outsiders. And we will not argue with anyone claiming this publicly, as these kinds of ideas have been prevalent among instigators for a long time. However, when a lover of his people who does not wish to talk his sons into converting to their faith, if this man would make that claim, we should tell him: you err and sin, because in doing so you won't succeed in promoting esteem for Israel, but what you will achieve is tearing apart its heart and weakening the pillars of love and brotherhood. Therefore, we conclude that removing the hope of future redemption from the prayer books is a bad change, bad for the faith and bad for the people's unity, and nothing good will come out of it for improving Israel's condition. And any man of understanding who loves his people must rise against this thing and hold on to this hope and teach it to his sons if he wants them to be Jews. [...]

2

Jews as a Spiritual (Cultural-Historical) Nation among Political Nations

Simon Dubnov

S. M. Dubnov, "Evreistvo, kak dukhovnaia (kul'turno-istoricheskaia) natsiia sredi politicheskikh natsii," in *Pis'ma o starom i novom evreistve (1897–1907)* (St. Petersburg: Obshchestvennaia Pol'za, 1907), 29–52.

Simon Dubnov (1860–1941) may be the only Jewish thinker to have constructed a coherent historical philosophy, ideology, and political program around diaspora nationalism. Dubnov was born in Mstislavl to a traditionally religious family (his grandfather was a prominent rabbi and head of the local yeshiva, and his father a lumber merchant), but at the age of thirteen, he refused to continue his yeshiva education and instead entered a government school. After numerous failed attempts to gain the necessary credentials to enter a university, Dubnov developed a reputation for himself in the 1880s as a Jewish journalist writing in Russian. In 1890 he and his family moved to Odessa, where he continued to write extensively on cultural and literary issues in the Russian Jewish press, first for *Rassvet* and then for *Voskhod* and *Khronika Voskhod*. It was in Odessa where, surrounded by other cultural and intellectual figures of the nascent Jewish renaissance, he became primarily concerned with the connection between Jewish history, politics, and nationalism. In 1891 Dubnov published a widely circulated call to establish a Russian-Jewish historical society to serve the express purpose of creating a new Jewish national consciousness based on history. Although Dubnov was not the first to call for such a society, he became a leading figure in the organization that eventually emerged, endowing it with an expressly nationalist mission: to chronicle the distinctive history of the Jews in Eastern Europe.

Dubnov devoted much of his life to researching and writing about Jewish history, and he became the most influential Jewish historian of the first half of the twentieth century. His historical writings stressed the autonomous nature of Jewish society, communal institutions, and self-government, arguing that Jewish religious and legal autonomy served mainly to preserve the Jewish nation in the diaspora. In Dubnov's view, Jewish history could be divided into periods of shifting "hegemonic" centers: as one center declined or was threatened, Jews moved to establish their autonomous religious, cultural, and political life somewhere else, thereby preserving the essence of Jewish national life.

The transition from historian to national political theorist therefore came naturally for Dubnov. In the ideological tempest of 1897, the year of both the founding of the Jewish Labor Bund and the first World Zionist Congress, Dubnov published his "Theory of Jewish Nationalism." In this essay, which would become the first in a series of "Letters" addressing Jewish national concerns, Dubnov sought to define the essential meaning of "nation," and explain why the Jews are still indeed a nation despite their dispersion and diversity of languages and why Jewish nationalism is both ethical and liberating. Employing his historical theory, Dubnov argued further that in each hegemonic center in the diaspora (including Babylonia, Iberia, Germany, and Poland) Jews created a framework for preserving their complete social and cultural autonomy, and in doing so preserved their nationality as well. Dubnov's second "Letter," "Jews as a Spiritual (Cultural-Historical) Nation among Political Nations," below, continues along similar lines. Yet a more important aim of the second letter is to articulate two points: the pitfalls of Jewish assimilation and the legitimacy — historic and legal — of Jewish claims to be a European nation. Dubnov continued his meditation on the meaning of nation and nationality, but here his intent is to prove why Jews cannot and should never assimilate into the Western nation-states, even if they received civil equality. While he had still not fully articulated the practical implications of his diaspora nationalism, Dubnov argued that Jews should demand not merely civic but also national rights in Europe.

In all of his "Letters," composed between 1897 and 1906, Dubnov developed his theory of Jewish diaspora nationalism and his political philosophy, which in his fourth "Letter" he named "Autonomism." He also sparred with a range of opponents on issues such as Zionism, emigration, journalism, education, the Jewish intelligentsia, and anti-Jewish violence. Dubnov and his family moved to St. Petersburg in 1905, and in the wake of the revolution of that year, he became the ideological spokesperson for a small political party initiated by several of the city's Jewish communal activists and wrote a letter outlining its objectives. Dubnov published the fifteen letters as *Pis'ma o starom i novom evreistve (1897–1907)* (Letters on old and new Jewry [1897–1907]) in St. Petersburg in 1907 to give an accessible and definitive ideological grounding to his new political party and program.

Dubnov influenced nearly all the intellectuals who defined themselves as diaspora nationalists or autonomists (many of whom were even called "Dubnovists"), and many others (including both Zionists and Bundists) who nonetheless absorbed his ideas into their programs. His view, expressed in this essay, that true emancipation required individual as well as constitutionally defined national rights reflected the spirit of the times, when other national minorities in the Russian and Austro-

Hungarian Empires were making similar claims and developing their own ideas about a multinational state. By disentangling the idea of national minority rights from territory, however, Dubnov created a framework for Jewish nationalism in Europe that was broadly influential in Jewish politics.

I

In the preceding letter it was established that the Jewish national idea not only does not contradict humanity's highest socioethical ideals, but is in fact conditional upon them. It is clear to us that all people devoted to justice and progress will support this idea, while those who promote violence and reactionary views will oppose it.

Once we contemplate this simple truth, we understand the distorted nature of the concept of nationalism that swayed circles of supposedly "progressive" Jews in the West and in Russia. They erred so bitterly when, in the name of progress, they condemned a principle as true and progressive as the right of *each* historic nation to its own free, independent development! They confused the two opposing concepts of national individualism and national egoism, forgetting that it is as great a crime to violate another's freedom of individuality as it is a moral duty to defend one's own right to this same freedom. While fighting for the principles of liberty and equality, they themselves paved the way for these principles' violation by rejecting their internal, national *freedom* in favor of foreign *tyranny*. When they acknowledged the right of surrounding nations to assimilate the Jews, these representatives of newly "emancipated" Jewry permitted such national egoism's legal codification; meanwhile, they did not allow their own people even the most natural right to national individuality. These Jews imagined themselves to be knights defending a universal concept, and believed that national abnegation and an obsequious display of servility would earn us greater love and respect. This remained their assumption until experience finally proved to them that respect is granted not to a docile being who allows himself to be depersonalized, but only to an *individual* who respects himself, to a strong personality.

Now that they have been found guilty of ideological bankruptcy, opponents of Jewish nationalism resort to arguments based on "practical wisdom." They say, "What are we to do? How can recognizing the Jewish national idea coexist with the fact that Jews live among other nations and depend on foreign political and social groups? Now that their rights match those of Christians in many countries and they still await equal rights in others, how can the Jews declare that they are not members of the nations that adopted them? How can they possibly proclaim that they are part of a unified, indivisible, though still scattered Jewish nation without being accused of dangerous separatism?"

This point constitutes a mainstay of anti-national politics among emancipated Jewry. We should allow ourselves to dwell on it at greater length.

I must respond to one of the previous questions with a question in return. In regard to the matter of how Jews can possibly claim that they do not belong in the nations that have adopted them, I ask: is it possible for Jews to proclaim, with a clean conscience, that they have really become members of the nations that "adopted" them simply because those nations are now ready to recognize the equal rights of the Jews as their citizens? One only has to recall the elementary definition of the term "nation" in order to grasp how thoughtless it is to assume that emancipated Jews in France have become French, that in Germany they have become Germans, and so forth. Members of a nation are not *made*, but *born* (*nascuntur*, originating from the words *natio*, *nativus*). One can be *made* into a member of a *manmade* legal or sociopolitical group, such as a civil society, state, corporation, or guild, for example. But it is only possible to *make* oneself a member of an organic group, tribe, or nation through a long process of extinguishing one's national individuality, and this can be accomplished only by physically blending with that group through marriage over a series of generations. It is completely absurd for Jews to formally enlist in the ranks of a foreign nationality and then immediately declare that they are German, French, or Russian. Changing one's nation is not the same as changing one's loyalties. An emancipated Jew in France, for example, may call himself a "Frenchman of the Jewish faith." Does this mean that he is a member of the French nation who professes the Jewish faith? Of course not. In order to be a member of the French nation, one must be descended from the Gauls or a kindred race; or else, over the course of several generations, have become close enough with the French to have adopted distinct traits produced during the course of their evolution. But Jews who were born and live in France remain members of the Jewish nation, and, consciously or instinctively, they carry on themselves and within themselves the imprint of Jewish historical evolution. The term "Frenchman of the Jewish faith" can therefore refer only to someone who was born and lives in France, or is a citizen of the French state who professes Judaism. Which nation would such a person belong to, if, as demonstrated earlier, he cannot belong to the French nation? He belongs, of course, to the Jewish nation. Which faith does he profess if his convictions prevent him from believing in Judaism or any other positive religion? None. Would he consciously or unconsciously cease to belong to the Jewish nation on account of this? No, because (as was shown in the preceding letter[24]), Jewish faith is not the only cultural and historic component of Jewish nationality; Jewish nationality cannot be reduced to religion alone. In *all* circumstances this Jew remains a *French citizen of Jewish nationality*. This is precisely the term that should be applied to all similar cases, instead of the vague and inappropriate "Frenchman or German of the Jewish faith" currently in use. Our use of shorthand expressions like *"German Jew"* or *"Russian Jew"* implies this underlying notion of a person who belongs to the Jewish nation and is a native or citizen of Germany (or Russia).

"But how can a person even be a citizen—and especially a good citizen or a patriot—of any state when he separates himself from the ruling nationality of that state?" It is odd that this kind of question is raised only in regard to Jews, and not Czechs, Poles, Irish, or other peoples that are part of multiethnic states. No one would ask whether a Pole, for example, can be a good citizen of Prussia or Austria. What else could he possibly be? He is and must be a citizen of the Prussian or Austrian state, since current historical conditions do not allow him the possibility of establishing his own state. And he will undoubtedly be a *good* citizen—not from a German-national, but from a Polish-national point of view. He will serve the common interests of the state as long as they do not violate his basic national rights, or restrict his people's freedom to exercise their internal autonomy and individuality. Every native-born person will remain a loyal citizen of his country as long as that country continues to protect his basic human rights (for the guarantee of this protection constitutes the very meaning of the social contract).

We must once and for all set in stone the fact that the state is a *formal* social and legal union whose task is to protect the interests of those belonging to it, while a nation is an *internal*, psychological, and existential union.[25] The former can be modified, but the latter will not change. At one time Poles and Czechs formed independent states of their own and even though they are now part of other, multiethnic, states, they have not ceased to be members of the Polish and Czech

24. [Dubnov's first letter, "Teoriia evreiskago natsionalizma" (The theory of Jewish nationalism), was first published in *Voskhod* in 1897 and reprinted in *Pis'ma o starom i novom evreistve (1897–1907)*.]

25. Herder previously distinguished *manmade* state groups from *organic* national ones. [Dubnov refers here to the influential German philosopher Johann Gottfried von Herder (1744–1803).]

nations, just as they were centuries ago. Let us assume that this is an anomaly, a consequence of international conflict; that it would be better for Poles today to have their own independent kingdom and not to be scattered among three states. Nevertheless, because a people lost their power of political independence due to unfortunate circumstances they should not then necessarily be deprived of their rights to a unique national identity. We have examples of nations voluntarily uniting within a single state, as in Switzerland, where the Germans, French, and Italians are three national groups that have created a single state, each preserving their own national individuality. If every national group is guaranteed rights of autonomy in *normal* multinational states, it follows that Jews can also consider themselves full citizens of the states where they live, only as long as they are recognized as members of a distinct nation with rights to its own national-cultural independence.

Some will say: "The Jews are in an exceptional situation. By their origins they are not a *territorial* people like the Poles, Czechs, or Irish, who are subordinated to foreign rule but still tied to their land, but rather are a landless people who were deprived of their territory long ago and now wander among foreign countries. Having no territory of his own, the Jew has either ceased to be a member of the Jewish nation and must be absorbed within the nations where his people have settled, or, if he stubbornly persists in regarding himself as a member of the Jewish nation, then he cannot aspire to the rights of a citizen in countries where he does not claim a single inch of land."

The belief that the loss of their ancient fatherland in Asia Minor has supposedly deprived the Jews of any moral or legal rights on European soil has become so widespread that it is not only held by antisemites, but is also unfortunately used in the propaganda of imprudent political Zionists, who dream of reestablishing a Jewish state in Palestine. Yet there is no delusion more dangerous or ahistorical than the view that Jews are allegedly "foreign" strangers in Europe. History tells us that Jews are Europe's ancient inhabitants, that they settled there even prior to the founding of civilization and the consolidation of Christianity. Ever since Alexander the Great's universal monarchy, Jewish fate has been closely tied to two Western powers, first Greece and later Rome. The displacement of a significant number of Jews from Judea under Greco-Syrian rule during the period of the Second Temple led to the establishment of "Diasporic" cultural centers in Syria, Egyptian Alexandria, and all along the eastern shores of the Mediterranean Sea. When Rome included Judea in its possessions, it also included the Jews there by granting them the status of imperial subjects with the right to settle in any lands belonging to the Empire—in most of Western Europe, that is (and moreover, without restricting them to a single "pale of settlement"[26]). Because Judean patriots still harbored hopes of liberating their homeland from the Roman yoke at that time, Jews made use of this right only to a minimal degree; but already by the end of the Second Temple era, Jews had formed their own settlements in Rome and in various Italian port cities. From there they began to penetrate into Roman provinces in Gaul, Germany, and Spain. Following Judea's great war for independence and the destruction of Jerusalem in the year 70, and again after Bar-Kokhba's failed uprising in the year 138, the Judean state's hope for rebellion vanished, and a great number of Jews resettled in the many provinces of the vast Roman Empire. Aside from the small semiautonomous center that remained in Palestine during the period of the Patriarchate, Jews formed their own colonies in both the western and eastern parts of the empire. They witnessed pagan Rome convert to Christianity; they anxiously watched the new faith expand under Constantine the Great, and then temporarily decline under Julian the Apostate;[27] they felt the iron fist of the first Byzantine emperors who yielded to the influence of clergy. Following the collapse of the Roman Empire, its lands were divided among the independent European states founded on its ruins, thereby also dividing the large numbers of Jews who had lived on these lands for many years. As Christianity spread to these various states Jews began to be persecuted—not as foreigners or strangers (they had lived there for centuries as Roman subjects, after all), but as the only *native* group that refused to adopt the new religion. It was solely religious, and not national, antagonism that lay at the core of Jewish persecution in Ostrogothic Italy, Merovingian France, and Visigothic Spain (it is characteristic that the persecution of Jews in Spain began only when the Visigoth kings rejected half-Judaic Arian forms of Christianity and embraced Catholicism at the end of the sixth century, for the Arian kings had not oppressed the Jews[28]). Charlemagne served as a protector for the Jews during his attempt to rebuild the fallen Roman Empire, not only in order to strengthen commerce, but also because of a vague sense that he had significant

26. [Dubnov here intentionally contrasts the legal rights of the Jews in the ancient Roman world with the residential restrictions governing Jewish residency in the Russian Empire.]

27. [As emperor, Julian "the Apostate" restored Hellenistic paganism to the Roman Empire in 362.]

28. [Dubnov refers here to the Visigothic kings who ascribed to Arian Christianity, a form of nontrinitarian Christianity condemned at the First Council of Nicaea, in 325.]

moral and legal obligations to the Jewish population he had inherited from the former Roman Empire. The subsequent fragmentation of the Western European continent into petty feudal kingdoms compelled European rulers and peoples to forget these responsibilities to ancient Rome's living legacy, the Jews. Medieval German rulers who bore the titles of "Holy Roman Emperors" did occasionally remember the Jews, but only for the purpose of making them *Kamerknechte* (serfs of the chamber), and slaves of commerce.[29] Harsh medieval regimes frequently subjected the Jews to expulsions—from Italy to France, from France to Spain and Germany, from Spain to Italy, from Holland to England, and from Germany to Poland. The forced wanderings of these ill-fated peoples from one European country to another was what prompted people to imagine Jews to be some sort of eternal wanderers, and primordial strangers in every country. In this way the legend of Ahasuerus, "the eternal *zhid*," became a part of people's collective imagination.[30]

However, all of this was the outcome of brute violence and the disregard of historic rights. Jews might have said to the Christian peoples of Europe: "You have no right to deprive us of land where our ancestors settled as subjects of an empire that had stripped us of our eastern fatherland. We are descendants of Europe's ancient Roman colonists of Jewish nationality. During the time of mass migration, when the European nation-states were still only nascent, we already possessed established settlements in many European countries. At a time when you were still backward pagans and your civilization was in its infancy, we lived alongside you as a civilized population professing an ancient universal religion. Can you say that we are inferior to the Huns, the savage Goths, or the other tribes of partially Asiatic descent that divided the legacy of ancient Rome among them? Can rights to this territory be acquired only by way of sword and conquest, rather than through the natural and much more humane process of

29. [The legal principle of *servi camerae regis* (*Kammernechtschaft*, in German) made the Jews the exclusive property of the crown for the purposes of taxation, but it also gave the crown responsibility for their protection.]

30. [Dubnov refers here to the legend of Ahasuerus, often also known as the "wandering Jew," who was believed to have been a Jerusalem shoemaker condemned to eternal wandering for having mocked Jesus on his way to the cross. After multiple editions of the legend in several languages were published in the early seventeenth century, the story—as well as reports of sightings of Ahasuerus—spread, and in the nineteenth century it made its way into a number of novels and poems. Dubnov uses the common Russian pejorative term for Jew, *zhid*, possibly to emphasize the negative connotations of this story.]

settlement and development of peaceful culture over many generations?" Of course, in an era when religious principles served as the foundation for state power, secular and religious authorities were able to ignore these legal demands. They were able to tell the Jews, "we persecute and destroy you because you are heretics who reject our religion, and your ancient rights in Europe are of no concern to us!" But now that church is to a certain extent separated from state, today's secular "democracies" cannot and must not ignore the historic claims of Jewish rights in European lands.

The case of Western Europe (the direct successor to ancient Rome) also applies to Jews in Eastern Europe. Slavic peoples began their cultural-historical life significantly later than Romance and Germanic peoples, but already at the dawn of their historic existence, they too encountered Jews as long-time residents of their lands. The Eastern Roman Empire in Byzantium furnished Jewish settlers for Russia's southern shores on the Black and Caspian Seas in the course of the very first centuries of Christianity;[31] the Khazar kingdom introduced the Jews to southwestern Russia during the era of the first Kievan princes;[32] and Germany and Bohemia sent Jews to Poland the moment a stable government was first established there. These Jews planted the seeds of industry and commerce in a country with a primitive culture; they taught the natives how to extract the earth's mineral wealth (from salt mines), and they connected remote Poland with the global marketplace, enabling its encounter with civilized countries. At a time when Muscovite Russia, isolated from the civilized world by the impact of the Tatar yoke and the legacy of Byzantine culture, prohibited entry to Jews, Polish rulers valued the services of the Jews and provided them with every kind of protection and support. Of course, the sad impact of the Catholic Church's medieval policies was felt here, too: Jews were often oppressed in Poland, and their basic rights that had been formalized in ancient royal charters were violated. They were degraded and artificially sequestered into a distinct social class defined by particular privileges and not by the general legal norms. Nonetheless, they were willy-nilly recognized as an organic part of the state, and were deemed necessary for carrying out certain social functions. In 1539, King

31. See the Greco-Jewish inscriptions in Tauride, relating to the first and third century of the Christian era, in *Regesti i nadpisi* [Registers and inscriptions] (SPb, 1899), 3–4.

32. [Between the seventh and eleventh centuries, the Khazar kingdom (also known as Khazaria) dominated the Ukrainian steppes, the Crimea, and much of the area along the Volga and Ural Rivers between the Caspian and Black Seas. At some point, probably in the eighth or ninth century, the Khazar king and leaders converted to Judaism.]

Sigismund I was overcome with horror after rumors spread about the intention of Lithuanian Jews to resettle in Turkey. He ordered a thorough investigation of the rumors and was appeased only upon ascertaining that the rumors were baseless.[33] Even when they were not treated with kindness, Jews played the role of peaceful culture bearers over the course of the several centuries before Poland was divided by its three neighboring states. Russia acquired most of the Polish lands densely inhabited by Jews, and thus shouldered certain obligations to the Jewish population in its newly annexed territory. The edifying history of the Jews in New Russia—with several million people still shamefully deprived of legal rights, with Judeophobic laws, expulsions, and pogroms during recent decades—illustrates just how well Russia has managed to fulfill its responsibilities so far. The treatment that Jews experienced in medieval Western regimes has repeated itself in present-day Eastern Europe. Supporters of this regime of course contest Russia's moral and legal responsibilities toward the native Jewish inhabitants of its current territories. But while legal rights can be suppressed, a sense of justice cannot. The state's "great robbery" of millions of its native residents cannot remain the social norm indefinitely.

Even from a formal perspective, then, the Jews possess indisputable historic rights to European territory. It is true that in contrast to other peoples who lack political independence, Jews do not form compact majorities in any one region, but rather constitute a national minority in all places. However, this fact does not compromise their right to call themselves native Europeans. Europe has served as the homeland for the majority of the Jewish people over the course of two thousand years. The bones of our distant ancestors rest in its soil. Here we witnessed, as ancient Roman colonists, the birth of Christian civilization and the forging of national and political unions. It is here that we independently developed an economic and intellectual culture that has also influenced our Christian neighbors. After this, we are still thought of as aliens and strangers, and there are even Jews who submissively accept the "wisdom" of our enemies, and thus justify their belief in an inevitable exodus of Jews from Europe! Rather than tirelessly protest this dismissal of our historic rights, we repudiate them ourselves! The conclusion is clear. If, according to the formal definition, the right to preserve national identity belongs to groups associated with a distinct territory (even if these groups are not politically independent), then Jews also possess this

33. See my study "The Jews and Reform in Poland," *Voskhod*, 1895, books VII–VIII; and also V*seobshchaia istoriia evreev* [The general history of the Jews], book III, 107.

right because they are in every sense of the word a "territorial" people, with the one distinction being that their territory in Europe consists of small slivers and does not constitute a single region. Jews are European aborigines, and they have established their rights here on the basis of centuries of settlement and cultural civilization, rather than ownership of land.[34]

How can Jewry preserve its national integrity and become a native part of the various political bodies where it belongs? In other words, how can we assume that a resident of a country who belongs to the Jewish nation will harbor love for the fatherland and devotedly serve its interests—that is, that he will exhibit what is known as patriotism? Will his *national* sentiments as a Jew conflict with his *patriotic* sentiments as the citizen of a given state? This circular argument was briefly mentioned above, and here I will subject it to a more detailed analysis.

Patriotism is a complex emotion composed of two elements: it is a *natural* sense of love for one's fatherland (*patria*) and a *moral* consciousness of the solidarity of interests among citizens in a particular state. When Jews lost their political center in Palestine, Europe became a second homeland for the majority of them. Over the course of centuries, then, they should have developed a natural sense of love for this second homeland. This love is an innate natural feeling, and it is not influenced by a person's life experience in that particular country. A person's love for the country where he was born and raised becomes an innate part of his soul from the time of childhood, tied to a relatively long line of familial and historic memories, be they happy or sad. The places where we suffered are no less dear to us than the places where we were happy. Who is unaware of that passionate centuries-old bond that Jews who were exiled from Spain and Portugal at the end of the fifteenth century have preserved for their homeland? Who has not heard about the exiles in America today—Jewish emigrants from Russia—who languish with nostalgic longing for their native land? It is not only landscapes but also precious national relics that bind us to countries that become our homeland over the centuries: our holy ancestors' graves, the sacred sites of our religion, and our historic monuments. These sites are connected

---

34. All that has been said about Europe can, mutatis mutandis, also be applied to America. Even if we exclude Columbus's Jewish companions who took part in the discovery of the New World, Jewish economic colonization in North and South America had already begun by the sixteenth and seventeenth centuries and continued to develop without interruption, parallel to European colonization. Jews played an active and equal part in establishing factories and urban industrial centers, and helped build American civilization alongside other nations.

with those poetic national traditions that we, with joy or sadness, absorbed from our youth, and only later learned to recognize as part of our people's history. Entire trajectories of our historical life are tied to the histories of Germany, Italy, France, England, Poland, Russia, and other European countries. How can one dispute the simple feeling of connection binding Jews to their homeland when all the factors that naturally create such bonds are evident and indisputable?

Jews born in a particular country are therefore just as predisposed to the primary, innate aspect of patriotic sentiment as are the Christians who were born in that country. The only question that remains concerns the latter, civic component of patriotism: the consciousness of mutual solidarity among members of a sociopolitical organization. This consciousness, which I would call "civism," depends on the individual's social status within the state. Feelings of civic solidarity and loyalty to political alliances can unite disparate groups within a state *only* if the state's laws apply equally to all citizens, and the fatherland does not divide its children into sons and stepsons. Furthermore, the internal freedom of each national and religious group must be guaranteed by the power of general consensus, and never sacrificed to the claims of the so-called "ruling" nations. Wherever this is not the case, civism will either vanish, or express itself in different forms among disparate groups. In Russia, for example, both the Jews and the "indigenous" Russian Dukhobors are persecuted for their nationality and their faith, respectively, and both groups are now abandoning Russia to seek a new, free homeland in the United States of America or in Canada.[35] In Switzerland, where each of the three nations that are unified within the state has complete autonomy, a sense of sociopolitical civism is reinforced and enlivened by a unique local patriotism. In Austria, however, sociopolitical solidarity is undermined because of the constant, seething struggle between various national groups that are competing for autonomy, and also often for hegemony over different regions. Thus, the sense of *shared* patriotism has vanished in Austria, where the German is patriotic in one sense, the Czech in another, the Pole in a third, and the Rusyn in a fourth. And in Ireland, although it is impossible for the Irish today to be British patriots, this would become entirely possible if Ireland was granted the broad national Home Rule for which it has been fighting for so long.

35. [The communitarian and pacifist Dukbobors, or *dukhobory*, were Christian spiritualists who rejected the authority of the Russian Orthodox Church and the state, to the frustration of several tsars.]

Jewish demands for national autonomy in various European countries do not, of course, go quite as far as those of the Irish and indeed the Poles. As long-time residents of Europe, Jews demand complete and equal civic and political rights for themselves; as members of a spiritual and cultural-historical nation, they demand the same form of national and cultural autonomy that any nation with aspirations for independent development deserves. Given their natural attachment to their second, western homeland, if the two requirements are satisfied then their patriotism in various countries cannot possibly incur doubt. A Jew who is content with his fatherland can be an English, French, or German patriot *and* a devoted, faithful son of the scattered, but still united, Jewish nation.[36] The state, as we have said, is a formal union, the nation a spiritual one; members of the former are bound by mutual interests, members of the latter by mutual sensibilities and customs. These two loyalties are distinct and do not contradict one another; therefore, one can be a good member of both unions. Adolphe Crémieux, for example, was a fervent French patriot who also boldly professed that Jews of all countries have similar interests by establishing the Alliance Israélite Universelle.[37] Of course, Crémieux remained far from embracing the Jewish national idea in its broader sense, but in that era of assimilation, his actions sufficed. In any case, the patriotism of, say, Prussian Jews is in no way less trustworthy than the patriotism of Prussian Poles. On the contrary, Jews might sooner be scolded for showing excessive patriotic zeal, at times at the expense of our national pride. We still remember the decision of Jewish reformers in

36. It is possible, of course, to have conflicts between general national feelings and the feeling of local patriotism. For example, the emotional drama of the Jews who fought in 1870 in the two armies—French and German—was not an easy one. The Poles would have experienced something similar in the course of a war between Russia and Austria or Germany, but such phenomena born of militarism, itself a relic of barbarism, cannot be considered the norm. Speaking of patriotism, I of course exclude that reactionary "patriotism" that originates in low chauvinistic motives and politics that have disgraced pan-Germanists in Austria, "nationalists" in France, and the "Black Hundreds" in Russia today. A Jew can never be this kind of patriot, because this sort of patriotism is usually associated with Judeophobia.

37. [Isaac Adolphe Crémieux (1796–1880) was a prominent lawyer active in defending Jewish rights in France and abroad. He was also active in the Central Jewish Consistory, becoming its president in 1843, but he retired when news of his children's baptism became public. Crémieux was a prominent figure in French politics, a member of the Chamber of Deputies, and briefly—following the 1848 revolution—minister of justice in the provisional government.]

Germany to eliminate all the poignant prayers from the liturgy about the restoration of Jerusalem, for fear of sinning against the German *Vaterland*.[38] These frightened people acted as if they were still living in an archaic police state, and failed to understand that a government based upon natural rights cannot violate its citizens' religious or national-historical ideals. Emancipated Jews in the West secured their freedom using slavish tactics, and they demanded equality with the timidity of a subordinate class. They believed that civism required internal sacrifice and a rejection of their cherished ancient treasures, and they were just as fearful after they were emancipated as they had been when they were completely powerless . . .

Therefore, Jewish spiritual or cultural-historical nationalism does not conflict with the social and civic commitments of various populations of Jews in different states. All people can be loving members of their own family *and* a citizen of their state; likewise, Jews who feel compelled to defend the interests of their national family can also participate in the civic life of the country where they live, and serve its interests, given of course that they have equal rights with other classes of the population. In this manner, Jews everywhere form not a *state within a state, but a nation among nations.* The Jews of Austria, Germany, and Russia all have distinct civic and political interests, but they share internal connections and collective national interests, just like the Poles who are scattered across these same three states. These mutual national interests are in practice expressed by specific forms of internal self-governance, in the independent organization of popular communal, educational, and religious institutions; in the autonomy of the school curriculum (including its linguistic autonomy); and lastly, by a united voice in parliamentary and social debates that results in distinct *national policy*.[39] Once a state acknowledges that Jews have rights as *citizens*, it must also recognize their rights as a *nation*—that is, the rights to independent internal development that flow from the broader freedom of self-determination. We must fight against the position that it is acceptable to demand that Jews renounce their national rights in order to gain civic rights. Our people *as a whole* will never sacrifice its national-cultural independence for the benefit of other nations. Only the notorious group preoccupied with assimilation can continue to believe that Jews must restrict their national individuality in order to gain civic rights, or

38. [See Smolenskin's essay, "The Eternal People."]
39. See further Letters IV, V, XII, and XIII where the questions relating to internal national organization are examined in detail.

preserve those they have already won. This is a theory of national suicide[40] that demands from Jews sacrifices not required of a single other nation, all in the name of "equal rights." This is a theory that contradicts the essential meaning of equal rights and the equality of individuals. Assimilation is the steppingstone from slavery to freedom only in the minds of former slaves and their former masters.

II

Let us closely examine the origins and essence of this doctrine called "*assimilation*," which only recently held sway among Jewish intellectual circles, and is currently undergoing a moment of acute crisis.

Assimilation occurred in the wake of an abrupt transition in which Jews went from having no civil rights to suddenly having equal rights. Assimilation in the West gained ground first following the French emancipation in 1791 and then the German emancipation in 1848. When the French National Assembly debated the Jewish Question in 1789, Clermont-Tonnerre, who supported emancipation, said that "as a nation, Jews must be denied everything; but as individuals, Jews must be granted everything . . . there cannot be a nation within a nation." Representing the Judeophobic camp, Abbé Maury based his arguments against Jewish emancipation on the idea that "the term 'Jew' refers not to a religious sect, but a nation," and that a Jew who is loyal to his national traditions "cannot become a Frenchman."[41] Liberals and conservatives both agreed that Jews would have to renounce their nationality in order to gain equal rights, that they could remain Jewish only in matters of faith and would become French by nationality. Liberals thought that this form of assimilation was feasible, and therefore supported civic emancipation, but conservatives did not believe it was possible and lobbied against equal rights for Jews. Neither party reached the point of acknowledging that a citizen's full and complete rights should also include national rights. Torn between fear and hope, the Jews themselves also failed to demand *full and complete rights*. In their minds, nationality was so intertwined with religion that it did not trouble their conscience to conceal the former beneath the latter in

40. [Dubnov uses the Russian word *samounichizheniia*, which might also be translated as self-abasement, self-humiliation, or self-degradation.]

41. See my monograph *The French Revolution and the Jews* (Voskhod [publisher], 1899); *cf.* the new revised edition *The Emancipation of the Jews in the Era of the French Revolution* (Vilna, 1906), 29–33.

order to save their equal rights. In 1807, when Napoleon I threatened the Jews with the loss of their recently granted civic equality, Jewish representatives in the "Great Sanhedrin" solemnly declared that "Jews today do not form a nation and prefer to become part of the great (French) nation, which they regard as a form of political redemption."[42] This public rejection of their nationality, or else a silent consensus (*tacitu consensu*) of this same principle, accompanied Jewish emancipation in other Western countries as well.

The majority of the Jewish population that had regained their basic rights viewed emancipation not as an act of simple justice for an oppressed nation, but as an act of charity that had been granted by the ruling Christian nations and stipulated by the requirement of national renunciation. Many Jews paid for this "gift" with the partial or complete obliteration of their national individuality through Germanification, Francification, and so forth. They did not *encounter* their fellow Christian citizens as distinct individuals with *equal rights*, but rather sought to *become like* them by imitating their national culture, and even *merging* with them. The first generation of emancipated Jews *simulated* foreign nationalism; the next generation appeared to have been *assimilated* in various ways. This tendency repeated itself, although on a smaller scale, among Russian Jewish elites after the liberating reforms of the 1860s. Jews throughout Europe who had either achieved or still desired emancipation sacrificed their national rights for the sake of acquiring civic rights. After centuries of slavery, degradation, and stifled thought it is completely understandable that Jews, like all other progressive European nations, would have felt drawn toward enlightened intellectual and social renewal—toward *humanization* in the highest sense of the word. In practice, however, they directed their energies to *Germanification* and *Russification*—that is, to artificially surrendering their national individuality to a foreign one. This form of "assimilation" was but a modification of their former state of bondage, but from an ethical perspective it placed them in a far worse position. Perhaps the Jew of the Middle Ages had bent his back before his Christian oppressor, but he never prostrated his conscience or departed in any way from what he regarded as his spiritual and national rights; the new type of Jew who can now hold his head high in Christian society has distorted his soul and his national character for the benefit of that society, which demands that he "resemble

---

42. "*Today the Jews no longer form a nation, and they instead have the advantage of being incorporated into the great nation, which for them appears to be political redemption ... [in French in the original]*" See L. Kahn, *Les juifs de Paris pendant la Revolution* (Paris, 1898), 333.

a Jew as little as possible." This is a form of modified slavery, a replacement of external with internal servitude.

Fairness demands mention of the fact that alongside *pragmatic assimilationists*, who were guided solely by opportunistic instincts of adaptation, there were also *idealist assimilationists* who saw this behavior as a condition for progress. Some of them became carried away with cosmopolitanism, and in the name of this ideal they began erasing their nationality, not seeing that in doing so they had simply become part of the nation to which they were tied by political and geographic circumstances, rather than members of an imaginary cosmopolitan society. Their theoretical rejection of the national principle led them in practice just to replace their own nationality with a foreign one, and wait for an "end of days" in which all nations will come together in one abstract "humanity." After passing through this phase, ideological assimilation became synonymous with the worldly interests that had dictated the necessity of "practical" assimilation. The corroded ideal became a transparent mask for a program of vulgar opportunism, gathering personal wealth, and launching brilliant careers. "Humanity's liberator" wore a thin veil to conceal the countenance of a slave who had abandoned his unrecognized nation for a foreign ruling power.

The ideology of assimilation merged with its practices on the basis of what one might refer to as "atavistic suppression of rights." The Jewish masses lived without civic rights for centuries; now they must live without national rights. Only recently have Jews begun to realize that no one is in a position to demand from them that they deny their nationality, that the denationalization of Jews is a rule just as crude and arbitrary as their prior state of civic degradation, that the essence of freedom and equality is not confined to the individual's exercise of his personal rights and must entail the freedom to exercise his national rights as well. This profound realization has already occurred to the majority of the Jewish intelligentsia, which no longer prostrates itself or its conscience before the ruling powers. Those who possess such inner freedom do not fear the kind of Western antisemitism or Russian Judeophobia whose demoralizing powers are reinforced by brutal police oppression. The only people who feel demoralized are intellectuals who have severed ties to their roots and their people, for in a healthy national intelligentsia, social antisemitism and violent state oppression (as in Russia) can only empower the growth of national self-consciousness and strengthen the opposition. Both historically and psychologically, it is precisely this process that had to replace assimilationist sentiment. Those who continue to support assimilation are cunning pragmatists who prefer to stick with the strong rather than be counted among oppressed or second-class citizens, or else the incorrigible ideologues of nonexistent cosmopolitanism. Of course, for many, assimilationism comes naturally and unconsciously as a consequence of bad upbringing, or because they had become estranged from Jewry at an early age. These wandering sons of the nation can still, with good will and under auspicious circumstances, return to the family. The everlasting tree of Jewry has never grieved over its rebellious, withered, or fallen leaves, and it has no reason to mourn for them now. National selection only reinforces the core of the nation.

Must Jews once again set themselves apart and create a kind of spiritual ghetto to replace the crumbled stone walls of the medieval ghettos? Not at all. I am not advocating any form of artificial isolation or separation. Isolation, in the sense of distinction, is necessary for each self-defined personality, whether individual or collective. It is necessary that Jews encounter their surrounding environment, but only on the basis of *equal rights*. A Jew who comes face to face with a member of a different nation need not *surrender* his national individuality; rather, both parties ought to *jointly submit* to the higher principle of the equal worth of all citizens. Should the non-Jew spurn the kind of social integration based upon equal rights, then the self-respecting Jew will declare that integration is neither possible nor desirable at that time. This may amount to separatism, if you will, but it is a necessary separatism, a separation with the intent to preserve one's personal freedom and national integrity. In Russia today, this is the position of what I might call *defensive isolation*, and it is occupied by the greatest Jewish intellectuals who wish to preserve the freedom of their souls. I bow before these proud and lonely people who prefer to stand outside the lively sphere of the national majority rather than participate in it on terms that degrade their sense of individual and national worth. Jews have lived in "splendid isolation" at many times throughout their history, but not in the sense of an armored fist, rather as an armored spirit . . .

And so, *assimilation is not only a rejection of Jewish national interests, but also a rejection of the unique freedom of the Jewish nation and its equal value within international cultural families.* It is wrong both in principle and in practice; it is a product of both *social prejudice* and a *moral flaw* equally common among assimilated Jews and those who demand Jewish assimilation. Regardless of his motives, an assimilated Jew—a Jew, that is, who subordinates his national self to a foreign one—will become an unconscious victim of an atavistic lack of rights, a psychic wound that turns into an ethical evil whenever a person abandons the oppressed in order to join the victors. It is possible that the non-Jews' demand for Jewish assimilation reflects the conscious, or perhaps unconscious, contempt of the strong for the weak, and a belief that Jewry, enslaved for centuries, must still pay for the "gift" of civic rights (that is, for the return of rights previously taken from them) by renouncing their national individuality. The demands of this sort as well as the submission to such demands repudiate the highest principle of all social ethics: the idea of the equal value of all nations.

Starting from the time of the first emancipation in 1791, we have sought only civic and political rights in the countries of the diaspora. Now the time has come for us to claim our national rights as well. As I have shown above, these rights are entirely compatible with the legal and civic status of the different groups of our people in the countries of the diaspora.

III

These are the general features of the practical conclusions of my doctrine of Jewish spiritual or cultural-historical nationalism. In the letters that follow, these general arguments will be explained in greater detail and applied to various aspects of our social and spiritual life. In conclusion to the present discussion I must address one remaining objection that has more to do with the tactics than the ideas of those who support the Jewish national idea.

The argument I have presented here may remind some of a dramatic episode from the life of Socrates. When the great philosopher stood before the Greek judges who had already declared him guilty of spreading "harmful teachings" and were preparing to pronounce the death sentence, Socrates made use of his right to mete out what he considered to be a more reasonable punishment for himself. Socrates requested that in return for his service to the state, he be "punished" with a life sentence in the Prytaneum—that is, by living out his last years at the state's expense in the state palace that housed honored Greek citizens, politicians, and famous military commanders. This kind of life, Socrates proudly declared, is highly appropriate for the type of person who needs leisure and freedom from worldly cares in order to instruct judges such as you in what is best. The judges, of course, were angered by the philosopher's audacious speech, in which he had demanded a reward for something that in their minds deserved stern punishment, and they carried out the fateful sentence that to this day continues to trouble the conscience of humanity.

Perhaps some will see a connection between this episode and my argument regarding the Jewish national question. "Yes!" people will say: "The Jewish nation today stands trial as the accused. In some countries it is treated like a pariah caste and denied basic civil rights, in others there are calls to repudiate its previously granted rights. The Jewish nation is judged and subjected to severe reprimand in all places. And on behalf of this accused nation, you proudly proclaim: 'We Jews are not satisfied with civic rights alone, we need national rights too. We demand respect for our national character, our history, our cultural achievements. We demand that our national autonomy be recognized!' This must be a joke. You have completely forgotten where we stand. Your demands may seem strange or offensive."

Yes, gentlemen, they may indeed seem strange or offensive. But to whom? To our accusers, to those who deny the Jew any of his human or civic rights, to those who cast him out or hold him in the position of a pariah? The kind of people who support inequality and oppression will not bend to *any* arguments in the name of justice and social ethics. Throughout history Judeophobes have not been able to forgive Jews for even existing, yet Jewry nonetheless continues to exist, defying the wishes of both the ancient and the contemporary Hamans.[43] When the self-appointed prosecutors put Jews on the bench of the accused, they often do not believe in the indictment they themselves have compiled, but the accused, proud with the knowledge that he is in the right, must hold his head high and declare that it is the criminals, and not the victims, who must stand trial. History's Nemesis has already placed those who judged Socrates, the leaders of the Inquisition, and the medieval oppressors of the Jews on the bench; it will place the new knights of antisemitism and Judeophobes there as well. We need not engage with the opinions of such ignorant people. In society there has always been and always will be a struggle with reactionary groups, and Jews will never be alone in that struggle: they will march in the ranks of the whole liberating army.

Is there anyone else who might find the national demands of the Jews unacceptable? Perhaps it is those false friends of ours who have "generously" returned our civic rights to us and demanded that in exchange we become part of the national environment, and not be Jews? Or else those who demand that we reject our cultural autonomy and preserve only our attachment to Judaic faith? To these people we reply: You, gentlemen, regard yourselves as magnanimous

43. [As recounted in the biblical Book of Esther, Haman—the Persian king's chief advisor—unsuccessfully sought to exterminate the king's Jewish subjects. The name became synonymous with villainy among Jews.]

and liberal, but how can someone be called magnanimous if, after keeping his innocent neighbor locked in a spiritual prison for many years, he feels at last compelled by an awakened conscience to free that neighbor, and then demands gratitude and self-renunciation from him? Can we call someone a true liberal if he defends the freedom to develop his own national identity, but denies this freedom to members of other nations? We reject the idea that "generosity" has compelled you to return our stolen civic rights, and we do not acknowledge the kind of liberalism that proposes such shameful conditions for emancipation. We will not barter our national freedoms for civic ones. Having lived in Europe since the dawn of its civilization, we have been naturalized by history itself, and we must enjoy all the civic rights enjoyed by even those nations that settled here after we did. When Europe is able to make amends for its thousand-year crime against Jewry, then the wrath of the oppressed will be extinguished from our hearts. A feeling of slavish thankfulness for the return of our previously abolished rights, however, will never arise in its place. As a historic and cultural nation, we have proved our capacity to flourish in all possible circumstances, and now we wish for our internal life to freely and independently evolve in a manner that contradicts neither our universal goals nor our civic duties. The progressive movements and spirit of these times will also influence our national way of life. We will strive to meet our own standard of perfection, alongside but not under the guidance of other nations. We will seek to improve the state of our inner life and to isolate its sad flaws. We will reform our religious, social, and cultural institutions; further, we must transform the Jewish school into an institution that can satisfy the requirements of our national life as well as our duties as citizens in each state. But we will accomplish all of this autonomously and in the context of our own evolution, not out of a desire to convenience, to mimic, or to win the high opinion of our neighbors.

It will be a long and hard road to autonomous development for our scattered nation, which clashes with every civilized nation in the world. Jews will not be granted complete national and civic rights at any time in the near future. Our awareness of this in no way compels us to put away our weapons but, on the contrary, fortifies us with the energy that will be critical for overcoming great obstacles in the long battle we will have to fight. Our history, after all, is measured in millennia. In Russia, where millions of Jews are still deprived of basic civic rights, our struggle will lead us to join other forces that oppose the despotic imperial regime. Our victory here depends on the ability of this broader social movement in Russia to replace the police state with a government based on the rule of law. Nevertheless, we will continue to insist on our national rights while fighting for civic emancipation, and we will not repeat the fateful mistakes of our Western brothers. The success of antisemitism in the West can be partly explained by the loss of self-respect among those educated Jewish classes that became obsessed with assimilation. They became trapped in the bodies of foreign nations, which they irritate like a foreign body irritates an organism. Once it lost its own sense of national worth, the Jewish community lost the respect of others as well. Now even the assimilated classes can sense the telling tremors from the outside that awaken Jewish consciousness. Sooner or later, this consciousness will lead to the struggle for our national rights, and put an end at last to the Jews' degrading encroachment upon foreign national hearths. If this does not earn us love, then it will at least earn the Jewish nation more respect from other nations. If we cannot make them love us, then we will do everything in our power to enforce their respect. The emotion of mutual love is necessary only among members of a tight-knit national family, whereas members of a civic union are tied together by social rights and responsibilities, and mutual respect is the result of the equal distribution of rights and responsibilities among all citizens.

History leads us to a resolute alternative: national disintegration or national rebirth. The process of disintegration has already manifested itself to such a degree that it is apparent where the danger lurks. Among the Jewish upper classes in the nineteenth century, the communal center shifted from our internal national life to the external surrounding environment, and into the sphere of foreign national interests. The pillar of our community moved from within our national circle to beyond it, thus creating an unstable equilibrium, a dangerous national vacillation. In order to stop the swaying, we must move the pillar back to its natural place within the circle of our national interests. Restoring our nation's lost equilibrium—herein lies the most important condition of our renewal. Now, we must take all of the strength, goals, and stores of energy that we have inherited from many generations of fighters and martyrs who heroically steered the ark of Jewry through the flood of world history, and we must direct them toward the great task of national renaissance.

3

"The Jewish Renaissance Movement"
and "Jewish Autonomy"
Nathan Birnbaum

Mathias Acher [Nathan Birnbaum], "Die Juedische Renaissance-Bewegung,"
Ost und West, September 1902, 576–84.
Mathias Acher [Nathan Birnbaum], "Juedische Autonomie," *Ost und West*,
January 1906, 1–6.

The articles "The Jewish Renaissance Movement" and "Jewish Autonomy" represent only one snapshot of Nathan Birnbaum's (1864–1937) varied ideological and political career. Though Birnbaum has not been widely remembered, Jess Olson has quite aptly suggested that he was clearly a figure of significance to his contemporaries. While a young man in Vienna in the 1880s, Birnbaum was an early and influential Zionist. He was among the founders of Kadimah, a Jewish nationalist fraternity at Vienna University; he founded and edited *Selbst-Emancipation*, the first Zionist newspaper in German; and he even coined the term "Zionism" (*zionismus* in German). By the 1890s, however, Birnbaum had become more concerned with Jewish national rights in Europe than with Palestine, and his difficult relationship with Theodor Herzl, the charismatic Zionist leader, probably fostered his shift away from Zionism (to Birnbaum, Herzl was a neophyte who was unaware of the movement's history; to Herzl, Birnbaum's resentment was a product of petty jealousy). In 1899 Birnbaum formally resigned his position in the World Zionist Organization, a move that reflected the culmination of his ideological shift toward a diaspora-centered nationalism as much as it did his dislike of Herzl. During the years following his break with Zionism, Birnbaum wrote a number of articles criticizing the Zionist movement's ideological resistance to the idea that Jewish nationalism could flourish in the diaspora through Jewish culture and politics. In particular, Birnbaum became increasingly interested in using Eastern European Jewish culture and the Yiddish language to craft a nonparty "Jewish Renaissance movement" rooted in Europe.

Following his departure from Zionism, Birnbaum clarified a definition of "Jewish Renaissance" independent of the prevalent Zionist one. Such a radical nationalist conception of renaissance arguably dates at least to Moses Hess's 1861 essay, *Rome and Jerusalem*, in which Hess, inspired by such nationalist contemporaries as Giuseppe Mazzini, had proclaimed that "only a national renaissance can endow the religious genius of the Jews . . . with new strength and raise its soul once again to the level of prophetic inspiration." Writing in 1902, and distancing himself from more romantic conceptions of renaissance prevalent among such cultural Zionist figures as Martin Buber (who had himself recently used the term "Jewish Renaissance" in the same periodical), Birnbaum offered a conception of "rebirth" detached from what he saw as unusable, remote pasts and grounded instead in political and cultural realities. This concern for the present is signaled by, among other things, his preference for Yiddish—bearing as it did the marks of recent diaspora history—over Hebrew as a national language. Birnbaum's modernist, pragmatic approach to the idea of renaissance appropriately accompanies his transition from Zionism—which, by 1902, he felt was an unrealistic solution to the Jewish question—to autonomism.

The political debates about national minority rights in the Habsburg Empire during the early years of the twentieth century provided an opening for Birnbaum to argue for Habsburg Jewry's political autonomy. It is the wrangling over Jewish exclusion or inclusion from new proposals for autonomy and political representation among the empire's nationalities that form the context for the article "Jewish Autonomy." Birnbaum became one of the leading advocates for Jewish national rights in the Habsburg Empire, in contrast to those people, both Jewish and non-Jewish, who believed that, unlike the empire's other nationalities seeking greater political representation, Jews should assimilate the political goals of one or the other of the nationalities among whom they lived. Though Birnbaum would move away from diaspora nationalism and eventually become a leading figure in the Orthodox political movement Agudat Yisrael, his writings, especially between 1902 and 1908, made a cogent argument for Jewish national rights in the diaspora.

The Jewish Renaissance Movement

In my article "Some Thoughts on Antisemitism," published in the previous issue of *Ost und West*, I mentioned the "Jewish Renaissance movement."[44] I now feel obliged to explain in further detail the meaning I ascribe to this term. If I substituted this word for "Zionism," one might think my intention was to coin a new word for the ideal of a Zionist party. That, however, is not the case. Rather,

44. [Nathan Birnbaum, "Einige Gedanken über den Antisemitismus," *Ost und West*, August 1902), 517.]

I wish to use it to counter the practice of the intellectual Zionists, who take "Zionism" to refer not only to the party, but also to the great spiritual movement behind that party. For this movement, however, the word "Zionism" seems to me at the very least too weak and too narrow. It is for that reason that I use the term "Jewish Renaissance movement," which, as it happens, I picked up from the intellectual Zionists, who themselves use it now and again.[45] I did not coin it. I wish to God I was as guiltless in introducing the word "Zionism" in the first place as I am now regarding the term "Jewish Renaissance movement"! I do, in any case, approve of the term and am able to specify what I mean by it.

Renaissance—that is, rebirth—is a mystical word that plays a significant role in various religious systems. In its narrower sense, it received its full world-historical significance in the Renaissance of classical antiquity, while nevertheless unveiling, in precisely this use, its inherent contradiction. For we are now all too aware—without having to refer to Houston Stewart Chamberlain—that the Renaissance was not a rebirth, for there is no such thing, neither in nature nor history, the latter being but one aspect of nature.[46] What is dead cannot be reborn, and that which is still alive does not need to be reborn. The perspective of the natural sciences reduces the notion of rebirth to absurdity.

Yet the term "rebirth" persists, and is constantly being reapplied to new areas. For it exudes a great poetic force, a force that does not deteriorate into lifeless romanticism since it is not being applied to aging, faded ideals, but rather to ones that have only just begun to reverberate. Modern man no longer employs the term it its literal sense. And where he has seemed to do so, it has only been in misapprehension of his own sentiments and desires. For the urge of modern man is not to link himself to a dead, ancient past, but to regain such lost happiness, such vitality, such richness as he had, or believes he had, in the past. His deeper longing is for rebirth not in the sense of a *second birth* of developments whose historic moment has already passed, but in the sense of a *new* birth of impulses needed to initiate new developments. This is the state of affairs, even if few will give it due credit.

It is with these reservations that I speak of a Jewish Renaissance movement. In fact, there is not a single, authentic rebirth to be found in it, past, present, or yet

45. [Martin Buber coined the phrase in the first issue of *Ost und West*, in January 1901.]

46. [Houston Stewart Chamberlain was a prominent German Romantic and nationalist thinker whose social-Darwinist, antisemitic ideas anticipated the racial worldview later proffered by National Socialism. Birnbaum explicitly sought to distance himself in the pages of *Ost und West* and *Die Welt* from Chamberlain's racial views.]

to come. Those aspects of Judaism that have died, that have internally withered, such as theocracy or its Asiatic disposition,[47] or indeed its entire ancient Hebraic character, will never be reborn. What thrives within Judaism—its drive to forge its own language and pursue a distinctive intellectual life, its longing for territorial community, its entire contemporary national character—all of this Judaism can experience and is experiencing, thanks to newfound strength enabling it to grow new wings for its youthful flight toward the sun.

Nothing could be more instructive for understanding this great process than precisely those enormous creative forces of language displayed by the Jewish tribe in exile. The course of this tribe's history has supplied it with two materials: the Semitic Hebrew and the Aryan German. It knew how to build upon both, when and where its young sprouts had sufficient time. The winter of the Hebrew language was long. But now it has ended. Young leaves sprouted out of the old roots and stems, and the greenery thickened and thickened.[48] Today it is a marvelous crown of leaves that will soon grant as much beautiful shade as it did during that great summer before the long winter. However, this did not satisfy the deep, inward drive toward "rebirth," which planted a foreign tree in the soil of the Jewish psyche, grafted onto it sprigs that the sojourning Hebraic tribe had collected from Hebrew and other languages, and fashioned a second language from that. This language, so unique and so suitable for expressing anything from the most glorious to the utterly common, has no reason to feel ashamed among the other languages of Europe, and yet this entire "rebirth" of twin languages has occurred so tacitly and modestly. No news of this was reported to the outside world. That is the way such things happen.

Language, however, is merely a rug that the soul of a people weaves for itself to tread upon when necessary. If, for some external reason such a thing cannot be woven, the nation must settle for foreign rugs. That does not mean it must lie or rest on them idly; it can wander around on them, display their beauty, develop their strengths, and realize their uniqueness just as well as on its own rugs. The Jewish "rebirth" has not shied away from such foreign rugs either. The Jewish spirit has been awakened by the kiss of the arts and sciences. The rumors, however, are even more silent about this than they are about the "rebirth" of the language. Whereas accounting for the latter requires only acknowledging inconvenient facts about its genesis, the former would require us to recognize and

47. [Birnbaum uses the German word *Asiatismus*.]
48. [There is a play on words here: *Stämme* can mean both stems and tribes.]

give up much-loved falsehoods, a reality that most would be "unable to bear." It is all the more exciting, for those of us who have abandoned these prejudices (once considered quite liberal views) to examine how Jewish scholars and artists managed to labor in the selfsame atmosphere of fundamental sentiments and values, despite all these heteronational elements within them.

The unconscious influence of individual national factors upon the creation of language and the artistic life of the mind, however, requires social life to be organized in groups in order to have any effect. This is why these factors' influence must be met by an indomitable urge for localization, for a place of gathering. And here, too, we observe the effects of the "rebirth." The extent of the current Jewish drive to concentrate in one place is unprecedented in history. The development and success of this drive is evident in the predominantly Jewish neighborhoods of central European cities and towns to the immense accumulation of Jewish proletarians in the Anglo-Saxon metropolises, and not least the great passionate quest for a Jewish homestead.

This entire Jewish Renaissance movement—creation of language, cultural genesis, quest for identity—is not man-made; it is governed by no one. None of the parties and personalities that we observe emerging from this movement are carving a specific path for it, unless it occasionally finds itself at an impasse due to some person's or some party's misguided efforts, from which it usually quickly finds its way back. On the contrary, the movement itself, impassioned and instigated by the overall economic and scientific developments within the Jewish soul, spouts out personalities from its mass, agglomerates the parties, and leads them in this or that direction toward its own still quite obscure goals.

No one should forget this, however much they might feel their deeds to be "theirs alone," even when committing to working within only one party. For only those who take this into account will remain in control of their actions and those of their party. Only those who remain able, in the midst of the daily routine of personal or partisan agitation, to contemplate the driving forces of history through a retreat into creative reflection, will be able to direct their own deeds—and those of their party—toward those decisive turning points that might otherwise go unnoticed. Of course it is especially difficult after such contemplation to reintegrate oneself into a party, for all the indignation and discontent it confronts one with. No one wants to hear from the grumblers and ditherers, from the theoreticians whose pallid thoughts ail each and every action. Action! Not the dull stubborn ways of the bovine, or those of skittish horses—action! Human action, distinguished from that of man's fellow animals by the sharp bridle of thought.

But alas! We cannot do without parties; I hear them shouting at me, and thus the Jewish Renaissance too must be incorporated into a party.

Slow down! There ought to be parties; certainly, there ought to be organizations to realize the will of history. But they do not have to be such hulking machines thrashing about with crude aim. There might be a time—and it will come sooner than one would expect—in which they prove to be the clockwork of society, with a fine sensitivity for the demands of progress within them. Well, I admit, this is not yet the case and the Jewish movement does not seem eager to get the ball rolling. But this does not mean that no constructive work is being done outside of the parties, especially outside of the Jewish parties. Please note: parties, not party. The Jewish Renaissance movement is not embodied in a single party, but in a multitude of past, present, and future ones. Not to acknowledge this fact is to underestimate the possibilities of operating beyond the confines of parties. Those whose nature is to fanatically pursue unity deny the possibility of and justification for organizational pluralism, which results from a multitude of perspectives on the Jewish Renaissance movement. And those who do not understand that diversity is a source of life, that it is the future, will never understand those who wish to help fulfill a great new realization of the Jewish people, without party affiliation.

Even at times when a nation stands in full spiritual and physical armor, when it has love and strength, such independent fighters are indispensable as conscious or unconscious supervisors to the so-called activist politicians and activist parties. Take the German nation, for instance, which could really make something of itself if not for individuals who by means of their critical or creative work save it from the shallowness of national liberalism, of liberalism in general, and to some extent of Social Democracy, who save it from the swamp of centrism and the crookedness of antisemitism.

And then take the Jews—who, despite impressive initial attempts, despite (or precisely because of) extensive insemination, cannot yet be referred to as a full-fledged nation, a people! All the parties are essentially premature infants with large embryonic heads and frail bodies. The nation has yet to be reared to maturity, there remain to be discovered a thousand ways to continually provide its mind and body with fresh nourishment, and to a thousand ends—that its language ability may grow, that its distinctive spirit can bloom, that its desire to gather itself together may continuously grow stronger, that it may adapt all such gifts to our modern age in which it is a joy to live. This is accomplished a thousand times more effectively by free people or by organizations of free people, unbound to a prescribed path, than by any party. Any so-called ghetto poet writing for his poor audience, any company publishing Hebrew and Jewish works or decent periodicals dealing with the Jewish Question, any Jewish workers' union that teaches its members to better understand the modern means of production, any Jewish theater that vividly portrays the current Jewish spirit to the Jewish people, any real, tangible colonial activism—any of these matter more to our future, matter a thousand times more for the "rebirth" of the Jewish people, than all the programs and deeds of all the Jewish nationalist parties combined.

Nobody denies the parties' right to see themselves as embodiments of the great Jewish Renaissance movement. However, they should remain proper and modest, not simply equate themselves with this great, forceful, historic phenomenon. They should approach this great work with a soft touch, not grasp at it vulgarly. Otherwise it might soon be time for their replacement by other, less demanding, more attractive parties. And anyone for whom the "rebirth" of the Jewish people means more than partisan dogmatism will be in his rights to shout at them with English blitheness, "*Hands off!*"[49]

Jewish Autonomy

Movements only appear to follow one another. In truth, the seeds of a new movement are already sown when the old one seems to have just begun to blossom. Thus the renaissance of the Jewish national intellectual movement—which, in essence, had never died—coincided with the childhood years of assimilation. Even then, emancipation was greeted here and there by a cry, unheard in the bustle of the masses, for national self-determination. Nevertheless, it took quite a long time until something like a chorus formed from isolated voices. It happened a mere twenty-five years ago. And only then, when goals were set and pursued, did the struggle for reality begin.

Where this concerned the idea of the rebirth of a state, distinctive images of the future soon emerged. And that, at least, always gave the movement renewed energy. Yet where this concerned infusing life itself with Jewish creativity, or elevating its Jewish creativity where it already existed, the question immediately posed itself much more unflatteringly. There were no aims, there could be none.

49. [*"Hands off!"* is written in English in the original.]

What was missing—until now—was a framework for activity. Now, however, a great opportunity presents itself, brought about by the idea of so-called national autonomy currently occupying Austrian minds.[50]

He who holds prejudice against everything Austrian may calm himself. We are not concerned with the idle contrivance of some activist, but with the final, intellectual result of certain facts and developments.

Austria does not exist, as so many tend to believe, because of the dynasty, but because of its peoples. Where they reside in their own territories, these are usually too small to become independent economic entities. Even more importantly, the jumbling and mixing of nations has advanced so far that their sharing a community of one state has become a necessity. Almost all serious politicians have realized this by now. At the same time, a refined understanding of the idea of nationality has gradually taken hold in wider circles. Its essence as cultural individualism has received renewed focus, and it shall no longer be abused for purposes of gaining and maintaining power.

The idea of national autonomy was born from these premises. In essence, it means the following: nationalities fill Austrian politics with their noise today because they do not have rights as such. Since each people can fulfill its cultural needs only by pushing them through in the Imperial Council [Reichsrat] and the state assemblies [Landtage], the result is a struggle of all against all. That is why national affairs, like religious ones, must cease to be a collective matter for everyone's deliberation and must instead become a matter for individual nations. Each nation shall administer its own cultural matters, schooling in particular. National associations at the imperial, provincial, and municipal levels shall take on this responsibility and receive the relevant rights of taxation. Representatives of the individual nations in the government, national contingents of civil servants, and the election by nation of deputies to the imperial council and to the state assemblies are meant to supplement and guarantee this system.

Known only to a few zealots a short time ago, national autonomy is now on everyone's lips. Even the prime minister spoke of its future in his last grand speech on electoral law.[51] Its essence and extent are still little understood; it is

50. [In November 1905, Austria's parliamentary advisory committee (Ministerrat) convened to propose ways in which Vienna would now be directly involved in electoral reform, specifically with regard to the ramifications of the newly established universal male suffrage. One of the government's main recommendations was the creation of the "smallest possible" voting districts along national lines.]

51. [Prince Konrad zu Hohenlohe-Schillingsfürst.]

mostly considered merely in its applicability in elections. In Moravia, it has even partly become a legal reality in this respect. But precisely for this reason it has introduced itself quickly into all strata of the people. And precisely for this reason it has suddenly unfurled the problem of the Jewish people.

If basic national rights are to be guaranteed to all Austrian peoples, why not also to the Jews, who need such a guarantee most urgently? This question, raised only by individuals in smaller circles so far, is now suddenly being voiced. It was raised in the house of deputies by the Jewish side (Dr. Straucher) and by the Ruthenian side (Professor Romanczuk).[52] In a Jewish mass assembly in Vienna, before which the author of this essay made a presentation, action was initiated. A committee—formed by members of various Jewish parties and groups and by individuals who have made early or special contributions to the cause of the Jewish people—will concern itself with the necessary steps for the time being. A functional organization has yet to be created.

One may well contend that these events have world-historical significance. Because for the first time, for a not insignificant part of the Jewish community and from a not-too-distant future, the legal and constitutional recognition of Jewish cultural individuality and of the rights issuing from it beckon the Jewish people. This must have far-reaching implications for both the general and the Jewish populace.

Certain people with tunnel vision have nothing better to do than to declare the granting of national autonomy to the Austrian Jews, which can be expected sooner or later, a victory of antisemitism. In reality, however, the granting of national autonomy can only weaken antisemitism, because it will for the first time acknowledge legal equality as an absolute principle independent of any preconditions, including assimilation. This is what is noteworthy, not the completely trivial support of the Jewish demand for autonomy by antisemites. What else is to be expected of them anyway? They would, after all, not be antisemites— that is, people who quite misjudge the direction of this development—if they did not call for the arbitrary (the isolation of the Jews) based on the inevitable (the acceptance of Jewish nationality). It is not they who call forth that which is

52. [In December 1905, Benno Straucher—a Jewish member of the House of Deputies, the lower house of the Austrian parliament—called for national electoral *curiae*, which would include a Jewish one. Each nationality would be represented as a group by a certain number of elected officials in the Reichsrat. Iulian Romanczuk, a non-Jewish Ruthenian, was actually the first Austrian parliamentarian to call for official recognition of the Jews as a nationality (*Volksstamm*).]

coming into being, but those non-Jewish friends of autonomy who are beyond any suspicion of antisemitism and of whom there are many, among them the most eminent intellectuals.[53]

National autonomy puts the Jews' legal equality on an unshakable foundation. It clarifies the relationship between Jews and non-Jews, which must in time evolve into a relationship between friendly neighbors. Most significantly, national autonomy makes possible a truthful image of the nature of the Jewish people, placing them among the civilized peoples of humanity. Who could, therefore, overlook for whom it is a blessing? For humanity, because national autonomy offers it the prospect of gradually paralyzing the most effective organizing force of reaction, antisemitism. For the Jews, because it not only offers this prospect, doubly valuable to them, but also completely different profoundly inward perspectives.

National autonomy faces its greatest challenge in the West. Here the Jewish community lacks a national language. Of course, language is not integral to the essence of nationality, but merely a form of its expression, which organizes the national spirit in a natural and unsurpassed manner, thereby enabling higher achievements and independent works. It is thus not language as such but its organizing force that raises culture and fosters creativity. If it were possible to replace this natural organizing force at least partly with a social, deliberate one, it would be possible to reinvigorate the collective soul of Western Jews. And what could be better than national autonomy, which, through national elections, is currently filling electors and elected of all parties with a sense of cultural responsibility? Which must—and this remains the most important point—necessarily lead, through national schooling and the concentration of Jewish intellect, to national cultural success? And one need not believe that only the Western Jews of Austria would be moved by this healthy change of affairs. National autonomy is not an Austrian principle, it is a new, national principle of humanity, and it is not at all inconceivable that it could, where the conditions are ripe, also mean a breakthrough for Jews elsewhere. Thus it is certainly possible in the United States, where the Jewish community already displays quite remarkably sympathetic tendencies toward Jewish nationals. Moreover, in those Western countries in which Jewish autonomy may not be feasible due to local circumstances, the

53. [For example, in December 1905, Romanczuk's Ruthenian National Democratic faction, Narodna Rada, voted unanimously that Jewish-national electoral districts be allocated to Galician Jews.]

repercussions are nevertheless valuable. They could achieve, at the very least, a more energetic Jewish tone in the lives of Jews in these regions.

For the East, Jewish autonomy does not have such a straightforward creative function. Yet it arises there with a much more immediate logic than in the West, and adds to language, which is not lacking there, as a further means of preserving culture. There it can reach its full potential. There, it is not a future wishing to be born that calls for it, but the certain, living present that seeks to continue living, to unfold more prosperously, brightly, and splendidly. And a present of which eight million Jews partake. For this does not concern only the Jews of Galicia and Bukovina, but the entirety of Russian Jewry for whom the question of autonomy has long been raised.[54]

In summary: with the idea of national autonomy, a new, providential star has risen for the Jewish people. And most auspiciously: all nationally conscious groups, regardless of their goals, have recognized this idea, and those further removed sense it with stunned amazement.

54. [Austria acquired Galicia from Poland in 1772. In 1774 Austria occupied Bukovina, a northern section of Moldavia that was part of the Ottoman Empire, and in 1787 Austria attached Bukovina to the province of Galicia.]

4 | Paths That Lead Away from *Yidishkayt*
I. L. Peretz

Y. L. Peretz, "Vegn, vos firn op fun yidishkayt," in *Ale Verk*, ed. Dovid Pinski.
New York: Farlag Yidish, 1920, 13:44–88.

Isaac Leib (Yitskhok Leybush) Peretz (1852–1915) is best known for his contribution to the emergence of modern Jewish literature in Hebrew and Yiddish. Peretz wrote poetry, short stories, plays, and "stories in a folk manner," and he is often mentioned alongside S. Y. Abramovich (Mendele Moykher Sforim, or Mendele the Book Peddler) and Sholem Rabinovich (Sholem Aleichem) as one of the figures who created a modern Yiddish literary culture. Peretz was born in Zamość, an important medieval Polish city, to a family that trained him to read Jewish texts while tolerating his European learning. While writing Hebrew and Yiddish poetry and verse, Peretz practiced law in Zamość, until without explanation the Russian authorities revoked his legal license, most likely for suspected socialist activities. Peretz found temporary employment working for a statistical survey commissioned by Jan Bloch, a railway magnate and Jewish convert to Protestantism, that was intended to prove the economic and societal productivity of Jews living in Polish towns and the countryside. Based on this experience, Peretz published his first extended work of fiction, the twenty-two pieces of fictionalized reportage that made up *Impressions of a Journey through the Tomaszow Region in the Year 1890*. Following his work for Bloch, Peretz moved to Warsaw and increasingly devoted his energies to Jewish literature and cultural and communal causes. Professionally, he worked from 1891 until his death as the record keeper of the Warsaw Jewish communal council, a position that provided him with both time and material for his writing. Peretz pioneered several Yiddish literary genres, including Yiddish modernism and a style of fiction intended to read like Hasidic folk tales. Perhaps his most famous short story, "Bontshe the Silent," satirized Jewish resignation to suffering and became a potent symbol in Jewish politics, especially among Jewish socialists.

Like others before and after him, Peretz called for a Jewish cultural renaissance. As Ruth Wisse has pointed out, however, Peretz was exceptional in being intellectually rooted in the Polish cultural world. Peretz was eleven years old at the time of the failed 1863 Polish revolt for independence, and his intellectual development was deeply affected by the spirit of liberalism and the sense of shared interests between Poles and Jews that permeated Polish intellectual circles in the several years following the revolt (Peretz wrote in Polish first, before turning to Hebrew and then Yiddish, and he published Yiddish translations of Polish literature in his Yiddish literary journals). Without political sovereignty, the Polish national movement turned to language and culture as the bases for national preservation, and Peretz saw the potential for a similar renaissance among Jews. When, in 1891, he first proposed a program of *bildung*, or Jewish education in this context, he held an optimistic view of a future Europe where nationalisms would be buttressed by culture instead of arms. By 1911, when he wrote "Paths That Lead Away from *Yidishkayt*," antisemitism had soured even the most liberal aspects of Polish society, and Peretz had become skeptical about the possibility that Poles would ever accept the Jews on equal terms. Nevertheless, he also doubted that the solutions offered by the Jewish parties and ideologies represented the panaceas their proponents claimed. Instead, he remained continually fixed upon using culture and language to build a sense of national consciousness and unity among Jews in the diaspora in general, and Poland in particular. By his death in 1915, Peretz had become a national figurehead for Eastern European Jewry, and his portrait and name graced (and still grace) schools, publications, and professional and communal organizations.

Peretz, Dubnov, and Smolenskin believed that the Jewish experience in exile had positively affected Jewish nationalism: the Jews' national ideal was more ethical than others' because it was not built upon violence. Yet Peretz was also rather astutely aware of the vulnerability of a national existence undefended by arms or political sovereignty, and for that reason apprehension as much as hope marks his literary *oeuvre*. In "Paths That Lead Away from *Yidishkayt*," Peretz argues that Jewish conversion to Christianity, at the time a much discussed issue, is symptomatic of a larger problem concerning what it means to be Jewish in the modern world. Though Peretz had personally labored for over thirty-five years to construct a secular and national Jewish culture, he still believed the foundations of Jewishness, or *Yidishkayt*, to be weak and its meaning unclear. Part of the problem lay in the erosion of the central place that religion played in Jewish national consciousness. To Peretz, the Jews, unlike other European nations, could not discard the key elements of their religion because their national survival in exile always depended upon their collective historical memory and hope for redemption. The central challenge, then, was to create a secular culture that would preserve those two essential religious elements.

Conversion was not the only path away from *Yidishkayt*. Many socialists and liberals advocated assimilation or a Jewish universalism that stripped Jewishness of all its distinctive markers. Meanwhile, Jewish ideologues further confused matters in their arguments about whether Jewishness is best expressed through Zionism or proletarian brotherhood (or even some combination of the two). The journalist, intellectual, and philosopher Hillel Zeitlin (1871–1942), with whom Peretz jousts in this essay, argued at this time that national revival had to have Jewish piety—not just culture—at its core. The following essay offers more of a meditation and critique of other intellectuals than a program for how to reaffirm *Yidishkayt*. To Peretz, however, the only means for Jews to navigate the challenges of the modern world must come through an internally driven Jewish cultural renaissance that would give meaning to what is *Yidishkayt*. The following essay first appeared as a series of thirteen columns in *Der Fraynd* and was republished in Peretz's posthumous *Ale Verk*. Columns 2, 3, 7, 9, 10, 11, and 13 are presented here.

IT MUST BE MADE CLEAR

—"*Yidishkayt* has become weak!"

But—what *is* "*Yidishkayt?*"

—"We're Jews!"

But—how so?

We often say:

—"We want our children and grandchildren to *remain* Jews ..."

But what is ours to pass on to them?

What should their *inheritance* be?

And yet when someone leaves us in defiance, we say to him:

—"You're a renegade!"

But then we have to ask the question:

—"*What* did he abandon?" "And *what* did he foreswear?" "*Whom* did he desert?" "What was the *Yidishkayt* he turned his back on?"

And so the stammering begins.

Each one stammers in his own fashion.

One stammers away at the other while each unclear answer cuts off another.

And this happens because each time, each place, each class, and very often each distinct person has its own *Yidishkayt* and wants a *monopoly* over it.

People take institutions that embody a certain place, a certain moment in the Jewish spirit, in place of the Jewish spirit itself.

People take symbols that vary according to time and place—the *language* of

Jewish religion, philosophy, worldview, morality, and the like—in place of living, creative content.

In place of the human being who lives and grows people take the lifeless attire that he changes according to time and place.

With their fists, people jam the *eternal* into a fleeting *moment*...

Here are people of common descent, living in various times and places, each have their own Judaism of their own "four cubits," of their own *brief* existence.[55]

And very often a foolish switch takes place: the foreign is adopted as one's own; and it is this, a foreign-influenced copy, that is accepted as the original, "from Sinai..."[56]

Hasn't the Polish gabardine cloak been made holy?[57]

Isn't *kapores*, for some, what Judaism is all about?[58]

Isn't refusal to believe in Persian demons and Babylonian angels considered by some to be worse than apostasy?[59]

. . . .

In striving toward our goal, we must once and for all renounce fleeting "moments," temporary signs and symbols.

We are searching for what is eternal, the "essence," the "fundamental matter."

Yidishkayt is the Jewish worldview.

And if you like:

It is the world idea that searches for its embodiment in matter, in shape, in that which knocks against the Jewish soul.

Yidishkayt is—

What in times of independence creates the freedom to fashion institutions to embody its revelation. In such times, it is the joy and happiness of this world.

What in times of conflict creates institutions to defend, protect, and guard itself and its adherents—and it is then the struggle and hero's song!

And that which must, in times of subjugated weakness, withdraw into itself,

55. [Four cubits is the farthest distance a Jewish man is permitted to walk without a head covering, according to Jewish law. A cubit is the length of a man's forearm and is therefore not standard.]

56. [A reference to "Torah from Sinai," the premise that the Torah was revealed to the Israelites directly from God at Sinai.]

57. [The long cloak that was the attire of Polish noblemen.]

58. [*Kapores* is the ritual, conducted a week before the Day of Atonement, of swinging a chicken around one's head to rid oneself of sin.]

59. [Peretz refers here to common Jewish beliefs (or superstitions) of non-Jewish origin.]

hide itself in the *"pintele yid"* [the essence of Judaism], enduring *silently*, awaiting better times—and then, it is hope, *pain and suffering* . . . messianic dreams and the "world to come."

And then *Yidishkayt* demands sacrifice . . .

And the *Yidishkayt* for which we demand this sacrifice must be defined clearly and precisely . . .

It was once thought that man is born as a tabula rasa and life comes along with its stylus and writes. Today we know that man plays a part, that life is a process, a struggle between man and milieu, between man and nature, that man comes into the world with a ready *inheritance*, with the seed of his *own* will, of his *own* individual power, with his aptitudes for life and struggle that determine whether he'll be victorious or fail . . .

The same holds true for the *nation*.

With what did *we* enter the world arena? What do *we* want? Which cultural thread do we weave into the web of the world? What is our tone in the world's harmony? What would the world lack if we were not here?—

What is "Jewish" and what is "un-Jewish"?—how do we differ from others? What do we have to *protect*? *Why* sacrifice ourselves? For *what* do we fight? What is our *life*, what is our *death*?

"MODERN"—A PARENTHETICAL COMMENTARY

The question "What is *Yidishkayt*?" has been asked, but to get at the answer isn't easy.

One is caught by the sleeve, stopped midway.

Our "modern," our modern person, doesn't want to hear the question . . .

The "spirit of Judaism,"[60] "true *Yidishkayt*," "Jewish ethics"—all of this is for the modern person—is old, hackneyed, and worn out . . .

"One Jewish God with all of his paraphernalia," the "You-chose-us nationalism"—mere dreams from the dark Middle Ages. . . . And the modern person needs light and color; be they stage lights or be they colors in a soap bubble, and in truth, only these . . .

Daylight and true colors are too banal; modern man's eyes are too weak and his nerves even weaker.

---

60. [Peretz uses *Yahdus* here for "Judaism," to distinguish it from *Yidishkayt*, or Jewishness.]

And so modern man creates for himself his own modern nationalism, saying: "The old must be thrown out. Soldiers must come, ripping out wire after wire, tossing out stone after stone, to reveal the mold to the world and show that it's in fact no fortress but an old ruin . . ."

"It is of no use to us in the hard, bitter battle for our survival . . ."

Here, the modern man has misspoken . . .

For modern man is totally unfit for war, unsuited for the army, even for the "nation," insofar as the nation requires work and sacrifice . . .

This, modern man is unable to give . . .

The "modern" folk, as modern man imagines it, must first of all demand no sacrifice; this is what the "herd" requires, that within the folk each individual is free . . . And whatever each and every free person of the modern free folk does, gather it all together and pour it into one sack, and you'll have the national culture you wished for . . . You don't need to define it; you need not do a thing . . .

. . . .

Who is he, our modern man?

The word "our" gets extra emphasis because we already know the modern European man . . .

He is known first of all in that he has long stopped being modern, even gone out of fashion . . . The best sign: he has just become fashionable among us and we are always late. . . . He has already become, it seems, tedious and wearisome. "The Moor has done his duty; the Moor may now leave . . ."[61]

Modern man found a few fine strokes of life, certain delicate nuances of color; he discovered several fine tremolos within the human soul, two or three small, very small, amplitudes of blood in the human heart, a near tear in the human eye, a near smile on the human face—and fled to the cabaret . . .

There were once great ideals for which people sacrificed themselves: "Fatherland" turned out to be—a prison where the poor classes do hard labor. . . . "Patriots"—contractors who supply provisions and then take the finished product. . . . "Family"—legalized human trafficking . . . and on and on. . . . So modern man ran away and had nowhere to go, busied himself with games and trivialities and was interesting for a while . . .

Examining, reevaluating values, placing something new in the overly scholas-

61. [This is the last line of the fourth scene in Friedrich Schiller's play *Fiesco* (1783), and is spoken by "the Moor."]

tic and worn-out vessels; creating new institutions, new symbols, this isn't for the squeamish, woebegone modern man with broken nerves . . .

But if one were to ask: is it real or not, true or false, this or that idea, this or that life purpose, this or that worldview???

When such questions are posed, modern man has *no* words. . . . He does not destroy, he does not build, he does not think, he does not philosophize . . .

And—here lies his greatest misfortune:

He is not free!

He has attacked his living god, and at every moment serves another bit of dust from that god, all the while believing that he has freed himself from God . . .

He believes he serves no one, and he believes this only because the things he serves are so small that he himself doesn't see them, and they change so often and lightning fast that they barely remain in his memory.

Modern man has no life, only individual moments; he therefore has no *character*, no *will*, only *caprices* and *"willing desires."* And this dances around in the kaleidoscope of his distracted mind . . .

He is an uncoordinated organism; beautiful perhaps, but so wormlike.

A row of loose segments, loose hoops in a sack. . . . And each hoop has its own bit of knowledge and needs—but only skin holds them together . . .

And for something that can't even organize itself, can't give its own life purpose, one can't expect it to organize world phenomena, or define the purpose of concepts such as class and nation . . .

Great men go their *own* way, not after the herd; modern man meanders without a path . . .

Is this what it means to walk free?

These are the paths followed by deserters, escapees of hard labor, and above all—people without a path . . .

"Tohu lo derekh," "to wander in the waste"—is not a path, not even to conversion.[62]

THE FIRST PATH

Zeitlin once wrote:

"Peretz has a heaven, but there is no God in his heaven!"[63]

62. [See Psalm 107:40.]
63. [Peretz misquoted Zetilin, who later corrected Peretz in an open letter. Zeitlin's ac-

The first half of the statement is certainly a compliment—and I acknowledge it with a friendly, brotherly smile. Better late than never.

As for the *second* half, *I positively and resolutely concur.*

I don't have so much as an inkling of where to look for Him:

Before the world's existence—as its Creator?

After the world—emerging from it?

Perhaps only in the world; He is its spirit; its universal will that reveals itself in various forms and clothed bodies; its regent, the subjugator of death and physical decay; its prisoner who struggles, breaks its chains, and tears down the walls of its prison to free Himself so that He can finally be revealed?!

Perhaps the earth is only clay and He—the artist who continually creates more beautiful and powerful forms, thereby fulfills His artistic dreams and— "ke'khomer b'yad ha'yotser," "as clay in the hand of the potter"—he shatters everything old in one stroke, creates anew, and finally grants to eternity the newest, most beautiful, the loftiest?[64]

Whatever it may be—He is the source of life!

To live means to have a godly vision and, to a degree, the godly will to implement that vision and change existing ideas and will according to it, constantly creating new forms, being a partner in His Creation!

I am alive; therefore inside of me is a divine spark! All living things possess it, and I feel that everything is alive!

Even the one who *denies* God's existence has the divine spark. His merely involves a misunderstanding, a small error: He denies the existence of foreign sparks that, in their vanity, are *disguised as complete gods*! But he can't free himself from his belief in them!

The blasphemer also possesses the divine spark!

---

tual words were: "Peretz's heavens are only a word, a noise, a hue—no God resides in them." My thanks to Michael Steinlauf, for making available his unpublished paper "'Paths That Divert from Yiddishkayt': Y. L. Peretz vs. Hillel Zeitlin, Warsaw, 1911," presented at the conference Warsaw: History of a Jewish Metropolis, University College London, June 2010.]

64. [The metaphor "as clay in the hand of the potter" comes from Jeremiah 18:6: "Behold, as the clay in the potter's hand, so are ye in My hand, O house of Israel." In this biblical text, God describes his power to build up and destroy nations at will. Later rabbinic literature interprets the passage as confirming that God is responsible for creating the "evil impulse" in man (Babylonian Talmud, Tractate Sukkah 52b and Tractate Berakhot 32a). Here, Peretz relies on the biblical metaphor to describe a divine role in the Jewish renaissance, adding an element of ancient tradition to a radically modern phenomenon.]

In an even greater measure, I imagine! Blasphemy is *frustrated love* that longs for the *source* of life but is unable to reach it!

It drives the mortified human *compassion*, which can't bear the pain and suffering meted out and divided up in God's name in such endless measure! Outrage verges on madness, seeing the blood that is spilled in His name!

Job screams out! Deeply shamed and mortally wounded justice . . .

And, if He is the sum total of all divine sparks, then love, mercy, and justice are the divine attributes of the human being!

Heretics and *blasphemers* are those who, animated by the divine spark, grow and in doing so outgrow the stultified norms and forms for dealing with the gods. They are loftier than the gods, more honest, and have grown so much better and more knowledgeable that they can no longer bow to them or their spines would break. So low has the *present-day* vision of gods become!

And yet the spark is too small, or the "body" it animates too lazy, too inflexible, and lacking in power to create new forms—lacking in courage and creative imagination!

So they become so many Abrahams, smashing idols but without receiving God; they uproot the evil that cannot create anything good, clearing the way for the new prophet who will come *after* them, find the space clear and clean, and build a new temple for a loftier idea![65]

But you are the ones who brought the renegade to life, placed destructive words in the mouth of the blasphemer—the ax in the hand of the destroyer; *you, the arrester, the fortifier*, you, who want thoroughly *petrified* ideas. Others want things of wood and stone, painted with brushes—you, children of the people of the book!—you satisfy yourselves with the quill, with the word inscribed once and for all time—but these are all arrested, static forms!

A different, indeed, a higher form!

The word is softer, more symbolic, but it is nevertheless—idol worship!

. . . .

If the godly sparks won't suffice and one must absolutely have an image of an absolutely personal God (Heine,[66] in the end, could not comprehend Him

---

65. [According to the rabbinic compilation Genesis Rabbah, Abraham's father was an idol maker. Left alone in his father's shop, Abraham smashed the idols in order to demonstrate their powerlessness. This midrash (rabbinic exegesis) serves to explain why Abraham left his home in pursuit of a single God (Genesis Rabbah, 38:13).]

66. [Heinrich Heine (1797–1856) was an influential German poet and writer. His *oeuvre* affected other literary figures, such as Peretz, struggling to balance their Jewish origins with

otherwise), then, like Moses, one must have an authentically Jewish (what was once a Hebrew) form, that is, no definite form at all!

"Remember—you did not see any image or likeness of me" was proclaimed at Sinai.[67]

Not there *exists* no image of me, because that would mean no personal God! But—*you did not see.* You only heard his voice! Because you know *no* definite image of him, you are forbidden to make one.

And one must feel the personal God as a *moving* one! Whatever stops, dies; God must be life! And He must walk ahead of man, who must yearn for Him, strive toward Him, be pulled higher and farther by Him! Gods that are carried and dragged along are *idols!*

"These are owned by those whom I chase away from you!"[68]

And He must keep *moving on!* In a moment of ecstasy and revelation, He shows Himself and is seen *from behind.* . . . Whoever sees His face can no longer live—he has lived to see everything! To live is only to seek! And He must be distant from man, so that man can never reach Him: his life is a step; gods one step further are idols.

God is found neither in the *past* nor in the passing present! *"Ehiye asher ehiye."* "I will be what I will be!" God is in the *future,* in the *eternal* future, in eternity! Seeking him must be eternal!

. . . .

And what do you want?

Do you, who preach *khumesh* with Rashi, want to bring back yesterday?[69]

Do you yearn, you hinderer of change, to stretch today beyond its limits and somehow prevent tomorrow . . . ?

Do you know what that means?

It is to take a viable seed whose shell has cracked and needs to be replanted so that it can blossom more beautifully and colorfully, and force it back into the

---

enlightenment ideals. Peretz refers here to the fact that Heine reluctantly accepted baptism in order to join the Prussian bar, but later in life he publicly professed his return to a personal god.]

67. [This is most likely a reference to Deuteronomy 4:15–16.]

68. [This may be a reference to Leviticus 26.]

69. [*Khumesh* is Yiddish for the Five Books of Moses. Rashi was a twelfth-century sage whose biblical and Talmudic commentaries, known for their simplicity and straightforwardness, were typically taught alongside the biblical texts. *Khumesh* with Rashi (or *khumesh mit rashe*) was the cornerstone of *kheyder,* or elementary, Jewish education.]

shell, bind it and wrap it with wire, and say an incantation: seed, grow in these narrow confines, grow in darkness!

This also means: not bringing the dead to the graveyard, but leaving them at home to poison the air!

What more can you do?

You want to push your grown children back into the cradle, wrap them in swaddling clothes with strings, or even better—push them back into the womb! It's warm and dark there! And if the younger generation begins to rebel, to tear up the cobwebs you thought were chains, breaks your straw "walls" and escapes from your poisonous prison, and leaves you and *your Yidishkayt*, you curse and shout without noticing that you, you hinderer, paved the first path leading away from Judaism—

Even if indirectly.

THE RAFT AND THE FORTRESS

I want to tell you a story about a great Indian recluse.

Once upon a time—according to Buddha—a wanderer walked along the banks of a river.

His path was long and hard, and the riverbank along which he walked was dangerous.

Robbers hid in caves and in the forest—wild animals roamed—danger lurked everywhere.

But the *other* side of the river was peaceful and quiet; on the other side there was certainty—Buddha's sole ideal!

But the river was wide and deep . . .

So the wanderer stopped, cut down a few branches from the forest, tied them together into a raft, crossed the river, and came to the peaceful side where his path would be sure . . .

But because the wanderer wasn't too bright, he did the following:

Having crossed the river, he said to the raft:

"Raft, dear raft, you have saved me from robbers and freed me from wild animals; you did not surrender me to the river's waters. I am *thankful* to you. You are holy to me, my savior, and I will not desert you! . . ."

And he placed the raft on his shoulder and carried it on the dry land . . .

Do you envy him?

Do you envy the man who carries the raft he made on his shoulders? How is his salvation, an idea, preserved eternally in a wooden raft?

And now, moreover, the path is uphill! And though the path is difficult, you've taken the knowledge that created the raft and thrown it *under* the raft . . .

"The small prayer house with its *minyen* of idlers!"[70]

. . . .

The "small prayer house with its *minyen* of idlers" is today—the raft on dry land.

Once, and this "once" was not that long ago, your *Yidishkayt* was great and beautiful and heroic!

A fortress for the Jewish soul!

A castle that, besieged by the entire Christian world, did not surrender!

All means to food and water blocked; the surrounding wells poisoned; all of the fruit trees uprooted—yet "*Yidishkayt*" does not surrender!

Starving, faint from thirst, exhausted shadows of men guard the walls within which the Jewish soul has taken refuge . . .

Temporarily taken refuge, "until this wrath shall pass"—

In other words:

If God's only name has not yet been sanctified on earth, we will not allow a compromise between Judaism and idolatry. We will wait!

In other words:

Messiah has *not* yet come. The world remains unredeemed. It's flooded with sin, overflowing with tears and blood! God's word does not reign, nor his justice. . . . We will wait!

You have taken the temporary fortress, "until this wrath shall pass," and made it *eternal*. You turned a means of protection into a *purpose* and an *end*! And when the siege ends, and tyrants cease attacking the walls, and no one is around, and the gates can be opened and one can walk about freely and reveal to the world that which is concealed, uncover what is hidden, and preach God's word, you have only a single statement for the world:

—Holy is the fortress.

Who is your God? What is His authority, His justice? How should the world and those who live on it behave so that both may be divinely pure? How would you redeem the world?

70. [A *minyen* is a quorum of ten Jewish men required for many prayers and rituals.]

You stand and murmur: *eyzehu mekomo* . . . "what is the place?"[71]

You have lost the *essence* and sanctified the ramparts of the fortress! You have forgotten the *intent* and continue to breathe into your lungs the putrid dank air of the prison as if it were holy incense . . . !

The soul is stale—one can't approach the world with dry words—so you hide your *Yidishkayt* from the world!

And what if the world that you must conquer comes to you falling on its knees to beg: reign!—you wouldn't leave your prison, or remove the decaying clothes from your body, or bow your head to receive the offered crown . . .

You would not, after all, say to the world: put away your antiseptic and use the ashes of a burnt cow!

Put away your medicine, and if a plague comes, erect a copper snake! End your agricultural system of field rotation and replace it immediately with a sabbatical year for the entire world![72] Would you erect a Temple with sacrifices and test adulteresses with the earth under the floor?[73]

You have killed the soul, and because you cannot approach the world with the dead body of the once great and proud *Yidishkayt*, so you hide it!

And so the young generation, which instinctively broke out of the prison and came into the world to live, had not so much as a Jewish word for "life" or "world"! The grandchildren of Jewish truth's proud defenders came to life and to the world as beggars, yearning for the *foreign* word! They came frozen stiff and naked . . . and barely managed to beg for foreign clothing to hide their shame! And they tricked their way to foreign ovens to warm themselves by a foreign fire! And for foreign truths they sat with wide open mouths and ears! . . .

And during this whole time the *best*, the most *beautiful*, the *strongest*, and the *most gifted* at life abandoned us! Our shadows grew darker and denser by the day and the air more and more foul, choking—

But even worse is that some of them returned—with the foreign word!

71. [This phrase is part of the daily prayer service. It comes from the Mishna and describes in detail the various locations in the Temple where ancient Jews brought their animal sacrifices. Its inclusion in the liturgy, despite its practical irrelevance to post-Temple Jews, has frequently been explained as learning Torah "for its own sake."]

72. [The term *shmite* (sabbatical) refers to the biblical commandment that all lands should lie fallow and all debts be remitted every seven years. See Exodus 23:10–11; Leviticus 25:1–7, 18–22; and Deuteronomy 15:1–11.]

73. [See Numbers 5:12–31.]

They opened a wide path that leads away from *Yidishkayt*, a wide and dangerous path—the *false national!*

AS ALL OTHER NATIONS

"Renaissance!" A single, small word, no addendum, no conditions of *place* and
time . . .

A small word, and yet it's the seed from which a whole *world, a Jewish world,*
must sprout . . .

And this word is mightily proud, and not new; it is the word of the Prophets
of old! The messianic word!

Ideas are eternal, changing only in form as they develop . . .

But the word, in its *purest form*, has not yet been uttered again . . .

When the Church withdrew weakened, when the walls of the ghetto, which
was at the same time our prison and our fortress, collapsed, *Yidishkayt* was too
beaten down, too weak—it was out of breath for a while.

One either feels for its pulse and can't find it, or is slightly deaf and can't hear
it, and so pronounces:

—*Yidishkayt* is giving up!

And so he expresses his deep regret:

—It was once so noble; it gave God to the world!

And he consoles himself: This *Yidishkayt* at least leaves an inheritance!

—A great pedigree! An everlasting *claim* upon the world for respect!

And he concludes resignedly:

—No one can live forever! The era of religion (and *Yidishkayt* is for him nothing more!) is mostly over . . . even the stronger and younger Church is in decline.
. . . One must do the right thing for "*Yidishkayt*" and sew some fine shrouds, find
it an honored spot in the mythology cemetery. . . ."Yahweh" is after all greater
than Jupiter!

Another, with more piety in his heart, counsels:

—It should not be "buried," but embalmed! Let it remain exactly as it is, petrified—forever! A historical monument for the antiquarian—an eternal joy!

In other words:

The Jewish nation has stepped aside, has renounced the world, so take *Yidishkayt* and place it like a headstone on its grave! . . .

But others aren't so ready to step aside. . . . A nation does not die so easily! . . .

"Blood is thicker than water"; it holds the national instinct.

It is sometimes confounded, shouted over by a bit of worldly screaming, and falls silent for a while—but then it reawakens stronger, and punishes more powerfully, more terribly.

And retreat to where?

Doors and gates are still not open! . . .

The gentile's stomach isn't that large or healthy. "Special individuals"—big bankers, politicians, famous scholars, singers, violinists—it can take in and digests as they are . . . but it can't digest all . . .

And so "the little people" are left behind, pulled back to it like a magnet, let no one rest . . .

And for the sake of their children and their children's children, one doesn't convert, and thinks instead:

We must keep moving; one can't simply remain within *Yidishkayt*; the stream of life carries us forward and we must *move with it.*

But not entirely!

It is so big, so awkwardly heavy—so unlovely!

It must be reduced, greatly reduced and ornamented . . .

And it submits to the surgery.

Dead forms are cut, and not a drop of blood appears, not a moan is heard! Perhaps the *shkhineh* groans from a ruin somewhere—but who hears it?[74]

And how easily the pages rip out of the prayer book! How pretty the holy books look in the archive! How beautifully clean the Jewish home has become, how perfect for a Christmas tree!

The remaining bit of *Yidishkayt* will stay in the *shul*, in the rabbi's care . . .

But the rabbi must now look like a *human being*. . . . The pastor's robes are so handsome; make something like them for the rabbi. . . . And the *shul* must become a synagogue, must become a temple. . . . Because at the moment it reeks of poverty, and poverty disgusts . . .

There are prayers without poetry, without sacrificial ritual and the Holy Land, and even translated into German; nothing "shocking . . ."[75] It is "*der Gottesdienst,*" the Lord's Mass, or it is at least once a year . . .

74. [The *shkhineh*, meaning that which inhabits or dwells in something, refers to God's presence, usually inside the Temple. It is a feminine noun in Hebrew and has therefore been taken by some to indicate the feminine aspect of the divine spirit. According to the Talmud, the *shkhineh* continues to dwell among the Jews even in the absence of the Temple.]

75. [Peretz here transliterates the English word "shocking" into Yiddish.]

True, it has no real attraction and has lost something of what once drew people—but the organ will lure people, and the girls' choir will pull the youth in by the hair. . . . And the quiet, heartfelt but poor melody of Sinai must be changed; it must—resound! As in a church!

And if people cannot come on Saturday, let it resound on Sunday!

Something must remain!

So they cut, change, perfume—and dead stays dead . . . the older ones hold on for a while . . . out of a sense of piety . . . but the younger ones flee—the reform is bankrupt . . .

A "new" person arrives, politely acknowledging the failure; he's opposed to any reform—Don't touch! The soul has departed and the form remains, but form is what's most important! . . . The wine has been drunk or evaporated on its own, but the barrel is eternal!

Hold onto the barrel and pour in fresh wine! It's easy to find! There is no dearth of wine merchants . . . only the winemaker changes; once it was Aristotle, today—Spencer, tomorrow—who knows . . .

Hold onto the barrel! . . .

Look for an empty and safe *cellar* to store it in! . . .

The "barrel idea" is also an idea—

But the time comes for ideas too, and they fall out of fashion.

Those who come back from "Europe," those whom "Europe" repulses, or who return on their own out of pity for the poor, suffering people, or out of piety, or a reawakened longing, have brought us news:

You are a people!

This we've actually known for a long time; no other language in the world has as many terms for race and folk as Hebrew. What was new was only the addendum:

"Nothing more!"

They did not feel anything more, nor did they see anything more while away among strangers!

"A people and nothing more"—here is where the danger begins!

THE DIFFERENCE

When one returns from somewhere and looks at our Jewish tragedy with a stranger's eyes, or at least through a stranger's glasses, one sees something outlandish.

This strangeness can't be understood, so the person says: Abnormal!

"Where the concept is lacking, a word takes its place!"

"Abnormal" can just as easily mean *below* as *above* the norm. Abnormal can mean *madness* and also *genius.*

Both the atavistic criminal and the prophetic revolutionary are equally abnormal.

We have always known that we aren't normal: A people that shall dwell apart[76]—one nation in the land—a single unit in the world . . .

But the abnormal needs to be evaluated . . .

Everything, ourselves included, must be examined freely and openly. Everything, be it man or nation, must be appraised, as far as possible, objectively.

When conducting an appraisal, one *compares,* but not in order to *make everything the same,* to make up a Sodomite bed, but in order to find what is *not the same,* what is *unique.*[77]

This is, in fact, what the exceptional individual does.

The more *advanced* the individual is, the more often he immerses himself in introspection, the more often he contemplates his own self, and asks: Why? What for?

He submits to no one other than himself, and seeks from no one justification for his life or approval for his existence; he will not base his raison d'être on usefulness to his peer or on similarity to him.

He immerses himself in introspection because he desires to find his self within himself, to *cleanse* it of what's worthless, to develop what's *worthy,* to take development as his goal and purpose, and for this he is ready to fight, to struggle until his last drop of blood, to sacrifice his life . . .

In this process, the superior being looks at himself from an even higher perspective: from above, to where he must, according to his nature, strive . . . from his "I" at the furthest point from his life's path.

This *imagined* "I" is his imperative, his judge.

He isn't bankrupt, and the past provides him only what he needs in order to recognize who he is. He doesn't liquidate his life, and his "I" in the present is not

76. [Numbers 23:9]

77. [A Sodomite bed is the Jewish equivalent to a Procrustean bed. In Greek mythology, Procrustes, the robber of Attica, forcibly fit people to his bed, either by stretching or by amputation. In Jewish tradition, the Sodomites are charged with the same crime.]

his judge or appraiser—his future "I" is his aspiration and faith and the justification for his life . . .

The same is true of peoples . . .

When I seek my *Yidishkayt*, I seek it *for myself*; I seek it in the future on the ground of its creative past . . .

I leave out the present, this "learned *khumesh* with Rashi"—this is our *decadence*, our refuse.

The judge of the exceptional individual is his superman; and the judge of the nation is none other than its national future—its stream when it flows into the sea—the sea of free humankind. . . . I place the *uniqueness* of my people before its national future (There is a "Thou" in His "Thou hast chosen us!") and ask:

Am I *worthless* or *worthy*? That I am different, this I know—

. . . .

My past reminds me:

You shall serve no other gods but your One God.

In the midst of your land, in Jerusalem, you shall erect your Temple.

Three times a year you shall come to the Temple, appear before God to offer up your sacrifice, to thank, entreat, and serve Him . . .

One people, one land, one Temple, one law, One God . . .

And everything is formed together in one breath . . . there can be no Temple erected anywhere else, and no altar. Nowhere else can sacrifice be offered, can incense be burned, even if to the One God—on penalty of death! The Temple is, however, open to all . . .

The stranger may come and *entreat*, and God will incline His ear and accept his sacrifice, and whoever calls the name of the One God is His child . . . and the law of all peoples will go forth from Zion . . .

The national—a world idea!

Do other peoples possess it?

Do the Germans, French, English, Russians, and other European peoples have a national *Weltanschauung*, a national religion, or national *world ideals*?

There is "German philosophy," that is, philosophical books written for Germans in German. . . . But there is no German philosophic idea.

There are *French* ideals for the French nation and for its sake: France is to be great and its fame widespread . . .

Here are England's ideals: I am the factory, the entire world my market!

And so it is with all . . . all . . .

They are "Christians"...

Yet Christianity has not united them. They didn't create their Christianity; they willingly accepted or it was violently imposed upon them. It didn't spring from their brains, it didn't sprout from their blood...

These are peoples subjugated by the Church...

The foreign floats above but fails to penetrate the core of their souls....It has no contact, no dealings with real life; it ceases to be a social phenomenon and becomes "faith."...It becomes a key to unlock heaven after death, not to subdue life; it is the "heavenly kingdom," not earth and not life on earth; it denies work and progress...

It is *faith*, not *will*; it is *resignation, severance, departure!* It is a means of redemption *from* life, not for life...

It is worn on top, like a coat, *over* life; in life, under the coat, *Roman* law rules, *Greek* art, European *technology*.

Four different sources of law—and the fifth is *nationality*, which sanctifies all crimes against others as—patriotism...

And so, if a European nation truly wishes to free itself from the international Church...if it wishes to progress in *life*, it must renounce heaven, religion...

We, a people without possessions, without a common language, with a striving for culture yet still without culture, we—as "a nation and nothing more" are nothing!

And how easy it is to walk away from nothing!...

THE ESTRANGED INTELLIGENTSIA

Nomadic blood; a family of wanderers in the wilderness.

In its blood—honesty and justice—and so in its God, who wanders with it and is therefore not fashioned of wood or stone, but a moving, living, God.

A lofty concept of God; a free and open world concept, without borders, without differences...

And when it leaves the wilderness and begins to wander through other lands, it can't mingle with the inhabitants; they are mutually repellent; and so it lives separately and escapes, finally, from pressure and oppression, and seeks a separate land...

The land is conquered. The familial God becomes the God of the chosen people in its chosen land. It wanders no more; it has a Temple in the land.

But its heart did not allow the extermination of the inhabitants; its honesty did not permit it to fence off the land from strangers, or to bind their lives to the land with an oath.

Their justice could not allow them to attack and subdue other peoples; a small people, a separate state—a state of priests and a holy people. . . . And with time, it fell . . .

But this people was the creator, not the product, of the state; the builder of God's Temple, not assembled and united by it; the arranger of the social, cultural, and economic forms in the land, not melted together in a crucible—this people outlives its freedom and its state, as well as its language and its Temple, with all of its cultural and economic forms, and goes once again to wander across the world. . . . And God once more goes with it!

The instinctive conception of God and of the world becomes clearer and more conscious; the people becomes a world people; its God, who does not abandon it and suffers exile together with it, a God of the world . . . the world, the entire state of exile—becomes the arena of conflict between the One God and the many *gods*. . . . God will triumph! . . .

The world isn't free of inequality and war, of forced labor, of robbery and anguish and oppression . . . because God is still *above* the earth, He has not yet *penetrated* it . . .

But the time will *come*, it *must* come. . . . God will judge the peoples and cleanse the world, Messiah will come . . . we will bring him. We the weakest, the martyrs of God's name! And wedged into all kinds of separate economic boxes, trapped in all sorts of sociopolitical bodies, suffering under the rule of a variety of provincial imperatives, patriotisms, wantonness, and unchecked power, and enduring all the trouble and weakness of a minority amid a terrible superior power—the people lives and remains true to itself!

It has its ancient state behind it as a golden memory of its youth, its future world state, the messianic world, before it as its guiding star. The people spin itself out of its two legends, weaving its symbols, illuminated by faith, by its sanctified belief it never falls into despair! If a wall is in the way, it bows its head for a while, but soon raises it up again, back toward God in heaven; if trouble comes—it endures, and soon easily forgets. . . . It doesn't want to remember, to recall its agony! Only to move on, only to survive, only to live to see the Messiah . . . at least the pre-Messianic pangs!

That's how this people lives, hopes, and believes!

And the intelligentsia? The "kidnapped child," that *nosher* in foreign kitchens! It is a tragicomic phenomenon:

We do not have a single *physical* barrier materially separating us from the world; and yet there are as many spiritual and moral barriers as there are nations among whom we are dispersed . . .

So our intelligentsia is the border population . . . and we take "pride" in them!

They provide us with other "peoples"—contrabandists who smuggle in foreign cultural values, sometimes "their father did not recognize their power"—a foreign web as a biblical-style agrarian law; often a bit of "duties of the heart"[78] chewed over by Count Tolstoy. . . . Above all, they are the bearers of culture between us and others—the mediators, the peacemakers and compromisers and defenders. . . . They count the medals that Jewish soldiers have received, the orders to which Jewish merchants belong, and the like and demand: rights! Not for *us* and not for *mankind*, but for those who are different—Russians, Poles, French. . . . Can we not shoot? Can we not kill, or swindle in politics?

And they come to us, these speakers of every language except Yiddish, with advice . . .

Absurdities:

—Mix the blood and disappear!

—Become Christian Jews . . . observers at the trial . . . or simply be "like all the nations" . . .

Seek your own rule, build your own *majority*, and let it be that somewhere law becomes your *mighty force*, your physical power—what do you care about the world and the God of the world?

. . . .

The petrified bourgeoisie on the one hand and the estranged intelligentsia on the *other*—these open the paths that lead away from *Yidishkayt*. . . . For these paths to be closed, a new *Jewish* intelligentsia must be created, one that will cultivate its own values and openly rally the folk!

Jewish *life* must bloom anew, the Bible must be brought to the folk as seed, and Jewish folk symbols and legends, newly refreshed, will be the dew and the rain![79] The field will revive, the folk will revive and awaken to suffer for truth and with unwavering faith in its victory! . . .

78. [A work of Jewish ethics by the eleventh-century philosopher Rabeinu B'hayei Ibn Pekudei.]

79. [Peretz uses "di bibel" here rather than "der tanakh."]

The flag of *Jewish* renaissance, of *Messiah and world-judgment*, of *world-libera-tion*—of a future free humanity must be raised again!

This is the mission of the eternal people, the world-people. This is what Jew-ish life must be, the Jewish home, Jewish school, Jewish theater, Jewish books, and everything that is Jewish must be.

March–July, 1911

II | Socialism and the Question of Jewish Peoplehood

5

"A Jew to Jews" and "Why Only Yiddish?"
Chaim Zhitlowsky

E. Khasin [Chaim Zhitlowsky], *Evrei k evereiam* (London: Fund of the
Russian Free Press, 1892).
Chaim Zhitlowsky, "Farvos davke Yidish?" in *Geklibene Verk* (New York:
Tsiko, 1955), 101–11. Originally published under the pseudonym Ben-Ehud
in *Forverts*, 1900.

Chaim Zhitlowsky (1865–1943) was one of a growing group of Jewish intellectuals
in the last years of the nineteenth century finding their way from Russian radicalism
to the idea of Jewish renewal in the diaspora. As a teenager, Zhitlowsky absorbed
the Russian populist and agrarian socialist critique of the Jews as a "parasitic" class.
His response, however, was to craft a particularly Jewish socialism rooted in the
culture and language of the people in order to correct what he saw as Jewish
exploitation of the peasantry. Zhitlowsky was born to a wealthy merchant family in the town of Ushatz, in the Vitebsk region of the Russian Empire. Although
both of his parents were from religious families, his father was a devotee of both
European culture and Haskala literature. As such, Zhitlowsky's father provided his
son simultaneously with a traditional Jewish religious education in a *heder* and with
private lessons in Hebrew and Russian, and Zhitlowsky went on to attend a Russian
gymnasium in Vitebsk. It was in Vitebsk that Zhitlowsky became close friends with
Semyon Ansky (1863–1920), who would later become a Socialist Revolutionary
and write the famous play *The Dybbuk*.

The dominant approach to the question of Jewish nationality among socialists
—both Jewish and non-Jewish—in the late nineteenth century was to press Jews
to disavow any kind of national or religious sentiment and assimilate into the working classes among whom they lived. Zhitlowsky, for his part, observed socialist
movements developing side by side with national movements throughout Eastern
and Southeastern Europe and the eastern part of Central Europe. He believed
the notion that the Jews' lack of territory disqualified them as a nation—and,
consequently, for an independent socialist movement—to be rooted in the personal views of socialist ideologists rather than in reality. According to Zhitlowsky,
his split with the radical agrarian socialist group Narodnaia Volia (People's Will)
stemmed from their executive committee's refusal to recognize his creation of a

Jewish faction. While living in St. Petersburg and later in exile in Berlin and Zurich, Zhitlowsky became increasingly convinced that Jewish socialists' equating of assimilation and cosmopolitanism was delusional and self-defeating.

In Zurich Zhitlowsky composed "A Jew to Jews"—whose first three of five chapters are presented here—as a distillation of his ideological position. In the 1880s Zhitlowsky blamed the Jews for their "parasitism," but by 1892, when he wrote "A Jew to Jews," he had decided that the Jewish people in Eastern Europe were in fact mostly laboring people. Because the Russian government resisted emancipating its Jewish population, Jews remained poorer and less acculturated than in the West. Zhitlowsky's central argument in this work is that the comparative lack of economic mobility in the Russian Empire preserved Jewish national cohesion; therefore, were revolution to bring liberal democracy rather than socialism to Russia, Jews would give up their national culture to join the middle classes, with disastrous results. Instead, Zhitlowsky called for socialist revolution and national renaissance. Like other agrarian socialists, Zhitlowsky idealized peasant life, and hence he sought to see Jews settle on the land in Russia (as he explains in the final two chapters of "A Jew to Jews," not included here). Yet, as a Jewish socialist critic of assimilation, Zhitlowsky was considerably ahead of his time.

Zhitlowsky saw the Yiddish language, Yiddish education, and the development of a new Yiddish culture as the natural foundation of a new secular, national, and socialist Jewish identity in the diaspora. He called—most famously in the essay "Why Only Yiddish?"—for Jewish intellectuals to end their estrangement from the Jewish "folk," to build Yiddish culture, and to build socialism in Yiddish. In a theme returned to repeatedly by other Yiddishists and diaspora nationalists, Zhitlowsky argued that only Yiddish culture could be the next link in the Jewish chain of tradition, replacing Hebrew and the stagnating religious tradition associated with it, because Yiddish was the language of the Jewish masses. Zhitlowsky wrote the article "Why Only Yiddish?" in 1897 (though it was not published until 1900), the year of both the First Zionist Congress and the founding of the Bund. The piece was intended to form the introduction to the first book in a series published by the Bund, but the Jewish socialist party's approach to Yiddish at the time was still utilitarian, and its leaders avowedly non-nationalist, so the party decided against publishing Zhitlowsky's introduction. Despite the fact that Zhitlowsky's overt Jewish nationalism made him somewhat exceptional in the organization, he nevertheless remained a member of the Bund until 1904, when he joined *Vozrozhdenie*, a group—and later a party—that melded the ideology of the Russian Socialist Revolutionaries with Jewish diaspora nationalism and Zionist territorialism (a goal that the group put off for the distant future). From 1908 onward, Zhitlowsky lived mainly in the United States and concentrated his political efforts there, promoting the principles of Yiddish culture, an autonomous socialist Jewish community, and Jewish agricultural settlement through his monthly journal, *Dos Naye Lebn*. Zhitlowsky's political sympathies in the 1920s and 1930s gravitated between socialist Zionism, Zionist territorialism, and eventually Stalinism.

Zhitlowsky managed to influence and even join a number of Jewish socialist and nationalist groups while remaining largely outside of party politics. Most significantly, he staked out an ideological place for diaspora nationalism on the Jewish Left and identified its tool: Yiddish. Yiddish could stand in for land until such time as Jewish geographical concentration became possible. The language also allowed the Jews their proper place as a separate national group within socialist movements. Socialist Zionists such as Nahman Syrkin, Ber Borochov, and A. D. Gordon believed that Zionism could return the Jews to labor. Zhitlowsky developed and promoted a Jewish socialism that was proudly nationalist and rooted in the diaspora.

A Jew to Jews

No time to weep, never despair,
Our fathers' sins we must repair.

I

The Jewish Question should be understood as a search for paths potentially leading to a radical transformation of Jewish life that does not currently correspond to an ideal of physically, intellectually, or morally healthy existence; and as fundamental legislative reform that does not correspond to current ideals of social justice.

It is unfortunate and shameful that in our times at the end of the nineteenth century, various reactionary groups have managed to move backward with respect to this question by nearly five centuries. They see the Jewish people as nothing but a pack of parasitic predators, and the Jewish Question merely as a weapon for fighting these predators. In Russia one can now find a particularly pure, evolved variety of this reactionary breed. Their interest, as well as the interest of their confounded followers in the matter of the Jewish Question, lies primarily in protecting the Russian peasant's fields from an onslaught of these voracious parasites. Unfortunately, such formulation of the Jewish Question in

Russia represents the extremely unfavorable condition of our people's struggle. Everyone silently accepts the fact that Judeophobes are responsible for formulating the important opinions about our question, while the main task of the friends of the Jewish people is to counter these opinions. Although we consider it unnecessary to engage in a critique of antisemitic views, we will briefly dwell here on one of these Judeophobic opinions, given that it is relevant to how the Jewish Question was defined at the beginning of this article. This is the question of what it is that the Jewish people in Russia represent: are they a toiling mass like all the other peoples of our fatherland, or are they exclusively a class of traders and merchants who are incapable of understanding the concept and demands of labor?

Not just Judeophobes, but Judeophiles as well, can be blamed, even up until recent times, for giving ambiguous and even false answers to this question. Neither group denies the commercial and industrial character of the great majority of the Jewish population's occupation: Judeophobes have claimed that Jews have a pernicious influence in this sector, while Judeophiles, in their turn, sought to prove them wrong on this point, preaching about the many blessings our people could bestow on a country if given the necessary space to practice their trade and middleman work. Judeophobes represent the interests of the Russian petit and middle bourgeoisie who otherwise have no means to compete with the more energetic and enterprising Jewish merchants; it is from these quarters that we hear cries of an "attack of the Yids." Judeophiles have in mind the entrepreneurial interests of the Jewish craftsmen and traders, who have to be content with lower profits than their non-Jewish counterparts given the pressure of internal Jewish competition; hence, we hear unremitting sermons from the Judeophiles about saving the fatherland by way of the Jews. However, the Jewish folk—the manual workers, diggers, porters, masons, as well as farmers, wherever they may be found—this entire class of the Jewish proletariat has completely faded from the horizon of the Jewish question, so much so that it had to be recently "discovered" by a Russian scholar, the well-known economist Subbotin . . .[1]

Now that this "discovery" has been made, we can at last systematically and

1. [Andrei Pavlovich Subbotin (1852–1906), a Russian economist, traveled in 1887 through the Pale of Settlement to study the economic life of Jews. He published his findings on the life of working people in the journal *Ekonomicheskii zhurnal* in 1887, 1888, and 1890. He published the serialized articles together in *V cherte evreiskoi osedlosti: Otryvki iz ekonomichaskikh izsledovanii v zapadnoi i iugo-zapadnoi Rossii za leto 1887 g.* (St. Petersburg: Severnago telegrafnago agentstva, 1890).]

clearly respond to the question before us: yes, the Jews of Russia are in fact a nation of toilers, for the great majority of them work in nearly every sector of manual labor. The author M. L. Peskovskii has written the following about this "discovery": in Mr. Subbotin's study *In the Pale of Jewish Settlement*, "we see such a striking picture of Jews engaged in intense physical labor, one can only marvel that this phenomenon remains known to so few readers."[2] Our usual notions about the role that Jews play in the pale of their settlement are overshadowed by this picture of Jewish labor to such a degree that on the basis of this research, Peskovskii categorically claims that "if there is indeed exploitation in the 'Pale of Settlement,' then it is above all the exploitation of unbelievably cheap Jewish labor. The notion of so-called 'Jewish exploitation' pales and fades to the background when confronted with the scale of this exploitation."[3]

It is not that Russian-Jewish publicists were previously unaware of our proletarian's existence. The appalling poverty of Jewish working people did not fail to draw the attention of conscientious scholars of Jewish life. However, in most cases our Judeophiles emerged from the ranks of the Jewish bourgeoisie, soaked to the bone with the interests of that class. When confronted with all of the people's bitter grievances they were only able to hear the complaints of merchants driving each other into the ground in the Pale, as well as the grumbling of all the potential lawyers, military officers, professors, and titular advisors (that is to say, those who simply never became lawyers, officers, professors, or titular advisors because of their unfortunate Jewish origins). "Unbelievably cheap Jewish labor," which is presumably used not only by Christians, or at least far less by Christians than Jews, has not managed to strike a chord within the harmonious choir of Russian-Jewish publicists who otherwise make fair demands. To counter all the ills of Jewish existence—the poverty, ignorance, oppression, and persecution that are bleeding the workers dry—they have only one prescription, one hope: complete legal equality for Jews with the rest of the population. How will the emancipated Jewish proletarian prosper physically and spiritually, given that his only possession is "unbelievably cheap" labor power? Who will support him in this endeavor, and will not his emancipated Jewish "employer" become the same villain that every employer is in relation to every proletarian? These are questions that have not been, and are unlikely to ever be, asked by the Jewish press in Russia . . .

2. M. L. Peskovskii, *Rokovoe nedorazumenie* [A fatal misunderstanding], St. Petersburg, 1891, 335.

3. Peskovskii, 347.

"This is not at all a Jewish question, but rather a labor issue," they will say. It is not a Jewish question, according to Peskovskii, who believes there can only be one opinion about the matter. The way to solve the question has been "indisputably and objectively determined; as in scientific theory, so too in state policy," that is to say, in the scientific theory and state policy of Western European countries.[4] But when was the Jewish Question in the West ever concerned with the Jewish proletariat?

Herein lies the problem, we respond: Judeophiles have simply slavishly imitated the manner in which the Jewish Question was posed in the West. Their sparkling image of Jewish life in Europe blinded them to the point that they forgot to ask whether equal rights actually benefited the Jewish masses. If Judeophiles truly had the interests of the Jewish proletariat in mind, they would not simply emulate the way the question was posed in Western Europe. They would be more cautious about the fatal mistakes that were made there in defining the Jewish Question, mistakes that have rendered the cultural, national, and spiritual (though not legal) conditions of European Jewry quite distant from the splendor that we are accustomed to imagining. Of course this does not mean we have nothing to learn from our Western European brothers. In fact we have a great deal to learn from the characteristic abilities of all Jews who have ever struggled on behalf of their people's rights—particularly their clear understanding of material circumstances and a reliable instinct for distinguishing friends of Jewish causes from foes.

In light of the great significance that the European example holds for our question in Russia, we will pause here to closely consider the history of Jewish emancipation in Europe. The digression that follows does not actually distract us from our theme, for nearly every aspect of the Jewish story in the West now also applies to the Jewish Question in Russia. The only difference is that in the Russian case our ideas remain relatively hypothetical or conjectural in nature, while in the West they are already established aspects of daily life, and processes that have clearly manifested themselves.

II

Jewish emancipation in the West has been characteristically marked by the fact that autocratic or even very conservative governments were always as op-

4. Peskovskii, 9.

posed to Jewish emancipation as they were to granting freedom to the general population. The Jewish Question has throughout history shared a similar fate with issues of political independence, limitations on autocratic authority, and freedom of thought, speech, and conscience. Monarchs and conservative regimes at the end of the eighteenth and beginning of the nineteenth centuries sometimes entertained themselves with the task of "improving" Jewish life by creating commissions, inquiring from experts, abolishing one or two of the countless restrictions on Jewish rights, or restoring a rare Jewish privilege. However, the Jews' complete emancipation had to be wrought from their hands together with their renunciation of autocratic power itself. They were just as reluctant to grant the Jews equal rights with the rest of the population as they were to grant civil rights to their subjects in general.

The connection between Jewish emancipation and political freedom is a thread that runs through all of modern history. Cromwell's revolutionary government took the first steps towards Jewish emancipation in England. Dutch Jews were emancipated only after the Netherlands freed itself from Spanish despotism. Liberation from the English yoke in North America brought equal rights to American Jews. In France, already during the reign of Louis XVI, there were debates about how to improve Jewish life and "make the Jews into useful citizens," but it was only with Abbé Gregoire and Robespierre's support in the revolutionary National Assembly that Jews were granted complete equal rights with the rest of the population.[5] Legal barriers between Jews and non-Jews in nearly all of continental Europe—Holland, Belgium, the German principalities, Prussia, and Italy—began to collapse beneath the force of the revolutionary ideas which France's revolutionary wars carried across European borders. As soon as continental Europe defeated the revolution, however, the majority of influential states (with Austria at the helm) sought to hastily reestablish the recently demolished barriers. The subsequent period of political reaction brought about renewed restrictions on Jewish rights and freedoms that only disappeared during the revolution of 1848. The same story ensued during the political reactions of the 1850s. Certain rights for Jews were of course guaranteed by constitutions in many European countries, but the autocracy's defeat of liberal

5. [The Abbé Henri Grégoire, a French bishop (1750–1831), argued alongside Mirabeau that Jewish "defects" were a product of the Jews' historical persecution and could be alleviated through full emancipation. Maximilien Robespierre (1758–94), known for his violent role as the leader of the Terror, also advocated on behalf of the Jews, arguing in favor of their full citizenship.]

demands has always meant a restriction of Jewish rights as well. The struggle for Jewish emancipation in conservative European regimes came to an end only after the decisive consolidation of European liberal institutions during the 1860s and 1870s.

There is nothing especially remarkable in the fact that liberals and democrats fighting for freedom failed to distinguish between Jews and non-Jews. It would be absurd to imagine a freedom fighter whose banner reads "freedom, equality, fraternity . . . and the status quo of all Jewish laws!" What is remarkably strange, however, is an innate, primitive Judeophobia that characterizes any autocratic and conservative regime and stubbornly surfaces at the first possible opportunity. As with everything under the sun, there are reasons for this peculiar phenomenon. Even if one dismisses a monarch's personal antipathy towards Jews as the product of a retrograde upbringing and the stifled atmosphere in which royalty must spend their youth, significant motives for royal Judeophobia still remain, particularly in regard to the internal policies of absolutist regimes. They include the following: first, autocratic authority rests in significant measure on religious fanaticism and widespread ignorance. The Christian Church, which has become an instrument of oppression in the hands of the king and clergy, sees the Jewish people as a living protest against itself. The Jews are an eyesore to religious leaders: they are fanatical opponents of the Trinity who deny the figure of Christ and have the nerve to look down on the Christian masses around them as a drove of bamboozled derelicts. Medieval Catholic policies were founded upon the desire to degrade and trample the Jews underfoot, to make them feel the power of the savior they had rejected. These policies were preserved even after the Protestant Reformation as a legacy of medieval times, though in a form that was relatively tame compared to the bright pyres of the Inquisition. During the nineteenth century, monarchs who had an interest in maintaining popular fanaticism had to continue to require these policies; autocratic regimes, after all, must take medieval traditions very seriously. Second, every component of the Jewish Question—its entire system of restrictions, statutes, decrees, special taxes and privileges, residence and expulsion decrees, synagogue closures—all provided the means for creating an atmosphere of religious intolerance and nationalistic enmity. Such an atmosphere, as we all know, is extremely conducive for producing subjects with slavish and loyal sensibilities. Third and last, the greatest Jewish intellectuals in Europe always felt two yokes of universal and Jewish bondage on their backs. For that reason they fought the system with twice the amount of passion and energy. The best individuals among the Jewish intelligentsia consciously joined the ranks of the most radical opposition parties, sometimes even serving as leaders. On account of this, they elicited even more hatred on the part of the monarchs toward the Jewish intelligentsia and Jewish people.

The relationship between the Jewish intelligentsia and the Jewish masses on the one hand and the general population on the other constitutes a second important aspect of the history of Jewish emancipation. Throughout the entire course of its historical existence the intelligentsia was always divided into two camps. Those belonging to the first group had been compelled for various reasons to cut themselves off from the spiritual life of their people, and for that reason, were able to represent Jews in the larger arena of European civilization. Those in the second group served as missionaries of this European civilization among members of their own tribe who lagged behind contemporary culture. Although those in the first group either had little in common with other Jews or had rejected their Jewish identity altogether, they never missed a chance to passionately speak out in defense of their people's rights as they stood on the front lines of the opposition. By the same token, those in the second group may have been purely devoted to cultural work, but they were very aware of how they stood to benefit from a favorable resolution of the Jewish Question and were ready to support the general population in its struggle against the demands of the monarchy and the aristocratic parties.

Finally, the relationship between non-Jewish society and Jews and Jewry constitutes a third important feature of our history. We have already noted that governments tended to be resolutely decisive in banning the Jews from their country's civic and social life. We have also noted an equally resolute but opposite desire to secure complete legal emancipation by every group within the Jewish intelligentsia. Unfortunately, the role that non-Jewish society has played in regard to our people has in practice not depended upon any such resolute principles. We emphasize "in practice" because in theory the attitude of different social groups toward Jews has been generally clear: conservative groups, with a few exceptions, are in principle opposed to Jewish emancipation, just as all liberal groups support it—but this is true in theory only. In reality, liberals lack the solidarity of basic principles and convictions that one finds among reactionaries. Many liberals have suggested that it is still too early to grant Jews full rights; that necessary and prudent measures have to be taken to gradually prepare Jews for their rights. The hypocritical attitude of various liberals regarding the Jewish Question is redeemed by the fact that almost every one of the greatest representatives of progressive social movements and philosophies has demanded equal rights for Jews without any provisions or limitations. The names of Mirabeau and Montesquieu, Gregoire and Robespierre, Lessing, Macaulay, and many others should clearly remind us which members of European society have given the Jews this kind of decisive support.[6]

III

In a time when they lacked political rights, every negative aspect of Jewish life could be explained by the Jews' exceptional legal status. As we have seen, this exceptional status was most strongly reinforced by conservative, reactionary states, and it was abolished when Jews joined their Christian counterparts in a struggle against systems of political injustice. Once the people had triumphed over their ignorant rulers, Jewish legal emancipation ceased to be a desire or hope and became instead an aspect of everyday life. It is therefore natural to ask how the legal component of the Jewish Question's favorable resolution has affected social and everyday life.

Prior to emancipation, most Jews lived in poverty, packed tightly together in infamous quarters and burdened by special taxes. Has emancipation improved the situation of the Jewish masses? Hungry Jews who were barred from many productive professions indiscriminately pursued any and all means of subsistence, regardless of how rotten or dirty they were . . . Has equality healed the sources of their material life? Prior to emancipation, a religious regime of rabbis and *tsadiks* kept the Jewish masses stifled in ignorance. Has Judaism managed to rid itself of this spiritual oppression? Has enlightened European thought penetrated the consciousness of the masses? Has this knowledge been absorbed

6. [The French aristocrat Honoré-Gabriel Riquetti, count of Mirabeau (1749–91), was an advocate for Jewish emancipation in pre-revolutionary France. After meeting Moses Mendelssohn in person, he composed a treatise about the political reform of the Jews of Britain. Charles Louis de Secondat, baron de la Brede and de Montesquieu (1689–1755), was another French political thinker who argued for religious tolerance, calling Judaism the "mother" religion of Christianity and Islam. Gotthold Ephraim Lessing (1729–81) was a noted German Enlightenment philosopher and dramatist famous for his close friendship with Mendelssohn. His play *Nathan the Wise* (1779), based on the life and ideas of Mendelssohn, made the case for religious tolerance. Finally, Thomas Babington Macauley (1800–59) was a British poet, historian, and politician. As a member of Parliament, Macauley used that forum to call for the abolition of all laws pertaining to the "civil disabilities" of the Jews. For Grégoire and Robespierre, see note 5.]

by the people's collective thoughts and ideals? In the era of their civic enslavement it was difficult to imagine the Jews being any worse off as a people than any other European nation. Have the Jews now attained a more esteemed and respected place for themselves among nations?

A mere glimpse at the material and spiritual condition of Jews who live densely packed together in Galicia and Bukovina—where equal rights were established long ago and where new foundations for national Jewish life should have clearly appeared by now—allows us to reply to all of these questions with answers that do not bode well for the Jews.

One would not find a relatively accurate description of the material life of Bukovinian and Galician Jews in the pages of local Jewish newspapers. These papers are occupied with supposedly higher callings, such as describing rabbinic jubilees, praising the charitable work of ladies' committees, polemicizing against antisemitism, and debating the question of which language should be used for conducting Sabbath services. Jewish poverty simply does not exist for these representatives of the satisfied bourgeoisie. The issue therefore seems all the more pronounced when it appears in any serious economic studies of eastern Austria. To give just a few examples of the scale of Jewish poverty—examples that at times surpass even the usual things we are accustomed to hearing about the blessed Jewish Pale, we offer a short passage from the work of Professor Platter, "Sociale Studien in der Bukovina."[7] He discusses the Jewish population in Czernowitz, the largest city in the Bukovina region. We have selected this particular region and city because Bukovina has for ages been known as the "Jewish Eldorado," while Czernowitz, with 50 percent of its population comprised of Jews, "can rightfully be called a Jewish city."

Professor Platter notes that the vast majority of Jews in Czernowitz are extremely poor, and that most parts of the city are filled with "wretched, dirty, stinking hovels." He then provides us with a description of street scenes that he himself witnessed:

The ideal filthy, ragged man, whose image can be conjured by the average Western European only in his wildest fantasies, really exists here and is visible at every step. You see pants made from twenty or thirty different scraps of material but that still consist mainly of holes; you see frock coats that lack

7. [Julius Platter (1844–1923), a German professor of political economy, was active in Zurich. Zhitlowsky refers to Platter's study of usury in Bukovina, *Der Wucher in der Bukowina* (Jena: G. Fischer vorm. Mauke, 1878).]

the entire back side and whose owners, unfortunately, are wearing neither waistcoats nor undershirts. I saw completely naked little girls between four and six years of age playing with half-naked boys in the dust of the capital's streets. But the main fashion one sees are large hordes of men in kaftans, and the sight of these garments alone can ruin even the heartiest appetite.[8]

This is a picture of the streets, but it is not difficult to guess what kind of image of filth and poverty he would have drawn for us had he looked inside the "wretched, dirty, stinking hovels." Platter's book was published fifteen years ago, in 1878, and perhaps the people of Czernowitz have become better dressed and more fashionable since then, out of concern that such "jolly landscapes" not offend the sensibilities of enlightened Western Europeans. But we have every reason to doubt that they have managed to escape from Jewish poverty, given that we have factual and relatively articulate descriptions of the impoverished, destitute condition of the Jewish masses not just from Czernowitz but also from nearly every town in Galicia and Polish Prussia (such as Poznan).

Living next door to this poverty are the notorious Jewish trading and banking firms and wealthy Jewish landowners who have begun the process of displacing Polish magnates from their inherited estates. The "Jewish landowner" is a new concept that the Jews have introduced into the sphere of finance and fortune after emancipation. The means by which a Jew can become a landowner will become apparent once we turn to examining the second question raised above concerning Jewish occupations and the sources of livelihood.

The existence of poverty among the Jewish masses provides sufficient evidence that emancipation opened up very few new opportunities for them. The fact is that the life of the masses has remained as it was before. The basic mode of economic existence for the overwhelming majority—the petit- and middle-trader, moneychanger, business agent, tavernkeeper, craftsman, mechanic, teacher, butcher, and spiritual proletarian—is that in the morning they have no idea how they will satisfy the hunger of their large families that night. How do the upper 10,000 employ themselves, then? They are traders *en grand*, as the so-called liberal professions refer to them . . . and . . . they lend money on interest! Galicia and Bukovina are almost exclusively agrarian regions. Peasants supply the main source of labor power, and Polish landowners supply the main source of exploitation. Agrarian culture is characterized almost entirely by abject peasant poverty and by the frivolous carefree incompetence of the landowners. The

8. Platter, 39.

rotten foundation of economic life on which Jews found one of the primary sources of their material existence, usury, was produced by the easy and loose lifestyle of the undisciplined magnates combined with the wretched drunkenness of the poor and ignorant peasantry. No one would deny that the current trend of both peasants and landowners transferring their land assets into Jewish hands was not entirely foreordained. The debts that landowners owe to Jewish banks have been a major factor in this trend. From an agricultural and economic point of view, the transfer of property into the hands of more intelligent and prudent owners might be considered a benefit for a country, as long as the majority of Jewish landowners refrained from bringing commercial principles into the agrarian sector, or converting family estates and peasant plots into objects of financial speculation. But from a social perspective, even an intelligent, capable, and exemplary Jewish landowner brings little joy to his country if the formerly free peasant landowner in practice becomes enserfed to a new lord.

Where then is the Jewish tiller of the soil whose appearance was predicted by all those proponents of Jewish emancipation? "The Jew," writes the previously introduced Professor Platter,

> can never, or at least, not in the near future, become a real peasant in Europe. He feels repulsed by exclusively physical labor because his active nature requires constant spiritual engagement, and he also realizes that because purely muscular labor brings such small wages he will never get rich from it, something which he for some reason considers his natural right. Insofar as he can, he leaves physical labor to the lot of those whose powers of intellect are inferior to his own. For this reason, in Galicia we see Jews who deprive peasants of their land and then rehire them as workers to till property that was formerly theirs. . . . In Galicia there are a few Jewish peasant families who work their own fields, but this is a rare exception, and there are none in Bukovina.[9]

We cast doubt on whether it is fair to extend the characteristics of the Jewish landowner to the entire Jewish population of Galicia and Bukovina. It is difficult to imagine that that "ideal ragged man" considers himself a contender for great riches. In order to explain the absence of Jewish farmers we need not resort to the hypothesis of "aversion to muscular labor," which has been so strongly discredited by numerous facts of life in our Pale and, in rare instances, even in Galicia itself. The matter can be explained quite simply as the result of poverty

9. Platter, 46.

and monotony in the everyday life of the Jewish masses. In order to effect a radical existential change such as transitioning the masses away from "baseless" pursuits to a life of agriculture, one needs money, and equally importantly, initiative. How were European Jews to get either of these things when after emancipation the best Jewish people, the ones whose spiritual and financial genius might have been able to help the poor, severed all their commitments to their people? These people failed to think of their less fortunate brethren, and instead threw themselves into leading positions in the liberal professions as doctors and engineers and as writers and publicists whose laurels now keep our own leading Russian-Jewish writers wide awake at night.

The flight of outstanding individuals from their people reflected in the most tragic way upon two other aspects of national life that we will now consider. Unfortunately, the size of this pamphlet does not allow me to dwell, even in the most general way, on questions of Western European Jewish nationalism and culture. In regard to the question of the enlightenment of the masses, I will limit myself to the well-known fact that the level of culture of the Jewish masses in Galicia, Bukovina, and Polish Prussia is significantly lower than it is among Russian Jews. That the authority of rabbis and *tsadiks* rages there with even greater ferocity than it does among us, where it has almost completely disappeared from most parts of the Pale. That the chasm between enlightenment activists and the masses is even wider there than it is in Russia. And the main thing is that all of this has occurred not in spite of, but as a direct consequence of, emancipation, or at the very least because the Jewish Question in the West was not seen as anything but a matter of legal rights. In Russia, where legal oppression has kept the Jewish intelligentsia connected to its people, such a total and decisive departure of the best people has not yet occurred as it has in the West, and the civilizing power of such people cannot have failed to positively influence the level of culture among the masses. In addition, Jews in Russia who understood that getting an education allowed them to bypass certain limitations on their rights agreed with the Jewish intelligentsia's devotion to European Enlightenment principles. But in the West, this powerful incentive did not exist, and religious obscurantists who encountered no decisive opposition were able to muster their forces and reinforce their power.

The horizon of Jewish national life in Europe is determined by a fateful constellation of poverty and ignorance, ambiguous and objectionable professions, obsolete religious fanaticism, the flight of the best people, and a growing gulf between the people and its intelligentsia. Given the influence of these factors it is not surprising that the Jews have failed to earn the position among the nations they undoubtedly deserve! The Jewish masses have been numbed to their degraded condition by poverty and ignorance that have dulled their sense of honor and national pride. Atavistic forms of religious fanaticism have translated national aspirations into the unrealizable dreams of a transcendent future. The practice of usury and exploitation of the peasantry have elicited a completely understandable hatred toward Jewish exploiters and provided Christian clergy and reactionary groups with fuel to stoke centuries of accumulated religious and national antipathy into fires of implacable hatred for the Jewish masses. This hatred sometimes sparks pogroms as terrible as those we have seen in Russia. For how on earth is a rural farmer supposed to know that the Jewish masses, who have abandoned the transparency of agricultural labor and concealed themselves in the cities, are not part of the same crowd as his exploiter; how, in the heat of the moment, can he possibly realize that he is venting his pent-up rage on someone just as poor and unfortunate as he is! There is only one rational and convincing argument for the Jewish people if they wish to resist antisemitic slander and insults. The existence of a toiling, agrarian mass would dull the shards of truth lodged in the foundation of Western European antisemitism; and the powerful muscles of a vigorous, vibrant nation of workers would hold the nation's enemies at a respectful distance. Yet, instead of concentrating on making the everyday life of the Jewish people more healthy, high-caliber Jewish intellectuals have left it to mediocrities (accomplices of the Jewish bourgeoisie) to engage in literary polemics with Judeophobes, to regurgitate for the thousandth time the arguments which have already been presented far more capably by Dohm, Bern, and Delich and other defenders of the Jewish people. Rather than inspiring people to build a national life on the productive basis of agricultural work and attach themselves to European culture, the best Jews have cut their ties to the familial tribe and hastened to join the Magyars and Poles, the Germans and Ruthenians: in a word, anyone but the Jews.

This has grown into a strange and, if I may say so, repulsive trend of Jews who imagine that they are Poles and fight in the name of the nationalist principle against their very own Jewish brothers who imagine that they are Ruthenians. The pseudo-Czech of Jewish origin struggles against his fellow Jew, the pseudo-German, while the pseudo-Hungarian considers it his duty, alongside the pure-blooded Magyars, to oppress weaker Slavic tribes. It never occurs to any of them that they have abandoned the nation to which they belong by virtue of flesh and blood, leaving them to decay under difficult conditions of urban life and the tyranny of rabbis and *tsadiks*. It never occurs to them that this nation has a far greater need for their intellectual powers than the peoples they have joined. By the same token, one should not overlook the fact that all of this is taking place in Austria-Hungary, a state like Russia, which is composed of many national minorities and whose leaders will preserve their rule only by granting complete equality to all languages and nations. If the kind of principles of complete national equality that have already been implemented to a significant extent in Switzerland and Belgium do not take hold in Austrian civic life, Austria will remain the arena where diverse nationalities contend on behalf of their own historical rights rather than on behalf of the principles of rational justice. When the Jews cast their lot with the general population they appear tragicomic in their adoption of certain positions and their support for obsolete principles that are of no use to their own people. It is equally tragicomic that while various Jewish intellectuals persist in their attempts to prove that the Jewish people as such does not exist in Austria, various leaders of Austria's national groups have already long grown tired of treating the Jews as a perpetual question mark, and in their own words before a parliamentary commission declared that "Jews, too, are an Austrian nationality, deserving exactly the same full rights as the Germans and different Slavs . . ."

The prize medal of Jewish emancipation has a very unappealing underside indeed, and if we simply adopt the Western European approach to the question, there is no reason to hope that we will successfully escape the sorry conclusion that Jews in the West have reached.

Why Only Yiddish?[10]

Five years ago, in a small Russian booklet, "A Jew to Jews,"[11] writing under the pseudonym E. Khasin, I accused the young Jewish socialists of ignoring the

---

10. I wrote this short article which I am now [1900] presenting for the American Yiddish-reading audience, three years ago. It was intended for the Russian Yiddish reader, and the title page contained only the following few lines: "A few words, which one can choose if one likes to read as a foreword to the booklet which we are now publishing and to all the additional ones we hope to publish."

As the reader can see, this article was to be the introduction to another work which was ready to go to print. There were also additional publications being planned by "a group of Jewish Socialists in exile." In this introduction to the introduction, I will not explain what goals this group had in mind, who the people in the group were, and why all of it ended

Jewish folk, of being utterly dismissive of the Jewish masses and of not coming to their rescue in their hour of need. "Do you," I asked, "even spend a tenth of your energy in spreading socialism among the Jewish working classes?"

Apparently I was not alone in this concern. It seems that these very young Jewish socialists had already been harassed for quite some time. Had this not been the case one would be very hard pressed to explain how the situation reversed itself within the span of a mere five years. Previously, a Jewish socialist advocating propagandizing among the Jewish masses was viewed as someone who must certainly be wearing Palestinophile *arbe-kanfes* beneath his socialist overcoat.[12]

Today there is not a single Jewish socialist in Russia who would deny that the Jewish worker, or for that matter the entire poor, oppressed, Jewish folk, has done nothing to deserve exclusion from the struggle for the greatest and holiest ideal of the nineteenth century, from socialism. Not only has socialist literature for the Jewish worker achieved high standing in London and America, but Jewish socialists are now hard at work on behalf of the Jewish worker in Galicia and Russia as well. And they are now expending not only the 10 percent of their energy which I had demanded of them earlier, but all of their energy in order to organize the Jewish workers and join them to the great army of the European proletariat. Booklets and newspapers are being published through which they seek to enlighten the Jewish worker about his sorrowful plight and about the means one must employ in order to improve it.

Hand in hand with the "secret" holy texts which require great effort to smuggle through the Russian censor, there are the "kosher" texts, the open literature in Yiddish which has been revived under the pen of Peretz, Sholem Aleichem, etc. This literature strives above all to awaken the human being within the laboring oppressed Jew. It seeks to arouse in him a desire for cultivation and knowledge. Most recently, a group of young Russian Jewish socialists have banded together

---

in nothing . . . I am printing this article here (for the first time) because I believe that these thoughts, which I wholeheartedly endorse, are still vital and can yet serve a purpose.

I had thought earlier to revise the article, and remove the anachronisms. Then I reconsidered and decided . . . to leave the article as it was written. I am therefore asking the reader to remember that the manuscript is dated: *Motsei rosh khodesh* [the beginning of] May, 1897.

11. Published by the Fond Vol'nai Ruskai Pressi, 1892.

12. [The *arbe-kanfes* is the fringed undergarment worn by religiously observant Jewish men. It is also known as *tsitses* (*tsitsit*, in Hebrew), the term for the knotted tassels on that garment or a prayer shawl.]

to produce socialist books for Russian Jewry. And here I am, sitting and writing the foreword for the first booklet which this group of young Jewish socialists wants to publish. Would this have been possible five to ten years ago?[13]

We Jewish socialists can rejoice. Our best people no longer deserve the scolding they once did. Nevertheless, as I write this foreword, I am filled with unhappy thoughts.

A new literature born out of the blue in a language "which until now was deemed worthy enough only to discuss the mundane" is no longer a novelty in our nineteenth century. Take for instance Flemish in Belgium, Ruthenian in Galicia, Latvian in Russia, and so on. Yet no Fleming, Ruthenian, or Latvian ever regarded the "holy texts" of his beloved language with such trepidation and hope as I regard the handful of "holy texts" in the new Yiddish language. These other languages were merely reawakened now to serve a higher purpose in the life of the folk. There is nothing left behind in the past for those speakers to long for. Flemings, Ruthenians, and Latvians have so much to look forward to in their future and their hopes are all built on real and solid ground. Their masses will only continue to grow smarter and improve their condition, becoming more "human," and their literature will continue to develop and help them in their development.

The new Yiddish language is, however, the first foray of the Jewish folk into its education. Behind it is a long chain of Jewish literature, and Yiddish is only one ring in that chain. One begins to remember and is reminded that the first step for the Jewish nation on the road to cultivation was the Tanakh. Its first "writers" were the authors of Psalms, and Isaiah, and Jeremiah, and the other Prophets that illuminate the Jewish and non-Jewish sky like eternal stars. Then came the Talmud with its giants who could move mountains and crush them into dust (*Rava oker harim*). The *Gaonim* followed after and then the great philosophers and then the beloved and resounding poets, Maimonides, Ibn Gvirol and Yehuda Halevi. They were followed by the Kabbalists who removed themselves from the real world to the other side of the clouds and there they built their own world. Then came the time of Mendelssohn and his disciples—and here in our Russia, the time of the Ribal and Lebensohn, then Smolenskin and Lilienblum. They were followed by the period of Russian Jewish literature, Orshanski, Levanda, Bogrov, and Frug.[14]

13. [It turned out to be still impossible in 1897, when Zhitlowsky first wrote the essay.]

14. [Maimonides—or Moshe ben-Maimon (1135–1204), also known as the Rambam—was a medieval Jewish philosopher. Solomon Ibn Gvirol (1021–58) was a medieval Jewish philosopher and Hebrew poet. Yehuda Halevi (1085–1141) was a renowned Hebrew poet and philosopher. Moses Mendelssohn (1729–86) was a German Jewish philosopher

And when one recalls that after this long and arduous journey we are now in the time of the Jewish worker and Peretz's *Yontef-bletlekh*, and that perhaps the last vestiges of Jewish folk life rest in this tiny handful of writers and their works, the heart begins to grow weak.[15] With what kind of certainty can we look to the future? How long ago is it since the others stopped proclaiming in every street that the Jewish folk is like a walking corpse for whom even the earth refuses to find a place, avoided by everyone who encounters him?[16] Who knows how soon they will start to sing that song again, and we will have to start from the very beginning? . . . No nation on earth should have to fear coming to such an end, and must we?

And another thing. All other nations have a single language and a single literature. They hold that one language dear and its literature sacred. Every writer of each nation knows that as long as he has talent and has something to say, he will sooner or later be heard . . . something of him will somehow remain and at least one drop of his blood will be incorporated in the building of his nation.

For more than fifty years well-intentioned Jewish intellectuals have been devoting themselves to the Jewish folk. They shed bitter tears over the grave misfortune of the masses and tried to put them on the right path to improving their lot through education and proper conduct and basic life skills. And what was the result of all these efforts? The Jewish literature they produced had

---

and leading figure in the Berlin Haskala. The Ribal is Yitshak Ber Levinzon (1788–1860), often called the father of the Russian Haskala, or the Russian Mendelssohn. The Russian Jewish Mikhah Yosef Lebensohn (1828–52) was a Hebrew poet and translator. For information about Smolenskin, see the chapter "The Eternal People." Moshe Leib Lilienblum (1843–1910) was a Russian Jewish scholar and author, Ilya Grigoryevich Orshanski (1846–75) a Russian Jewish essayist and journalist, and Lev Osipovich Levanda (1835–88) a Russian Jewish journalist and fiction writer. Grigorii Isaakovich Bogrov (1825–85) was a Haskala writer of short stories and novels. Shimen (also known as Shmuel or Semion) Frug (1860–1916) was a poet and essayist in Russian and Yiddish.]

15. [The *Yontef-bletlekh* (Holiday pages), published by the Yiddish writers I. L. Peretz and Dovid Pinski from 1894 to 1896, was a serial publication that billed itself as a series of fliers for the Jewish holidays in order to evade the oversight of the Russian censor, who was responsible for approving the content of all newspapers. The *Yontef-bletlekh* played a major role in creating a popular readership for Yiddish literature. All seventeen issues, which contained short stories, poetry, essays, and political articles with a socialist bent, were immensely popular and widely distributed across the Russian Empire.]

16. [Zhitlowsky refers here to the chosen metaphor of Lev (Leon) Pinsker in his influential tract *Auto-Emancipation: An Appeal to His People by a Russian Jew*, published in German in 1882.]

absolutely no impact on the hearts or minds of the Jews. Not only the literature of the Shomers, Blausteins, and other depraved writers of the old *"zhargon"* but also the Russian Jewish literature of the Levandas, Orshanskis, Bogrovs; even the old-Hebrew literature of the Lilienblums, Gordons, and Smolenskins—none of them could boast of having won over the Jewish folk, or its masses. Not one of those writers could claim that the folk took his words to heart or that it even considered that giving him a hearing was not such a terrible thing.

Jewish thinking and particularly that of the simple Jewish masses remained essentially the same as in the time of *Kol mevaser, Te'uda be-Yisrael*, or the *Razsvet* of Odessa.[17] True, the larger cities were witnessing a whole new life for Jews: Gymnasium students, doctors, horse-drawn coaches, dyed mustaches, bow ties, fine ladies wearing their own hair, walking sticks, cigars on the Sabbath. There are no longer any celebrations of the accomplishments in Hebrew learning and Torah study as in bygone days when the *kehile* was the sole ruler over the Jewish soul. Actually, even now pious fathers and mothers would gladly bribe their son to partake of a bit of Torah study—not, heaven forbid, out of piety ("who today is, *borkhashem* [thank God], religious?") No! He should do so out of a sense of respectability, a sense of personal accomplishment.

We are not talking about "bow tie–Haskala" and "quadrille education." We are discussing the highest and most important ideals in the world, the enlightenment of the folk, the masses, and of improving their intellect and emotions. In this arena we see that, until quite recently, everything was stuck in the old order. The same thinking, the same feelings and aspirations endured, despite our *maskilim*'s repeated attempts at purification and elevation . . .

We, Russian Jews, have three literatures and three languages: *loshn koydesh* (the holy tongue), Russian, and Yiddish.[18] All three literatures endure a miserable existence among us. There isn't a single Jewish writer, regardless of how talented he is, how passionate he is about his ideals, or how honestly and earnestly he is devoted to them, who can with full confidence claim to have accomplished something of merit and left his readers in awe. I am not talking about the usual Jewish reader here, the petit-bourgeois "distinguished readers," with their *pilpul*-trained business minds and hearts covered with the dust of the trading floor.[19]

17. [Haskala publications of the 1860s.]

18. [Throughout the essay Zhitlowsky uses *"loshn koydesh,"* the traditional Hebrew and Yiddish term for the Hebrew language.]

19. [*Pilpul* refers to a method of Talmud study and reasoning dominant in Eastern

The bourgeoisie looks down on the Jewish writer as a jester, a crossword-puzzle writer, a street entertainer who creates rhymes, an acrobat who can twist and bend and play strange tunes . . ."—He does that excellently!"—He says it with the same tone, the same indifference as when reading *To'eh be-darkhe ha-hayim*, the *Zapiski evreia*, or the *Yidishn far peysakh*.[20] Do not think that the fault lies with the writers or their poverty-ridden existence or the fact that the Jewish bourgeoisie has nothing but disdain for them. If the writer happens to be a man of means it is even worse. He is regarded as a strange creature, a ne'er-do-well, an incompetent. No, I am speaking now neither of the writers nor of the readers. I am talking about the folk, about the masses, and about the devoted offspring who have taken upon themselves the improvement of its lot.

In *Voskhod*, in the September 1881 issue, there is an article by our late well-known writer Levanda.[21] There he describes the founding in Odessa of the first Russian Jewish newspaper *Razsvet*.

"Actually," Levanda says, "there had already almost been a newspaper for Russian Jewry. It was however published in Prussia, and in *loshn koydesh* to boot. In addition it was a for-profit business venture and thus had to cater to the level of education and tastes of the 'blind' Jewish folk masses. It would flatter them and support their archaic views and ideals, and lull them to sleep with the most foolish old wives' tales. In short, this publication followed the masses and did not lead them. In this manner it brought even more darkness into the dimly lit minds of our brethren who were so in need of light, cultivation, and rebirth. That is why it was necessary to have not merely any Jewish periodical, but one that would be a vital honest representative of healthy ideals and real cultivation. It also had to be in a language which our Russian neighbors could comprehend. In short, what was needed was a Jewish publication printed in Russian."

European yeshivas that became the source of considerable criticism from educational reformers.]

20. [*Ha-To'eh be-darkhe ha-hayim* (The wanderer on the road of life), first published in Hebrew in 1871, was Peretz Smolenskin's best-known novel, a sprawling and vivid semi-autobiographical account of contemporary Jewish life. Bogrov's *Zapiski evreia* (Notes of a Jew), published in Russian serially in *Otechestvennye zapiski* from 1871 to 1873, was another autobiographical account and the first full-length work by a Jewish writer to achieve recognition in the mainstream Russian literary scene. *Yidishn far peysakh* (Before Passover) was a quasi-anthropological study of Jewish life by A. M. Tchatchkes.]

21. [Levanda published frequently in *Razsvet*, *Sion*, *Evreiskaia biblioteka*, *Russkii evrei*, and *Voskhod*.]

Osip Rabinovich took it upon himself to get a permit from the Russian censor for such a Jewish newspaper.[22] It would be written for the Jewish folk, but could also be read by its "neighbors." This is what he wrote to Levanda regarding his requests: "I began by pointing out to them that the crippled *zhargon* which Russian Jews speak is unsuitable for 'cultivation' because it is impossible to express a clear thought in it, let alone anything philosophical" (!).

All of Rabinovich's good friends were of like mind. Just imagine—the very "neighbors" from whom he had to beg permission to write in their language for a Jewish audience did not want to "lend" him their language! Instead, they allowed him to publish *Razsvet* not in Russian, but in Yiddish, or as the "neighbors" wrote, "In the Jewish-German language which is used by the Jews in Russia and Poland."

At the time this was a tragedy. Once again they sent submissions and requests to "appropriate" places, and permission was ultimately granted. "To work!" Rabinovich wrote to Levanda and his friends, "To work, young and old. Our own field awaits the plowmen: Until now we have watered it with our tears, let us now water it with our sweat! God will bless our toil. The stalk will be strong and healthy. I feel it, of this I am certain!"

No one considered using *loshn koydesh* because, as Levanda expressed it, "No one wanted to look at the squared letters any longer." He tells us: "Within six months, using the power of truthful, searing, words, we were able to reform the entire reading public. We set a brand-new head filled with new thoughts and ideas on its shoulders."

For twenty-five years Levanda wrote for Jews in the Russian language. And even though he wrote what he did about the Odessa *Razsvet*, he was still quite pleased with his work. Then the pogroms began. In the midst of it all, the twenty-fifth anniversary edition of Levanda's newspaper needed to be readied. While others wanted to celebrate the occasion, Levanda refused and even called into question the accomplishment of his twenty-five years of work. He specifically wrote that he wished that this endeavor had never even existed. He ran back "home" to the folk masses with the "dimly lit minds" and was happy to find the old head, with the old thoughts and ideas, still sitting on its shoulders. It is no

22. [Osip Aranovich Rabinovich (1817–59) was a prominent writer and editor. Known as the Jewish Grigorovich for the sentimental naturalism of his writing, Rabinovich published essays and fiction about Jewish life in the Russian Empire. He served as the editor of *Razsvet* from 1860 until it was shut down by the government in 1861.]

wonder that he found what he did. The "new head" filled with new thoughts and ideas did not manage to rest on the shoulders of the folk masses for even a minute.

The following is an example of the great accomplishments of *loshn koydesh*. You probably remember the anniversary celebration of Yehuda Leib Gordon. If you have never heard of him, ask someone to tell you about him and for a translation of his sad, sad poem, *"le'mi ani amal."*[23] You will then understand how much tragedy lies in every line of his verse. A man has worked a lifetime for the good of the community. In the end he realizes that it has all been for naught. The folk masses do not want to hear him (not yet!!), and he goes on to bemoan that the younger generation has flown too far away and may not ever return.

I often reflect on these two moments. They come to mind, bringing sadness with them.

But I have a way of driving my sad thoughts away. I say to myself: this was all in the past. It will be different now. Since we have begun to write socialist material for Jews in Yiddish we have turned a new page in the history of the Jewish people.

The socialists do not speak to the people in a language that they have long forgotten. They also do not borrow the language of their neighbors. They speak *mame-loshn*[24] and bring ideas that mothers could have learned by heart and repeated to their children every day—ideas that teach us how the poor, oppressed, and abused segment of human society can free itself from its pitiful situation . . .

Socialism is a strong bond which will unite the folk masses with the youth, and the youth of this generation will no longer have to flee to places from which they will not return. Our young people will not have to search for respectable work to do among our neighbors: they will have enough to do at home. There were also many socialists among the older writers: Lieberman, Ben-Nets, and others.[25] But for whom did they write? To whom did they pour out their bitter hearts? Whom did they hope would help them?

Their audience was the well-to-do bourgeoisie or the few perennial yeshiva students, who were more awed by the beauty of the language in which socialism was garbed than by the power of the ideas themselves.

23. ["For whom do I toil?" (1870–71), a Hebrew poem in which Gordon voices his fears about the language's demise.]

24. [Yiddish, the mother tongue.]

25. [Because of his literary and political essays in Hebrew and Russian, Aharon (Aaron) Lieberman (1843–80) is sometimes referred to as the father of Hebrew socialism.]

Our present-day socialists have little to do with the Jewish bourgeoisie. They speak to the masses, the workers. For the worker, socialism is not a matter of mode or fashion. It is a matter of life. Of course he will pay attention to the words showing the way out of his desperate situation.

Let us tell the plain truth; the socialism of our older Jewish socialists was very strange. They sang the praises of socialism but wrote very little about it and studied it even less. Their socialism was a flowery socialism in rhymes and free verse, in poetry and prose. They knew *what* was needed, but not *how* to accomplish it.

This is no wonder. The best teacher of socialism is the life of the workers, or, put better, their battle for existence, their struggles with their bosses. As long as this teacher was absent from Jewish life, our socialism was totally ephemeral. Our present-day socialists are learning from life and can therefore exert control over life. They come to the Jewish worker with more than mere words. They bring their own experience as examples of what is needed and how it must be done; not eventually, when all the other nations will come to the social revolution, but now, at this moment—in order to improve our own condition even by a tiny speck until the glorious time will come for all workers of all nations.

If Osip Rabinovich could dare in the 1860's to hope for "strong healthy stalks," then we—knowing the mistakes of the past—certainly have the right to cast off any doubts and to proclaim to the new generation: "To work, old and young! Our own field awaits the plowmen! Until now we have watered it with our tears, let us now water it with our sweat!"

6

The Worldwide Jewish Nation
Vladimir Davidovich Medem

V. Medem, "Vsemirnaia evreiskaia natsiia," in *Teoreticheskie i prakitcheskie voprosy evreiskoi zhizni* (St. Petersburg: Trud, 1911), 90–105.

As a leading ideologist of the Jewish Labor Bund, Vladimir Medem (1879–1923) was one of the key figures responsible for guiding the largest and most important Jewish socialist movement in the Russian Empire and independent Poland toward a platform for national-cultural Jewish autonomy. Medem grew up in a Christian family in the town of Libau, his parents having converted to Lutheranism. As a university student in Kiev, Medem joined first the Russian Social Democratic Workers' Party, then its Jewish section, the Bund. Medem became a leading figure in Jewish socialist politics in the Russian Empire, spending time both in prison and in exile, and eventually was one of the more important leaders of the Bund in independent Poland.

The Bund began as an effort by Jewish Marxists to integrate the Russian Empire's Jewish workers into the Polish and Russian revolutionary movements. Although it later became a proponent of cultural Yiddishism, the movement remained continually opposed to "bourgeois nationalism," which it equated with Zionism. The Bund crept toward becoming a national movement, but it never fully resolved the difference between nationalism, which it opposed, and the demand for national-cultural rights, which it came over time to support. Medem's *oeuvre* encapsulates many of the tensions inherent in the development of Jewish socialism in the Russian Empire. He was personally opposed to all forms of nationalism and at the same time resistant to all efforts by Russian and Polish Social Democrats to delegitimize any kind of separate Jewish socialist movement. Medem—unlike Zhitlowsky—did not grow up in a deeply Jewish environment; however, he was cognizant of the fact that Jewish workers were unlikely to join a movement that did not seek to protect their national rights.

Medem was responsible for developing the Bund's "neutralism" in his 1904 essay "The National Question and Social-Democracy," when he argued that the Jewish workers' movement should stay neutral in the fight between assimilationists and nationalists, as both served the ends of the bourgeoisie. More important, to Medem, was defending the Jews against national oppression by others. With the

Bund's plunging popularity following the failed 1905–7 revolution, however, and the broad efforts by all Jewish parties to reorganize the Russian Jewish community, Medem actively debated with Dubnov and others the nature of Jewish nationality and nationalism, shifting toward the idea of a cultural yet avowedly secular nationality (Medem later dismissed his publications in nonpartisan journals during this period, especially 1908–9, as written only due to financial necessity). In the essay below, published in the volume *Theoretical and Practical Questions of Jewish Life*—a collaborative effort by a number of socialist, autonomist, liberal, and Zionist thinkers, which appeared in 1911—Medem questioned the idea of a unified Jewish nation, a cherished assumption of the Jewish national movements and an idea at the very heart of Judaism. Where others sought to determine how Jewish unity might be preserved in the absence of religion, Medem simply decided that such a thing was impossible: with secularization, there can be no "worldwide Jewish nation." Yet at the same time Medem did not oppose seeing the Jews in national terms nor building the foundation for a secular Jewish nation in Eastern Europe. He opposed treating the different Jewish communities of the world as a unified nation, either politically or institutionally. In the context of an increasingly transnational Jewish political life, he dissented in favor of localism.

Medem became one of the earliest and most influential leaders of the independent Polish Bund, founded during World War I, when much of Poland was under German occupation. Once again Medem edged the party toward acknowledging the Jewish public's desire for autonomy and continuity, while providing a response to the growing popularity of Zionism. Medem became a proponent of *doikayt* ("hereness"), drawing a clear distinction between the Jewish socialists, who sought to improve the life of Jews in Poland and elsewhere, here and now, and the supposedly utopian program of the Zionists. Written in 1911, the following essay in some ways offers a bridge between neutralism and *doikayt*. Medem here continues to promote neutralism through his third way between assimilation and nationalism. Yet, as Medem is astutely aware, the basis of Jewish nationalism is in the unity of Jewish peoplehood, embodied in its religious tradition and given secular meaning by Jewish nationalists. Therefore, even as he argues that many Jewish nations might evolve in different locations throughout the world, his underlying message is one of opposition to Jewish nationalism. Medem's efforts to define Jewish nationality as locally as possible represent a change in emphasis toward practical cultural work, a relatively new development reflecting the Bund's precipitous drop in relevance and popularity in the years following the end of the 1905–7 revolution and its desire to rebuild a base of support. In stepping into the debate about the meaning of the Jewish nation, Medem inveighs against "abstractions" such as self-consciousness and suggests fanatical cultural work instead. But perhaps most important, because Medem is far more concerned with Jewish socialism than with Jewish national questions, his efforts to push aside the debate by questioning any attempt to coherently define the Jewish nation reflect the fine line walked by Jewish socialists leading a national movement, who were themselves more cosmopolitan than nationalist in outlook.

Time and again one hears the reproach: "Why does the Jewish nation end for you with [the border towns] Eydkunen and Alexandrov? Why do the Jews living on the other side of the border not exist for you? Why this fetishism of the boundary cordon? Is the customhouse more important than the living nation?" And so on.

Unfortunately, we still have not had a thorough conversation with those who issue such reproaches. But meanwhile the subject deserves as much. And the subject is interesting: who is it we ultimately have in mind when we utter the words "Jewish nation"? These words are uttered at every turn, after all—it would seem they ought to have attained a quite certain meaning. But this is not the case. Their amplitude is extremely imprecise. And this leads to inevitable confusion. We have to try and explain things. For this is not a theoretical question of scientific terminology; it resounds at every turn in the social and political movement, and acquires on account of this a quite tangible meaning.

I

As a theoretical question it is extremely thankless, like any question having to do with terminology, classification, or naming. What is it to give something a particular name? What is a nation? What a loathsome subject! And to a tremendous extent it is a futile one, for it operates not on the living dynamic of a defined thing, but on its scholastic "characteristics." It is futile because there is, in essence, nothing to prove: any designation is a purely relative thing, and is kept in place not so much by the reason as by the consent of all—by the tacit consent manifested in the traditional use of the word. And the so-called proof is reduced time and again to nonproductive whirling in a vicious circle. And indeed, two people argue on the subject of, say, whether language is a necessary feature of a nation; one says yes, the other, no. The proof? "Let us take Switzerland," says one of the disputants, "and we shall see, by example of the Swiss nation, that there can exist a single nation without one unifying language." What does the other answer? It is not difficult to guess: "It is true that Switzerland does not have one single unifying language, but nor is Switzerland one nation; it is three nations living under one government." It is obvious that the argument is futile, for each proceeds on the basis of what it needs to prove. Build the definition of a nation on the basis of its characteristics, and derive the sum of these characteristics from the definition of a nation . . .

No, we shall not get into such things. But that does not rule out still one more. Even if the question of an exhaustive sum of characteristics is futile, it is nevertheless possible to find an acknowledged minimum of generally recognized features, that common factor that can be derived from all of the definitions, about which there is no argument, and that is inseparably linked in everyone's mind with the very concept of a nation.

It would seem that such a common, universally recognized factor exists, and that it can be expressed most precisely by the German term *Kulturgemeinschaft*: a cultural community, a common cultural milieu.

I repeat: this is only a common factor, perhaps not even (continuing the arithmetic comparison) the greatest factor. It is by no means an exhaustive definition, nor is it even a definition at all: for a definition must capture that which distinguishes a given object from all others, whereas the notion of *Kulturgemeinschaft* can be applied to not only a nation, but—to one extent or another—a whole array of human collectives. Professions and classes are also to a certain extent *Kulturgemeinschaft*. But then, I am not seeking a definition; a minimum on which everyone could agree would suffice, so that we might thus find common ground for further debate. It would seem this minimum is common to everyone—inasmuch as one can judge from literary statements, at least.

I will cite at random several quotes from Jewish writers. I deliberately refer to people belonging to currents with which I disagree regarding the matters concerning us here; it is especially important to me to come to terms with them about this minimum. Take any one of them; each will, one way or another, acknowledge the principle of cultural communication. I open Zhitlowsky's pamphlet "Socialism and the National Question" and read: "A nationality is a group of people that over the course of several generations has solved all the cultural problems of humanity *for itself*, with a number of them having done so *differently* from how it is done by different groups of people . . . as a result of which the group developed special 'national' forms of creativity." The Zionist A. Hartglas (I just came across his brochure "Territory and Nation") tries to define a nation as a phenomenon of economics, but he too says: "a nation is an economic unit consisting of social groups that are engaged in class struggle but *are united by a common culture* that exists owing to economic development on a particular common territory."[26]

S. Dubnov sympathetically cites Renan: "A nation is a soul, a spiritual principle. Two things, which in truth are but one, constitute this soul or spiritual principle . . . One is the possession in common of a rich legacy of memories; the other is present-day consent, the desire to live together, the will to perpetuate the value of the heritage that one has received in an undivided form . . . A nation is a great unity" and so on.[27] Dubnov for his own part adds that what maintains Jewry's national bond is a "common historical destiny." He explains further that in speaking about this "commonality," he is thinking "about our former glory, our centuries of suffering," about "the endless chain of shared impressions experienced by our ancestors, accumulated over centuries in the Jewish soul and leaving behind a certain lasting residue."[28]

This is all the same cultural discourse. To my great dismay, I do not have S. Dubnov's latest work at hand.[29] However, his views on the "spiritual," and thus cultural, character of the nation are so well known that there is no need for further quotations. Indeed, we have quoted him enough. We see that for Dubnov the idealist, Hartglas the "materialist," and Zhitlowsky the eclectic, the concept of nation is consistently connected with the notion of cultural commonality. And so it is for everyone. Depending on the general outlook, this element will figure in some fashion: for one it will be a self-contained thing; for the second, it will be derived from economics; for the third, it will be yet something else. But it will *be* there for all. Without this there can be no nation.

But this is only while we are speaking about the nation in general. We need only turn to the Jews and the seemingly mandatory prerequisites lose their force.

After all, if a prerequisite such as *Kulturgemeinschaft* remained in force, would it really be possible to speak about a worldwide Jewish nation? Not under any circumstances. For what cultural commonality can be found between the Jewry

26. A. Hartglas, "Territory and Nation," 1907, 23. Italics mine—V. M. [As a Zionist and deputy in the Polish parliament between the world wars, Apolinary Hartglas (1883–1953) also fought for Jewish cultural autonomy in Poland.]

27. [See Ernest Renan, "What Is a Nation?," in *Becoming National: A Reader*, ed. Geoff Eley and Ronald Grigor Suny (New York: Oxford University Press, 1996), 42–56.]

28. S. M. Dubnov, *Ob izuchenii istorii russkikh evreev*, St. Petersburg, 1891.

29. [Medem is probably referring here to Dubnov's "Letters," published in St. Petersburg in 1907 as *Pis'ma o starom i novom evreistve (1897–1907)*.]

of the Pale of Settlement and French Jewry? Or German? Or Dutch? Or Bulgar-
ian? Where are those elements in the dynamic of cultural life that would join
them together? Where is that "common culture" that Hartglas demands? Where
is that common creativity of the culture "for itself" of which Zhitlowsky speaks,
where is the "chain of shared impressions" that Dubnov cites? There is none of
this. There are no real threads that would stretch from individual to individual,
from group to group, interlacing in an intricate complex of constant psychic interaction and reciprocal cultural influence. There is no collective life, thus there
is no national life. Is a nation conceivable without a national life?

Admittedly, they may say to me: does there truly, within the bounds of a regular "real" nation—let us say, the Russian or German—exist in full measure this
commonality of cultural life? Are the lower classes not cut off from the national
culture? Indeed, [Otto] Bauer demonstrates that in each given historical period,
the national culture is under the monopolistic control of one or several of the
upper classes, and the realization of a true *Kulturgemeinschaft* can occur only following a radical turn in the entire social structure.

I do not intend to challenge this obvious fact. But I believe we must keep in
mind the following two conditions. First, while the lower classes have indeed
only weak and limited access to the culture of the upper classes, the latter are
under the constant influence of the culture (or quasi-culture) of the former.
Without enjoying the riches of the national culture, the lower classes still exert
a tremendous influence on its entire character; the "lower" life flows in a wide
stream into the cultural creations of the intelligentsia, permeates all of its pores,
leaves its imprint everywhere, and it is this imprint that ultimately gives the culture its national character, creates its particular physiognomy. Thus, commonality, even if unidirectional, still exists, and the internal coherence of cultural
creation is apparent.

But more important is a second consideration. Perhaps the lower classes are,
to a tremendous degree, cut off from national life. But they are cut off from it
inasmuch as they have no cultural life at all. To the extent that their cultural
life exists, it does so within national forms. Beyond the national relations there
remain only places empty of culture—black, unadorned stripes on the cultural
spectrum. Every cultural ray that penetrates this spectrum is nationally colored.

The matter is completely different among the separate groups of Jews. Take
the West European Jews. If they are cut off from the cultural life of Eastern Jewry,
then not in the same way as the Russian *muzhik* [peasant] is cut off from the Russian intelligentsia. They are by no means located off the spectrum of cultural life;

these are extremely cultured people, more cultured than we. Thus they are not a black mark; on the contrary—extremely colored. But they are colored with a *foreign culture*. They are not simply located outside the Jewish *Kulturgemeinschaft*, they have departed deep into a foreign cultural milieu. The French Jew shares a common culture with the French, the German Jew, with the Germans. He speaks their language, not simply "speaks," but claims this language as his *own*, he knows no other; and language is at once an indicator of cultural exchange and, more importantly, a necessary condition for this exchange. He grows up on their literature, lives on their science, their art, all the cultural creativity of their world. For him it is not "their" language, not "their" literature, not "their" art, but "my" language, "my" literature, "my" art. He speaks of them in the first person, and cannot do otherwise. For if not about this, then about what will he speak in the first person? About the "*zhargon*" [Yiddish] which he does not recognize? About the Hebrew language, which he does not know? He speaks of the French, the Germans, in the first person. For he comprises a part of their collective whole. It is with them he lives—not only geographically, but also in their entire way of life. Whether or not he lives with them amicably is a special question; though they persecute him, he still lives by the culture of his persecutor. Whether it is ethically or otherwise dubious, it is nevertheless a reality, one we will not evaluate right now.

With them he lives, about the Jews he remembers—in the best case, dreams. To the Jews he reaches out—in the same "best case"—his arms. But these arms reach over a chasm dividing one from the other into two cultural worlds. It is a bridge over the chasm. As to whether such a bridge can hold there are various opinions, but still it extends across the chasm, and the never-ending conversations about the bridge only confirm once more that the chasm exists, that there is no single unified Jewish milieu.

All of this, it would seem, is so clear. But the idea of a worldwide Jewry persists with exceptional tenacity. It looks for all sorts of props, resorts to a variety of crutches just to survive.

The usual prop: a reference to national consciousness. National consciousness, a national idea unifies the dispersed Jews! I am at a loss to find sufficiently polite words with which to answer the bearers of this crutch. Indeed, I do not even know that it is necessary. The antediluvian notion that national consciousness forms the basis of a nation is so compromised that there is no need to stop and address it right away. One need not be a historical materialist in order to put this stagnant historical spiritualism to rest for good. It is enough simply to shake from oneself the hypnosis of the phrase and ask: what does it mean that national consciousness constitutes national unity? This consciousness must, after all, have some sort of object. Otherwise it is not consciousness but hallucination. The object of national consciousness should be the nation! And it is this very nation about which we are asking: on what is it based, what is it, how is it expressed? And if it is expressed only in national consciousness and national feeling, how then is this consciousness and feeling sustained? Where do they come from? What keeps them going?

With those who are unable to answer these questions, we have nothing more to discuss. But others will give an answer. And we must consider their answer all the more seriously, for it issues from the lips of very serious people, and among the weeds of an idealistic view of history, it is not difficult also to gather some valuable wheat of sound sociological thought.

For an answer they resort to the very same idea of cultural commonality about which I spoke previously. But they perform on it meanwhile an operation of vital significance: they shift from the present to the past tense. They declare: now there is no commonality, but there *was*. It is by virtue of this *past* connection that the Jews have been united until now. I shall permit myself to cite a more extensive extract from an old work I have already quoted by Dubnov, in which the point of view interesting to us is formulated with tremendous definitiveness. I do not know whether its author would subscribe to it at the present time. But for me this is not important. What is important is that here a specific idea is spelled out with full clarity, consistency, and purity.

> Wherein lies the essence of the Jewish national idea? In other words, what constitutes that cement which connects and unites us into one complex organism? We have not had the material signs of a nation—territory and state—for a long time. They are replaced by abstract foundations: religion and ancestry. Unquestionably these are two powerful factors, but are they alone in sustaining the national connection of Jewry? No, for, assuming such were the case, we would have to also allow that a weakening of the religious foundation among freethinking Jews, and of the racial particularity among "cultured" groups of Jews, must correspondingly weaken or even completely shatter our national foundations—which, in fact, we do not see. On the contrary, we usually see progressives, and at times even religiously indifferent people and *libres penseurs*, at the avant-garde of all our national movements. What is it that binds them to a people with whom an affiliation, in a majority

of cases, constitutes a feat frequently accompanied by martyrdom? Indeed, there is something common and all-embracing that connects people of the most diverse views and cultural positions into a unified whole. This "something" is the *common historical destiny* shared by all the fragmented parts of Jewry. We are connected by common memories of our past, rich with events, memories of our former glory, of our centuries-long suffering, of our calamitous exile; uniting us is an endless chain of similar impressions experienced by our ancestors which have accumulated in the Jewish soul and left there a certain lasting residue. In a word, the universal Jewish national idea is founded chiefly on *historical consciousness.*[30]

It would be foolish to question that distinguished place that is occupied by a "common historical destiny," both in the concept of "nation" and in the very fact of the existence of a nation. On the contrary, it is precisely we, those coming from the materialistic point of view, who constantly try to place the live dynamics at the center of attention in place of the dead statics. But what is the dynamics of national life, if not a common historical destiny?

It is self-evident: only in this way is a nation formed, only on the crucible of history is it forged, and when Renan, whom Dubnov quotes, says that the "idea of a nation" assumes an absolutely certain past, this sounds to us like a simple truism. Of course, without a past there is no nation.

But can a nation be based on *only one* past? Indeed, herein lies the entire question. There was a unified Jewry. Does that mean it now exists? After all, Dubnov's ideas clearly result in the following formula of national existence: "I was, therefore I am." The historical past is "the social capital on which the national idea is based," says Renan himself: it is a "common heritage." This is undoubtedly true. But a common heritage can be preserved in whole, can be kept jointly, but it can also be divided. Herein lies the entire question: Is it divided or not? And if it is divided, then the nation, too, is divided.

The meaning and role of a common historical destiny is tremendous. Peculiar historical destinies continue to speak to us long after they themselves have become things of the past. And they "let us know about themselves" not in the form of historical vestiges, not as historical ballast dragged on the way of the nation like a ball chained to its leg; no, their role consists chiefly in what the national collective created by it *in its own way* perceives and in its own way processes

---

30. S. M. Dubnov, *Ob izuchenii istorii russkikh evreev*, 6.

all that it has to perceive subsequently, when it already drinks from the chalice of "common," or rather strange, culture. A specific national prism is created, and thanks to this prism, the same factors of a country's social, political, state, and economic life, which diligently exert their influence on the entire nation—let us say, Russia—one and the same factors permeate into every national milieu in refracted form. Concrete historical values can die off, but this formal moment of historically original refraction—that which Bauer aptly described using the term "national apperception"—remains.

But already from this one thing is clear: we are dealing with two elements—a subject that exists as the result of "historical fate," and the new life perceived by it. Further evolution is determined by the interaction of *both* elements. Two children, having received the same upbringing, similar in character, having a common heredity, finding themselves in two different environments, will become different people, despite the identity of their apperception. It is that simple. Historical legacy is not a forever frozen form. History does not stand still; "historical fate" is not only what *was*, but what *is*, and what *will be*.

A common history left us as a legacy a series of "indelible marks"; but since then we have diverged in various directions and lived though our subsequent history, not common history, but history nonetheless; and it too leaves its "indelible marks" which layer upon the old, introducing a new integral part in the old perceptive apparatus, modifying it, reworking it anew. The common heritage evolves. And since it evolves piecemeal, in the hands of different successors, on different ends of the globe, in different states, under different ways of life, in the atmosphere of different cultures—it is quite obvious what fate befalls it. One successor or another may lose his heritage completely and pass to a strange house; of these we do not speak. But even those who preserve their capital can diverge from one another along completely opposite paths; each of them will have his house, but they will be strange to each other.

We have seen few such examples in history when from a once common organism there are created, either by way of division or budding, wholly independent new beings. I will point to the Dutch nation as an example, which Bauer also cites, by the way. They originated from among the German people, but "completely different from the Germans, the Netherlanders' national economic destiny gave rise there to a distinct culture; detached from the Germans in economic and cultural relations, they severed relations (*Verkehrsgemeinschaft*) with the German tribes; alas, the threads that connected them among themselves were too tight; those connecting them with the remaining German tribes were too weak; in this manner they created their own special language as an instrument of their culture, and ceased taking part in the process of cultural integration of the German nation through a common German language."[31]

Indeed, this is occurring at present within Jewry. And if in our times one cannot *yet* speak of several Jewish nations, one can *no longer* speak of one unified Jewish nation. We are obliged to recognize this by the historical process occurring before our eyes.

More precisely: not occurring, but concluding. For it would be strange if it had only begun to occur after twenty centuries of dispersion. It has been in preparation throughout this entire gigantic epoch. But its conclusion required the arrival of that critical epoch signified by the nineteenth century. It was necessary for the rebuilding of all national life to begin on new foundations.

A life of twenty centuries in dispersion undoubtedly prepared all the elements for the division of a once united nation. But that was not enough. It was also necessary that the ice of the Middle Ages, which had forged together something that without it would have disintegrated, melt. This was the ice of *religious culture*.

The "common heritage" was frozen, preserved, sealed off from the influence of the outside world; individual moments, such as the Jewish-Arab period, were only exceptions. Religious culture engaged in self-assertion, self-fortification, self-protection, created from itself; but it did not know evolution. The Jewish world was closed unto itself; closed with two locks: one with which it locked itself off from the outside, strange world and another with which this strange world in turn locked it into a ghetto. Individual Jewish cells, closed unto themselves, scattered across the entire world, did not absorb the external culture, reduced to a minimum its influence, had to do without the outside world and could do without it. It made the preservation of their mutual connection that much easier. It is comparatively easy to preserve in whole that which does not move. Religious culture is static, and not only that: itself static, it stopped movement. To the extent that cultural life even penetrated from the outside, it had to huddle in the backyard; the place of honor belonged to the religious foundation—immovable and unifying. This was the case not only among the Jews. It was the same with the international dominance of the Catholic Church, scholastics, and Latin. The same iron ring of universalism, weighing on the folk, and hence national, culture.

It took the hot wind of the nineteenth century to melt this icy ring. The ghetto

31. O. Bauer, *Nationalitätenfrage und die Sozialdemokratie*, 100–101.

fell, and the influence of the outside world gushed forth. Cultural creation began, and this creation threatened the Jews with destruction. The old foundation of Jewish unity—the chain of religion—suffered a blow from which it would not recover. Secularization of the culture put the existence of the old collectives at stake.

And so in its critical form this process is still new. It began at the point when the question of a new foundation of national existence entered the agenda, and when Jewry was examined from this point of view, as a whole and in its separate pieces. And it became immediately apparent: the old ring ought to drop off— no, not drop off but at least loosen—and no unifying links remained; there remained individual bricks. A whole series of these bricks had already fallen away, for they had held on only by force of the ghetto. It alone contained that integrating strength that fixed Western bricks to Eastern ones. The dam is broken—and the chasm gaping.

At the same time, we know that there too, on the other side of the chasm, a hangover set in, and a national feeling began to speak, with assimilated Europeans being drawn to their "suffering Eastern brothers." But this does not change matters. In place of the warm wind of liberalism there blew the icy wind of anti-semitism and pushed it away. But it has nowhere to go. The connection with Eastern Jewry is severed; creating an independent national life is beyond them. There remains only a longing for national life. And the absence of it. This is truly a tragic conflict: there is national consciousness and no national existence. But from this conflict there is no exit. For in essence they are not part of the Jewish nation, but small pieces of the French and German nations wishing to become Jews again—but unable to.

Whatever the intensity of these desires, it is fruitless. And it is no wonder that they are either Zionists or . . . assimilators. There is no third possibility for them. The idea of unity never can replace unity itself.

If they, these Western Jews, or at least a significant part of them, constituted a compact, large mass, comprising a more or less closed milieu, having a common language unifying them among themselves and distinguishing them from other peoples, we could then expect that among them there would begin the very same process of true national revival that we observe in our own country. And then in the West there would emerge a special Jewish nation, distinct from both the surrounding peoples and Eastern Jewry. But that is only "if." Not one of the indicated conditions exists, and therefore their national aspirations are the galvanization of a corpse. To say that they together with us constitute a united

Jewish nation is in any case impossible. For even if they had not died, they would still be a foreign organism to us.

It is largely the same with those small groups of Jews possessing their own special "jargon"—the *españolski*.[32] Whether they are capable of cultural revival, I cannot presume to say. But they, too, face the same alternatives: either become part of the surrounding nations, or form a separate Jewish nation that will be a special cultural collective, completely separate and distinct from Eastern Jewry.

Matters are more difficult with this "Eastern Jewry"—Russian, Galician, Bukovinian, Rumanian; it also concerns the branches separated from it in the process of emigration: the Jewry of North America, London White Chapel, the Paris Jewish Quarters, South Africa, Argentina, and so on, and so on. Approaching the question from the static point of view, you immediately reach a dead end. No one will be such a fetishist of the state border as to claim that the Jews of Krakow and the Jews of Warsaw belong to two different Jewish nations, the Jews of London to a third, the Jews of New York to a fourth. This would sound like a joke, as would the assertion that the day after the partition of Poland, Jewry, united the day before, awoke and saw itself divided into three Jewish nations. All of this is very funny, but only while we hold to a static point of view. The moment we have a look into the dynamic, the matter takes on a different appearance.

The day after the partition of Poland there was no difference between Warsaw and Krakow Jews. Visit Warsaw and Krakow *now*—and you will see that there is a difference.

True, the difference may be minor, but it is greater than before. Hence it has grown, and grows. And it will grow, since the "historical fates" have ceased to be common. It could not grow more because the Galician-Bukovinian Jewry still to this day has not come out of its immobility, from its state of cultural marasmus, indeed, Russian Jewry too is only beginning to come out. But who can guarantee in which direction or in which directions the intensive pace of historical development can push it. I do not want to make predictions; for there are also many circumstances indicating that unity can be preserved or revived: territorial contiguity, likeness of the surrounding milieu and—perhaps most certainly of all—unity of language. With the presence of linguistic unity, with an existing trend toward expanding the foundation of cultural life to the expansion of the cultural market owing to a *similarity* of way of life, there can be a *commonality*

32. [Speakers of Judeo-Spanish, or Ladino, most of whom lived in the Ottoman Empire.]

of life, in other words, national unity. Whether or not this will happen, I cannot undertake to guarantee, and if I posed this question, then it is in contrast to those who see the very posing of it as blasphemous infringement on its grand national idea.

Things are different with North America, Africa, Argentina. True, here too, thinking statically, one arrives at the same curiosity: can it really be that these same Russian Jews with whom we not long ago lived side by side, worked together, developed together, with whom we are connected by thousands of cultural threads, all of these close, known, familiar, our own people, after crossing the ocean, become nationally estranged from us? Cease to be members of the same real Jewish nation, *our* nation, which we experience as a living collective? Isn't it funny, after all?! Of course. But take the same Jews who left thirty years ago and look at their children. And you will stop smiling. This is no longer the realm of curiosities; this raises a serious question. And it is regarding the second generation. And what will be with the third? At the present moment, while the overwhelming majority of American Jewry consists of people newly arrived from Russia, and the hypertrophied stream of immigration pours yearly in huge streams of "greenhorns," a commonality of national life exists, maintained nothing less than physically. But this is now, while American Jewry is—historically—still in its youth, after all. A second generation will grow up, a third, a fourth; on the other hand, immigration will subside; and even if it did not subside completely, the percent of new immigrants in relation to the native American-Jewish core population would fall, the new arrivals would dissolve. The ideological connections to Russia are already weakening before our eyes. The tremendous American life with its frightening intensity seizes and grinds. This does not mean that the American Jews must without fail turn into Yankees, but it means that a type of American Jewry is taking shape that is moving further and further away from Russian Jewry and that can turn into a new national type.

Already in the Jewish-American way of life there is so much that is frightening and strange to us; one should have a look at their newspapers! Already the language is changing, becoming heavily Anglicized. And that is only within a few years. What will be next? Will this process not go further, and will it not reach to the end?

Again, I dare not make predictions. But I see that the trend is now precisely such. This is where things are going. Such is the dynamic.

The same is happening in Africa, the same in Argentina. Everywhere the same two alternatives: assimilation or a distinct new nation. The third possibility—

preservation of national unity with the old metropolis—is becoming increasingly unreal. Under these conditions is it possible to speak of worldwide Jewry as a dynamic reality?

Worldwide Jewry has become a fiction. It is its individual components that are truly alive. It lives by its laws, yielding to its destiny, and what new combinations are made from them depends precisely on the destiny of these pieces. Here are the real values with which one must operate, here is the basis for work, here is the cornerstone. The individual pieces—these are the real collectives on which it is possible to build. Worldwide Jewry—this is an abstraction, and an obsolete one at that. On an abstraction one can build only castles in the sky.

II

But where we come from they love to build castles in the sky. Both assimilators and nationalists build them. And herein lies the fatal lot of one and the other, that they are doomed to this sad building. And even when they make something useful, it issues from "airy" premises. How much harm comes from this!

I have no intention to engage in purging assimilationism. Nor do I hope that the nationalists will be brought to reason. A certain intellectual bourgeois milieu comprising the primary nursery for contemporary Jewish nationalism is in need of certain, more or less hazy, idealistic foundations, and cannot do without conventional abstractions that embellish its ideological existence. But still this nationalism occupies a visible place in the contemporary cultural movement of Jewry—not in all its forms, but embodied in a few trends. I foresee that in fact, despite all the differences in premises of principle, we will be allies in a number of matters. In these matters their success will be our success. But there is a precondition for success—at least a partial removal of the ballast.

The principle of a worldwide Jewish national organization is one of those weights that the nationalist ballast, it seems to me, could easily do without. And as to the need to sacrifice it, I will not have to say very much.

Whither pulls this weight? By strange paradox, it pulls not down, but up. Such is the gravity of the nationalist weights: they pull away from the earth into the cloudless sky of abstraction.

What is dear to the nationalist, the person who bases his work on the national idea? What is dear is that which constitutes national value. And this is usually what unites a nation, what is common to it, what can be designated as the common denominator. It is commonly cultivated, becomes an object of concern, a subject of public service. And it is clear that completely different things are considered common (and, consequently, placed on a pedestal) depending on which circle the bounds of the national collective appear in. If the movement issues, for example, from the task of the national rebirth of Russian Jewry, let us take it even further, let us suppose "Eastern" Jewry, one will consider such common cultural factors as the folk language ("*zhargon*"), literature created in this very language, and at its base the folk school, folk art, theater, and so on—all factors, frightfully important and necessary factors, to which cultural and educational energy should be wholly devoted. But as soon as we expand the object to the magnitude of the *worldwide* Jewish nation the matter changes sharply. All that which we just enumerated can no longer be considered common. For these are not elements that unify all. They do not unify, but divide, and hence they cannot claim a common national role. It is necessary to search for others. And these others will be religion and the ancient Jewish language (Hebrew), plus an abstract idea of Jewry in general. And thus all perspectives shift. What was important retreats to the background; that which was behind assumes the first place. Religion and the ancient Jewish language serve as *common national* factors, hence, from the point of view of nationalism they play a paramount role. The Jewish (not ancient Jewish) language,[33] Jewish literature, Jewish folk culture—all of these are things on which they continue to work, which they continue to both love and value, but which one can nevertheless not view as common national wealth. They cannot sustain national unity! It is not for them to play the role of national palladium. And if they retain the rights of citizenship, then it is only of the second class. Thus a terrible opposition is created between the *national* language and the *folk* language, between the language of national *unity* and the language of folk *life*; the contrast between the national idea and the national culture. It is evident, meanwhile, that the "national" occupies the first place, the "folk" retreats into the background. And the national sanction is not awarded—that which is awarded is in fact a different, higher sanction, which can only be the sanction of true life.

This dualism of the "national" and "folk" extends everywhere.[34] In the best case the two are both put on the same plane. Usually the "folk" must *pietätvoll*

33. [That is, Yiddish (not Hebrew).]

34. [There is an important distinction in Russian between folk or people (*narod*) and nation (*natsiia*) that made its way into Jewish debates over nationality and language during this period. This distinction is much less clear in Yiddish (in the case of *volk*) and Hebrew (in the case of *am*).]

[with reverence] kneel before the ancient fetish. And one dares not declare a struggle against it. One dares not, and yet it is needed most urgently. For the fetish holds tenaciously to its fruitless existence and defends it with all its energy. He has no shame. He inflicts blow after blow on his enemy, who respectfully receives a battering of jibes and insults.

This dualism eats away at the core of the national movement, paralyzes its strength, kills its resolve. It creates a cult of fossils, it extends abominable hypocrisy, on account of which unbelieving freethinking people don the mask of the churchgoer; it brings the living language to sacrifice to the dead one; it needs for this living language not to be able to get out of the swamp of disdain into which it was trampled. Just consider the necessity to carry on the fight for a native language in the Jewish milieu! Of course, this fight is not due to only one dualism, but to what extent is it aggravated by it! Take the sheer fact that to this day the folk language does not dare be called the national language.[35] One must understand: the thing is not the titles. But the title has a symbolic meaning. And this denial of title symbolizes a certain attitude: it is still not a language, they say; it is still "not it"; still a helot. And so it goes in all matters. Life's true needs are neglected; shadows occupy honor's corner.

I repeat, only in the best case is true life awarded a place *next to* the shadows. And this best case is also fairly bad. For given the poverty of Jewish cultural life, and the chronic crisis that it suffers, and the multitude of obstacles that it has to suffer, success is conceivable only if all of the cultural movement's might is focused on one task; a concentration of attention, of maximum effort, is essential; monism is essential. Everything must go through one channel. The greatest perseverance is needed. Fanaticism for cultural work is needed—militant, uncompromising fanaticism. Relentlessness that knows no fetishes and strikes everything that stands in its way. And that which stands not in the path, but *next* to the desired path, must be passed by. Hats off to him, if he is a respected elder and if he is not in the way—and keep walking! "He who is not with us is against us."

35. [The Czernowitz conference, held in 1908 in the town of Czernowitz (Chernivtsi), was the first international conference on the Yiddish language. Its founders sought to avoid political disputes and focus on the practical advancement of Yiddish, but the conference quickly became a forum for debating the centrality of Yiddish in national Jewish culture. The conference delegates ultimately adopted the formulation of Yiddish as "a national language," alienating both Hebraists who rejected its elevation and Yiddishists who viewed it as *the* national language.]

III

In the realm of social organizational structure the same fetishism can be observed, the same impulse from the earthly to the heavenly. Here in this realm
one has occasion most often to hear the reproach regarding Eydkunen and Alexandrov. It is still the same contrast between the living reality and the revered
spirit. The living matter for one—the abstract national idea for another.

From the point of view of the abstract idea the matter is simple: when you
build, try to build on a common national foundation. If only there is an external possibility. Building on a different scale—it is in essence opportunism, a
leniency of discipline, a compromise with one's conscience, a tolerable evil, but
no more.

From our point of view such a simplified system is utterly impossible. Any
organization must serve certain vital needs. It is in accordance with this goal
that it should be built: *expediently.* And in accordance with this both its circle and
its forms are determined. Depending on which organization is in question.

For example, if we take the purely cultural society, here there is no need what-
soever to always keep within state limits; a certain amount of cultural work is
possible on a joint basis for all of "Eastern" Jewry. For example, in the realm
of philology, work on the development of the Jewish language, the establishment of a commonly recognized universal grammar, and so on. Indeed, nobody
denies this. But even such a society would not be an all-Jewish organization, for
it would include only those Jews who speak the "*zhargon.*" And so: neither state
fetishism nor fetishism of worldwide Jewry!

Even in the purely cultural realm, however, such international unions can
have only extremely limited significance. There is little in which they can find
application for themselves. Even such a simple thing as a common book publishing house is hardly possible on a large scale for two or more countries, too
different are the cultural practices, market conditions, tastes, except in the realm
of belles-lettres, the least of all dependent on state boundaries.

Outside the purely cultural sphere, some organizational unity is possible and
necessary in the area of the regulation of immigration. Again, not for the sake of
the idea, but in the interest of practical results. Perhaps if we probe we can find
some other examples still. I have no need to go through them. What is important to me are the examples for explaining the method.

And so, if with this method you approach the realm about which you
most often hear rebukes, the realm of *political* organization, you will be truly

perplexed. They talk about worldwide Jewish parties, call for their formation, demand that party building be carried out on this basis. Yes, but what is it such a party will engage in?! Usually political parties engage in . . . politics. But politics is determined above all by state conditions! After all, a political party is a unity of people that has assigned as its task a particular impact on the state system, on the system, that is, of a given country. Political parties of individual countries come closer together, provide support for one another—of course! But again, each will do this within the bounds of its state unit. It is downright awkward to talk about it.

I could understand if, let us say, the PPS formed a united Polish party in all three partition regions.[36] It would be understandable, for in all three parts there is a common political goal—the restoration of a unified government. But even they are limited to close relations, not creating a united party. Perhaps they would in fact create it, though, were it not for reasons of legality and law enforcement. I am even ready to understand the Zionists, who want worldwide unification. They, too, have a particular concrete goal, capable, in their view, of unifying all.

For them the entire *golus*—as considered from a bird's-eye view—is none other than a single episode in the history of the Jewish nation, united in the past and united in the future; it follows as obvious that this temporary, albeit long, episode, does not justify severing the unity. But even for the Zionists all ground for unification disappears, inasmuch as their activity encompasses not only Zionist, but also political tasks, since it takes place in the form of a political party's work. And indeed, united in the sphere of actual Zionist work, Zionist organizations of individual countries acting as political parties operate completely independently and completely autonomously; each in its own way, according to the conditions of the country. The same applies to the various types of proletarian Zionism conducting, despite all talk of unity, completely independent political work in each individual country. But nevertheless, I repeat, I can still understand Zionists and territorialists of all and any types. But they demand also of non-Zionists that they too follow in their footsteps. They stake a claim on us—and this is beyond any common sense.

This is again the same cult of absolutes. It is the same lack of political culture that knows only one type of adherence to a principle—idolatry. It is still the same idealistic nationalism that knows only one form of national work—service to national abstractions. And if the talk of worldwide parties brings no

36. [The PPS is the Polska Partia Socjalistyczna (the Polish Socialist Party).]

great harm in and of itself it still causes confusion—for in the end the matter ends with talk. But more important is their symptomatic significance. This is the product of the same old scholastic mode of thinking permeating every variety of Jewish nationalism, rendering it so sickly and anemic. And if I were a doctor, I would prescribe to Jewish nationalism: less dreaming by the moonlight, fewer visions of ghosts and apparitions! And more living work among living people!

7

Jewish Autonomy Yesterday and Today
Jacob Lestschinsky

Yakov Lestschinsky, *Di Yidishe avtonomye amol un haynt*. Kiev: Central
Committee of the Fareynikte Yidishe Sotsyalistishe Arbeter Partey, 1918.

Like the many other ideological nomads in this volume, a belief in socialist autonomism and diaspora nationalism marked but one stage in Jacob Lestschinsky's
(1876–1966) long and varied political career. Lestschinsky was born in Horodische,
near Kiev, where he received a traditional education before moving to Odessa,
then Bern, and finally Zurich in pursuit of higher education. In Odessa, Lestschinsky became a Hebraist and devotee of Ahad Ha'am, but in Switzerland he
transformed himself into a Marxist and returned to the Russian Empire a devoted
socialist Zionist. Over the course of his life, Lestschinsky moved from socialist
Zionism to territorialism, then to socialist autonomism and diaspora nationalism,
and finally back to socialist Zionism.

Lestschinsky is best known as a pioneering Jewish sociologist and demographer.
He began publishing sociological studies as early as 1903, with an economic and
demographic study of his hometown, and wrote the first work in any language
to attempt to detail the impact of industrialization on Russian Jews. *Der yidisher
arbeter (in rusland)* (The Jewish worker [in Russia]) was one of the first scholarly
monographs in Yiddish, and in explaining the disadvantages faced by the Jewish
proletariat, it made a Marxist argument for territorial concentration. During World
War I, Lestschinsky worked for a Jewish relief agency based in Warsaw, and with
the fall of the tsar, he moved to Kiev to participate in building Jewish autonomy
there. He helped organize the United Jewish Socialist Workers' Party (Fareynikte),
the Kultur-Lige, and its publishing wing, the Folks-Farlag.

In "Jewish Autonomy Yesterday and Today," Lestschinsky analyzed Jewish economic and communal life in Poland before and after partition in a manner combining Dubnovian autonomism and Marxist history. Lestschinsky argued that Jewish
self-government preserved Jewish autonomy from the beginning of the Jewish
diaspora, but as a holdover from feudal autonomy and a stand-in for territory,
the Jewish communal government could not survive modernization. According
to Lestschinsky, in the nineteenth century Jewish self-government became a tool
of oppression in the hands of the wealthy, and with increased economic and class

stratification, the bourgeoisie and middle classes sought to separate themselves from the Jewish nation. In contrast, the newly emerging social classes — Jewish workers and artisans — reinforced national identity and created their own form of autonomy. By concentrating geographically, he wrote in a section of the essay before the part included below, the Jewish laboring classes in effect "create a new Jewish 'territory,' and urban and modern Jewish domain." The Fareynikte published "Jewish Autonomy Yesterday and Today" in pamphlet form within the context of the competition between Jewish socialist and liberal parties to define, shape, and control the institutions of Jewish autonomy in Ukraine. Thus, the pamphlet was clearly intended to give a historic underpinning to the Fareynikte's claim to Jewish national leadership. Lestschinsky went to great lengths in his argument to dismiss all efforts at Jewish national cultural construction preceding the revolutionary period. If Jewish autonomy has been historically preserved by the working class, then the Fareynikte must be best equipped to lead the way to Jewish autonomy in the future.

Lestschinsky was known as a romantic who got carried away with ideas, but he never joined another party after the Fareynikte. In 1921 he became Berlin correspondent for the New York daily *Forverts*, and he wrote for the paper for the next forty years. Between 1923 and 1925, Lestschinsky was one of three editors for the journal *Bleter far yidisher demografye, statistik, un ekonomik* (Papers on Jewish demography, statistics, and economics), and with other émigrés from the failed autonomous experiment in Ukraine, he helped found the YIVO Institute for Jewish Research, in particular its economic statistical section. After being expelled from Germany in 1933, and making brief stays in Prague and Riga, Lestschinsky lived primarily in Warsaw until 1938, when he moved to the United States. During the 1930s, Lestschinsky returned to socialist Zionism, seeing Israel as the only place where Jews had the combined freedom and insularity necessary to return to the cohesion of premodern diaspora Jewish life. Lestschinsky moved with his family from the United States to Israel in 1959. Below are the concluding two chapters of "Jewish Autonomy Yesterday and Today."

4

All that remains is to examine the processes in Jewish life that led to new ideas of autonomy, which in turn enabled the organization of Jewish national life on a newly conceived foundation.

In previous chapters we demonstrated that the negative processes—the processes of decay—really only trapped the uppermost strata of the bourgeoisie and intelligentsia. The middle classes remained in the Jewish social milieu, and cultural assimilation did not leave deep roots in its midst.

At the bottom there remained a large dense mass with great historical national inertia, with a hardened, petrified, and obscured heritage, yet rich with high, in a certain sense almost refined, cultural values and cultural practices, and with relatively highly developed cultural needs and cultural preferences. This same dense mass was also rich in as yet undiscovered *primitive* forces and was nourished by deep roots found in the subterranean foundations of every national culture. These fed the emotional experiences and primitive understandings of nature and man, beauty and ugliness, good and evil, wealth and poverty, power and powerlessness, rulers and oppressed, etc.

The confluence of these two different cultural strains, the meeting between a refined three-thousand-year-old culture with the subterranean primitive one would, under ideal conditions, have created a uniquely sculpted national culture. Tragically, we are nowhere near the birth of this meeting, as the road to this harmonious confluence is strewn with great obstacles that cannot easily be removed.

One thing is clear, the hidden primitive powers needed to be discovered and the hidden roots had to be raised to the level of a national multibranched cultural tree. In order to access its historical treasures and inherited wellsprings, the primitive Jewish people and folkways[37] had to evolve into a modern nation and a modern national culture. We are interested here in the social processes that created the conditions for the emergence of a modern Jewish nation, for autonomous Jewish life and creativity.

Before the nineteenth century the social physiognomy of the Jewish folk underwent a complete change. Until then, the center of Jewish economic life was in various forms of middlemen's work—from the small-time trader who chased after a sack of wheat to the court banker who financed kings' wars. In the course of the nineteenth century, the center shifted to labor. Labor began to play the main role in Jewish life. We can briefly characterize this process numerically. At the beginning of the nineteenth century the working classes constituted no more than 10 percent to 12 percent of the Jewish population and now they are more than 50 percent. In America, particularly in New York, they represent up to 75 percent.

37. [*Folkshaft un folkstimlikhkayt.*]

This one fact created a complete change in organized Jewish life.

The middleman, the trader, the *luftmentsh*,[38] the stargazer, and to a degree the small shopkeeper constituted a class suspended between the classes. It was constantly shifting between other social groups and earned its living through serendipity and unrealizable dreams. This group lived in constant tumult and achieved little. The middlemen lacked stability and continuity, security and steadfastness, factors equally necessary for the individual as for the group in order to create, to achieve, and to give birth to something new. Mendele, the child of the Jewish middleman and of the Jewish fair, was completely surprised by the Jewish worker, in whom for the first time he found artistic spirit, unmediated love of nature, and innate love for God's creatures.[39]

As long as the Jewish middleman lived isolated as an individual, he drew from his own past. He lived on the merit of his ancient forefathers. He was sustained by refurbishing the same old values. So lived the Jewish folk during nearly all of the Middle Ages. A few exceptions serve only to reinforce the rule. When the Jewish middleman was drawn into an alien life he ceased to be an individual and discovered himself through competition, a partner in the same class of the surrounding nations. He began to live on the back of someone else's efforts, partook of the general resources and became not only a social but also a cultural parasite. It was now alien values and cultures that sustained him.

Such was the life of most Jewish middlemen to this day. They had already long settled in Yehupets along with Sheyne Sheyndl and no longer ran to Kasrilevke.[40] They had in fact almost entirely forgotten Kasrilevke.

Had the Jewish social structure remained as it was at the beginning of the

38. [The Yiddish word *luftmentsh* (literally, a person of the air) refers to a person with no defined occupation (also an idler or a dreamer).]

39. [Mendele Moykher-Sforim was the pen name of Sholem Yankev Abramovitsh (1835–1917), known as the founding father of both modern Yiddish and modern Hebrew prose. Abramovitsh grew up in a middle-class family in the town of Kapulye (Kopyl).]

40. [Lestschinsky uses the characters and geography of Sholem Aleichem's stories and novels as a means to describe the transformation of Jewish life through urbanization. Kasrilevke was the name of a fictional place used throughout Sholem Aleichem's *oeuvre* to indicate the quintessential small Jewish town, or *shtetl*. Here Lestschinsky is also referring to Sholem Aleichem's *The Letters of Menachem Mendl and Sheyne Sheyndl*, an epistolary novel in which a beleaguered wife, Sheyne Sheyndl, left behind in Kasrilevke exchanges letters with her impractical and chronically unemployed husband, Menachem Mendl, in Odessa and Yehupets, Sholem Aleichem's fictional city landscape that roughly corresponded to Kiev.]

nineteenth century—one of middlemen, traders, and shopkeepers—we would certainly have had a strange folk creature; one with a cultural hunchback, a masked face, a rich but dead legacy, and living small on borrowed capital.

The transformation of the largest part of the folk from mediation to labor resulted from objective conditions. It rescued the Jewish nation from the aforementioned terrible end—from its old tragic history. It refreshed the old strengths and poured new blood into its weakened and dried veins. It infused dry branches with fresh sap and the national tree began to grow and bloom again.

Differentiation played no small role in the renewal of Jewish national life. Differentiation: the splintering of a nearly monolithic, social, mediator-led organism into opposing classes and conflicting social groups.

There were also occasional small social conflicts in Jewish life until the nineteenth century. The strong wealthy classes waged war against the rabbis for control of Jewish autonomy. Later, these same groups joined forces to battle the weak worker and to deny him voting rights in the *kehile*.[41] The rich large *kehiles* choked the smaller ones by imposing heavy taxes. There were no crystallized social classes that would transfer their social privileges and political power to future generations as an inheritance. On the other side, there was also no crystallized oppressed class that would, in like manner, pass on its hatred of the oppressor and its dream of freedom. Our wealthy classes therefore did not create a rich and colorful culture that results from plenty, as did other nations. The poor also did not create a culture of longing, protest, anger, and revolution, which is usually born out of need, suffering, oppression, and slavery.

The social map of the Jewish folk was gray, and therefore so was its culture. Only in the nineteenth century does the salaried worker appear on the Jewish street as the factory worker, the artisan, and his assistant. Handcraft was divided into cottage industry and handwork in the strictest sense of the word. Commerce was also differentiated into large trade, the middle bourgeoisie, and small shopkeeping. A financial and industrial bourgeoisie was created. The intelligentsia was divided between the professional bourgeois intellectual and the folk intellectual. Only in the nineteenth century did new colors appear on the Jewish social and cultural map. New sounds began to be heard, more precisely, the social choir of different classes and groups. This choir, struggling and striving, gave birth to the harmonious national culture.

41. [Jewish communal government.]

Together with the two social processes just mentioned, there was also a third development—the concentration of the Jewish masses in large cities. A few figures will clarify how much this concentration grew in the last century.

At the beginning of the nineteenth century there was not a single Jewish community in Eastern Europe of ten thousand. Now there are twelve, each with more than one hundred thousand Jews. More than a third of all of Eastern European Jewry is concentrated in these twelve communities, totaling more than three million Jews. In New York alone there are now close to one and one half million Jews. A typical Jewish community at the beginning of the nineteenth century consisted of three to four hundred Jewish souls. A typical Jewish community in our time consists of ten thousand.

Jews lived scattered throughout the Middle Ages as small islands, isolated from each other. In our time Jews live in large concentrated and dense masses. Uprooted from the small *shtetl* with its static and measured life, its limited needs and concerns, its narrowed horizons and perspectives, the masses now found themselves in the boiling caldron of the big city. Minds were immediately bombarded by new ideas and concerns. Hearts beat with new emotions and longings. Wider horizons appeared and new stars lit up the heavens. These masses were not like isolated grains of sand cast about, but were rather compact groups that from the beginning inhabited a specific quarter of the city and a specific cultural and social milieu functioning in its own ideological and psychological atmosphere. These transplanted masses not only bore the imprint of their inherited legacy, but also a new class structure founded in the new Jewish space, bringing about a particularized culture struggle. The concentration in the larger cities sped up the transformation from middleman to laborer and deepened and sharpened class differences and class conflict. It hastened the tempo of the change from a ghetto life to a modern, European, universal, humanistic life style. It uprooted the masses from their medieval existence with its inherited limited views and joined them to the universal political and social ideals and movements. The modern Jewish nation was born in the big city, with its European life, with its European concerns, with its universally human social, political, and cultural aspirations.

These three processes discussed, the transformation from middleman to laborer, the differentiation into classes, and the concentration in large cities, established the conditions for an independent national life and unique cultural creativity. In this manner, these processes enabled the birth of ideas of autonomy, which captured the imagination of almost the entirety of the Jewish people.

Not all classes, however, were equally interested in Jewish autonomy.

5

We have demonstrated the *social* forces which gave birth to the strivings for autonomy and which established the historical foundations for autonomy. Now we will deal with the *political* forces called upon to bring these ideas to fruition.

If we first examine the upper bourgeoisie and upper elements of the bourgeois intelligentsia we must conclude that they are so far removed from the Jewish social and cultural milieu that, at present, they have little interest in Jewish autonomous institutions. They are assimilated and drawn to Great Russia, and will probably in time move to the central regions, in so far as Ukraine, White Russia, and other federative nations will share the predominant local culture.

Undoubtedly part of this bourgeoisie and bourgeois intelligentsia, the part most tied to local trade and commerce, will try to accommodate itself to the local national majorities and will in time become patriots of Ukraine, Moldova, etc. During this process this group will also be erstwhile supporters of Yiddish culture. For a while, this group may get lost and temporarily return home, but at the first opportunity, they will embrace the culture of the ruling majority.

Understandably, in this new stage—that of Jewish national autonomy—it will be much more difficult to leave the Jewish community. It is bound by civil, psychological, and social difficulties, which will impede and greatly reduce the process of assimilation. These difficulties, however, will not be able to stop the process entirely. The organized Jewish community is the best armor to protect us against splintering, separation, and assimilation. It cannot, however, fundamentally change our social status as a national minority, which under even the best and most liberated social conditions must make concessions to the national majority. In truth, *political* moments will arise to restrain and tie the discussed social groups to the Jewish body. These groups [the bourgeoisie and bourgeois intelligentsia] will surely strive to exploit the Jewish masses during general political elections, in state and regional elections, and to do so they will be forced to participate in Jewish autonomy and position themselves closer to its life. These moments will certainly cement to the Jewish nation those desiring to leave it. All of this will be the *consequence* of Jewish autonomy: this influence will be felt only in the period after Jewish autonomy has already organized the Jewish community into a single political organization.

Currently, one cannot count on these groups [the bourgeoisie and bourgeois intelligentsia]—in fact, we see that they do not participate in our political life, they are uninterested in what is happening. Moreover they do not even know that there is a movement for Jewish autonomy, and if they do know something, they have no clear concept about this trend in Jewish life. This group will be absent from building and solidifying the structure. They will not oppose the democratic forms or the progressive ideas of the Jewish autonomous organs because they do not yet appreciate the power of them. Rather than benefit Jewish autonomy this will, of course, greatly harm it.

Because these groups stand apart from Jewish social and cultural milieus, they make these milieus weaker, poorer, paler. This weakness can be felt in the efforts on behalf of national autonomy. It also colors the struggle for the form and content of Jewish national autonomy. The political tensions, the cultural conflicts which give concrete meaning to class struggle, split the national movement but do not tear it asunder. They bring the classes into battle but do not drive them apart; rather, to the contrary, these tensions push the classes to forge a broad structure in national life. We lack all these things that nourish and enrich national movements, from the voice of the mass bourgeoisie to the higher strata of the bourgeois intelligentsia.

The situation of the middle classes and the lower strata of the bourgeois intelligentsia is very different. These social groups remain within the Jewish social and cultural milieu. They remain, but not securely. They strive to join the upper bourgeoisie and expend great energy to catch up to the upper classes, to overcome the national barrier, and escape from the Jewish milieu. The Jewish middle classes including the manufacturers, merchants, storekeepers, and intellectuals who are professionally involved with the Jewish cities and towns all are to a great degree still economically bound to Jewish labor and to the Jewish middlemen who distribute their wares. *Culturally*, they are still close to the living Jewish street.

In so far as they found assimilation attractive, their conversations about it could only occur at the local level, and these groups are actually hardly assimilated because no opening existed to do so. The uppermost strata, already a large segment of this group, are closely affiliated with the greater bourgeoisie. This assimilated segment makes a large imprint on the political face of the middle class.

The lower elements keep the middle classes securely within the realm of Jewish interests, tying them to the Jewish community and forcing them to become interested in the national political organizations and social structures. However, the upper elements we speak of pull this group away from the national milieu, break its ties to the Jewish body, and make the middle class passive and indifferent to the Jewish national institutions. This unstable situation, being suspended between worlds, created the two-faced and duplicitous politics of this class.

This two-facedness manifested itself in the following: living an assimilated life but having a national dream; actively creating institutions that foster assimilation while at the same time passively building Jewish autonomy; discussing Jewish autonomy with extreme chauvinism while actually hindering its growth; supporting clerics among the masses while living assimilated and atheistic lives; preaching nationalist maximalism while not even minimally adopting Jewish nationalism in their own lives.

To this we must add that more than all other groups the middle class suffers from antisemitism, and fears it most. Like other elements in Jewish life, over the last thirty to forty years, when the upper classes were already overtly assimilated and the lower classes were as yet unable to provide a Jewish education for their children, the Jewish middle classes were almost the only ones teaching Hebrew and sustaining the fire of the study hall while preserving the old legacy. Then the double bookkeeping of the middle classes became clear. On the one hand they hopelessly climb assimilation's ladder, while on the other hand the prayer for messianic redemption still hangs on their lips. They shred the living national threads connecting all parts of the folk, whose hearts still long for the national absolute, for a state, for their "own" land and the old language.

Besides the working class these social groups are the only politically active groups on the Jewish street. Their activity, nonetheless, is laden with danger. If they gain the upper hand in the organs of national autonomy they will bring with them the double bookkeeping and the two-facedness. They will use the organs to create the illusion of national rebirth rather than the facts of national life. They will speak more of the bright future than work through the dark today. They will distract the thoughts of the masses from the immediate task of building national fortresses out of the accumulated material of Jewish life, by looking to forces somewhere outside of Jewish life to gather strength for a time yet to come.

Objectively, these social groups contain enough elements interested in national autonomy. The more these elements demonstrate their abilities to protect their own interests, the more they will prove their ability to create a factual national milieu. The more equality Jewish culture is granted, the less it will be seen as an impediment to Jewish economic life. The more Jewish national identity will stop being a factor in the social lot of every Jew, the stronger will be the attachment of these elements to the facts of Jewish life and they will play a more positive role in the Jewish national organs.

At this moment, the political life of the middle classes is governed by the uppermost strata, ultimately capable of undermining the process of Jewish autonomy. The struggle against them must be sharp and clear, and they must not be given any ground.

The Jewish petit bourgeois classes—the small shopkeepers, merchants, traders, *luftmentshn*, and self-employed artisans—make up the majority of the Jewish folk. These social groups create the foundation of Jewish autonomy. More than any of the previously mentioned classes, these groups need the institutions and organs of Jewish autonomy. These are the weakest and are, in the social and political sense, a transitional group and in time they will also become the most *reactionary* and conservative part of the Jewish autonomous organization.

These groups are, at this moment, little prepared for an independent political struggle for autonomy. Moreover, they do not yet possess the creative forces to participate in the building of the autonomous structure. They are, however, more interested than any other group in the national autonomous institutions and it is therefore no surprise that they support the proletarian party in elections. To the extent that they lean toward Zionism, they nevertheless force it to accommodate to the socialist parties' demands for diaspora existence.[42] In the not too distant future, the Jewish petit bourgeoisie will no doubt have its own political organization. The petit bourgeoisie about whom we speak consists of very varied strata, from the simple, strong, and primitive craftsmen to the wheeler-and-dealer inheritors of the Jewish marketplace, the little *luftmentshn* and small middlemen of all kinds. There are also manual laborers who feel secure in life and tend toward radical slogans and to real and concrete national ideals. The small-time middlemen and *luftmentshn* are dreamers living on miracles and therefore lean toward pessimistic theories. They are politically passive and nationally utopian. All these strata have much in common. They all remain within the framework of the Jewish national, social, and cultural milieu and add to the national atmosphere in which national institutions arise. That is to say, they build the physical *national mass* that is the foundation of national life.

The remnants of the old *kehile* along with elements of the new *kehile*, the *heders* and Talmud Torahs, trade schools, hospitals, old-age homes, emigration offices, workshops, children's homes and, to a certain degree, the Yiddish press, Yiddish theater, and Yiddish literature—all these institutions and organs are given life by the petit bourgeoisie. They are supported by it; they are built for it and, in no small measure, at its expense.

42. [*Golus-lebn* in the original.]

The Jewish working class also emerges from these social groups. The closer the petit bourgeoisie stands to the worker, the greater is the demand for modern culture and education. The broader the social and political perspectives, the more real is the national striving. The more conscious and active the participation in political life, the freer the petit bourgeoisie is from the burdensome national and religious legacy. The "Folks-Party" relies on the laborer and so it must therefore put forth a somewhat radical political program and yet be realistic in national terms.[43]

But even this segment of the mass of our petit bourgeoisie, the most progressive and politically active among them, was not only unable to become the avant-garde of our national liberation, it could not even play a significant role in the revolution. The peasantry claimed that role in the general Russian Revolution.

We will not deal with the details of why the Jewish petit bourgeoisie did not play the same role in the Jewish revolution as did the Russian peasant petit bourgeoisie in the Russian Revolution. We will deal only with the primary cause.

We believe the primary cause is that the Jewish petit bourgeoisie consists of too many differing social elements. They are so varied and opposing that they weaken their own political activity and energy. In the future autonomous organs, the Jewish petit bourgeoisie will be the most reactionary force, striving to impose on them a conservative and backward economic policy in order to rescue its own insecure social situation. There is also no doubt that a political split will occur on this very issue. The more conscious and organized this mass will be, the sharper and clearer the conflict between its various factions will become; between the middlemen on one side and the working class on the other. This will result in the rapid crystallization of two separate political streams of petit bourgeoisie.

One of the most important tasks of the Jewish proletariat is to hasten this process, to remove the working masses from under the influence of the mediating aspects of the petit bourgeoisie and to utilize, to the fullest measure, the political potential which the working masses carry within them. We can and actually must lean on the working elements in the struggle for Jewish autonomy as well as in the struggle for secular culture and for a real national policy.

---

43. [In 1917 a number of local parties of liberal and moderately socialist autonomists were created that went by the name "Folks-Party" (also Folkspartay, and, in Russian, Evreiskaia Narodnaia Partiia) and followed the ideology of Simon Dubnov.]

It is true that the Jewish laboring class has little political culture and even fewer political traditions and political organs. It is, for the time being, very backward. This class played a very small and passive role in the organizations created in the Pale; for example, it allowed the merchants and middlemen to head the cooperatives. Yet it does not have the flaws the others have, whether attachment to the moribund religious tradition, or dragging itself after the utopian Zionist policy, etc.

In the avant-garde of the movement for Jewish autonomy stands the Jewish proletariat, the most progressive class in the nation. This is quite natural. The Jewish proletariat suffers from disorganization more than the other classes. Before any of the others, the working class felt the need for a culture, felt the power of education, and recognized the weakness and the poverty of the old Jewish *heder* training and study house culture. Involved in the social struggle, the working class felt every step of the way how far removed it was from the old Jewish spiritual world with its narrow and limiting religious atmosphere. It felt its access blocked to the wells of humanistic culture and the treasures of universal ideas and ideals it carried within itself as part of the universal proletariat. There was no bridge, no continuity, neither in content nor in form between the old *beys medresh* world, or even the new Hebrew literature, and the ideas which began to inspire the Jewish working class at the beginning of the nineteenth century.

In no other nation was the plight of the working class as tragic in the above sense as was the case in the Jewish proletariat.

When the working class of any other nation appears in the historical arena, it encounters vast cultural treasures. Large stores of accumulated revolutionary thoughts, memories, traditions and their value cannot be underestimated. The proletarian does not reject this legacy. He takes the best and the most beautiful from the creations of the bourgeoisie. The proletarian finds quite an adequate and developed cultural apparatus whose functions he enlarges to suit his needs and ideals. Schools, the press, theater, politics, the arts, science, all these organs of culture used by the bourgeoisie for its power are also used by the proletariat in its struggle against this power. If truth be told, the bourgeoisie created a very rich culture. It created a more beautiful and comfortable world, more multifaceted and colorful. The legacy, which the working class will receive, is much richer than the one that the bourgeoisie inherited from the feudal world.

The proletariat of every nation has its separate legacy. This inheritance has a very strong influence on the entire character of the class struggle of the proletariat and places its stamp on the destiny of every nation's working class.

The Jewish proletariat when it emerged in Jewish public life did not find an entirely barren field. The legacy was, however, very impoverished and unenticing. The traditional historical national legacy was in Hebrew and practically inaccessible to the proletariat. While the bourgeoisie played an active role in creating the modern culture of the nations among whom we live, it did not create a modern Jewish culture. The only attempts made by the Jewish bourgeoisie to do so, Russian Jewish schools and Russian Jewish literature, were unsuccessful and remained alien to the masses.

At its birth the Jewish working class received no inheritance or legacy of revolutionary thought and traditions. It found no cultural apparatus and no large cultural organs.

It found no modern bourgeois schools which could be made accessible to the broad masses and free it from religious study by creating a good folk school.[44] The Jewish worker found the ruins of a medieval *heder*. He also found foreign schools whose mission was to further culturally impoverish the folk masses by removing the educated individual from the collective. He also found attempts to connect millions of the masses to our old Hebrew culture. These actually had the same results as the foreign Russified schools. The Jewish worker does not have the task of reforming or rebuilding a school structure, readying it for the broad and progressive needs of a new class. Rather, he has to build the structure itself; laying the foundation, hewing the stones, and mixing the mortar and loam for the bricks. The Jewish working class found no political organs and traditions, practically no press, no scientific strengths, and few organized public institutions.

The little bit of theater that existed was and continues to this day to be so far from art that its existence need barely be acknowledged. There is little consolation in the fact that other nations also have this lowly form. They, however, also possess true art theater alongside it, and thus infuse new thoughts and new literary and theatrical materials into the baser forms. In no time, this base form is transformed into the new reality of a folk theater. We however lack the channels through which the bourgeoisie and its intelligentsia can create spontaneously for all classes.

The Jewish working class did receive a meaningful inheritance in one cultural

44. [The creation of open, democratic, Jewish "Folk schools" was a major goal of socialist and liberal autonomists. See the chapter on the Kultur-Lige regarding those created in independent Ukraine.]

branch, literature. There the Jewish masses exhibited their raw creative power. Mendele, Peretz, Sholem Aleichem, Asch, Reisen, Nomberg, Bergelson, Morris Rosenfeld, and a large array of young talents constitute significant cultural capital enhancing our impoverished little world.[45]

This was the creation of the broad Jewish masses with the active and perhaps most energetic participation of the working class. The most salient characteristic of our entire Yiddish literature is that it nearly does not represent the Jewish bourgeoisie. The main protagonists of our literature are the lowly mass, the middleman, the shopkeeper, the *luftmentsh*, the student, and the early *maskil*. It is true that Asch writes about the Jewish bourgeoisie, not the modern assimilated one but the old Hasidic one. The intellectual who appears in our literature seems like an uprooted limb, a stranger, a guest in the Yiddish world and not as an organic part of the folk organism. Only in the writings of Bergelson do we see an attempt, for the first time, to render the assimilated or rather the half-assimilated intellectual within the natural framework of the Jewish family, within the borders of the national collective and not on the margins of Jewish society or on the threshold of the old Jewish world.[46]

The inherited cultural and creative legacy was small and impoverished. This was not so for other elements of the legacy such as medical and social assistance, immigrant aid, etc. In place were institutions, accumulated experience, and traditions—many good beginnings overgrown in the mold of charity. Everything was concentrated in the hands of philanthropists and do-gooders, saturated with the spirit of the moribund charity box.

To extricate these institutions from the hands of the plutocrats and rid them of the spirit of charity so that the masses would not feel themselves to be beggars, to give democracy authority over this national treasure, is far from an easy

45. [Here Lestschinsky lists eight well-known Yiddish writers, all of whom were instrumental in establishing a thriving Yiddish literary culture in the late nineteenth and early twentieth centuries. In addition to Mendele, I. L. Peretz, and Sholem Aleichem, the other figures are Sholem Asch (1880–1957), Avrom Reisen (1876–1953), Hirsh Dovid Nomberg (1876–1927), Dovid Bergelson (1884–1952), and Morris Rosenfeld (1862–1923).]

46. [Dovid Bergelson's most famous novel—*Nokh alemen* (The end of everything), published in 1913—was said by the literary critic Shmuel Niger to mark the birth of the Yiddish novel. In *Nokh alemen* and his other early works, Bergelson focused his attention on the alienation felt by Jewish intellectuals and children of the middle class in provincial small towns. Until the 1920s, Bergelson was politically active as a socialist autonomist and played an important role in the creation of the Kiev Kultur-Lige (see the next chapter).]

task. This represents a long struggle and a huge and difficult task of education because both sides are not yet ready. The bourgeoisie is not ready to cede power, certainly not to democracy, and democracy is not yet developed enough to seize it.

The Jewish working class restored an old Jewish national idea: the idea of independence, of an organized Jewish body, and a strong political organization. We are standing on the threshold of this revolutionary thought's realization. For the time being it will only have a legal face, which will be filled in the future with true life and progressive content. Such is the lengthy struggle in front of the proletariat.

A new page in Jewish history begins with the realization of Jewish autonomy. The Jewish working class and the Jewish proletariat will write the first lines etched with blood. They will stand on guard and will not give up the struggle to ensure that this new page in Jewish history does not separate the Jewish working class and does not put us into a new ghetto. Together with the working classes in general they will struggle for a new and free world and make national autonomy the basis for the struggle for the highest human ideals, for socialism.

8

"The Founding Tasks of the Kultur-Lige"
and "The Kultur-Lige"
The Kultur-Lige

Di grunt-oyfgabn fun der "Kultur Lige." Kiev: Drukeray fun di yorshim
Y. Shenfeld, 1918.
Kultur-Lige (a sakh-akl): zamlung. Kiev: Central Committee of the Kultur-Lige,
November 1919

The League for Culture, or Kultur-Lige in Yiddish, was founded in Kiev in April 1918
by a group of political and cultural activists intent on using the opportunities aris-
ing from the independent Ukrainian government's granting of Jewish autonomy.
Following the February 1917 Revolution, Ukraine, while remaining part of the new
Russian Republic, created its own Central Rada, a parliamentary-style government
that operated parallel to the provisional government in Petrograd (St. Petersburg).
In order to gain support from minorities for some form of Ukrainian independence,
the Central Rada proposed Jewish, Polish, and Russian nonterritorial autonomy
within an autonomous Ukraine federated with Russia. In January 1918 the Rada
passed the Law on National Personal Autonomy, granting minorities the right to a
constituent assembly and internal government with the right of taxation. The Law
on National Personal Autonomy occurred nearly simultaneously with the Rada's
declaration of independence from Russia, ushering in both legally sanctioned Jewish national autonomy and a brutal civil war. In the subsequent years of civil war
and rapid changes of government, Jewish autonomy in Ukraine moved ahead,
only coming to an end with the Red Army's victory and the consolidation of Bolshevik power in Ukraine.

Despite the anarchic conditions, Jewish intellectuals and political activists attempted a genuine experiment with Jewish autonomy. Kiev happened to be a
logical place for such an experiment to occur. The earliest and most comprehensive platforms for socialist Jewish autonomy emerged there among dissatisfied
socialist Zionists who formed the group Vozrozhdenie (meaning renaissance, or
rebirth) in 1903. The group advocated complete political autonomy for the Jews
in a revolutionary state, and in Kiev in 1906 many of the same individuals founded
the political party most closely associated with socialist autonomism, the Sejmists.
Finally, following the October Revolution and Bolshevik coup in Petrograd, many

of the Jewish political activists who had attempted to establish the institutions of Jewish autonomy in the Russian Republic moved to Kiev, pinning their hopes for Jewish autonomy on Ukraine.

The Kultur-Lige professed to approach culture as what it called an "organic whole" and sought to involve itself in all of the components of Jewish cultural, educational, and communal life. As the first item of its founding principles, below, makes clear, the Kultur-Lige was not merely Yiddishist but saw itself in direct competition to the new, and flourishing, Hebrew cultural scene and its key organization, Tarbut. The Yiddishists of the Kultur-Lige sought a near total reconstruction of Jewish secular culture and the creation of a Jewish high culture in Yiddish. Its leaders were simultaneously radical revolutionaries, socialists, and Jewish nationalists, and they therefore saw their cultural work as a key aspect of Jewish politicization. Yet at the same time, the "Jewish culturalists," to borrow Kenneth Moss's term, whether Yiddishist or Hebraist, also sought the separation of culture from politics in the construction of their new Jewish renaissance. Perhaps the best example is Dovid Bergelson, a prominent Yiddish literary figure in Kiev and a devoted socialist autonomist who was also one of the leading figures of the Kultur-Lige and a literary editor in a number of publishing houses. As Moss points out, despite Bergelson's commitment to revolutionary politics and diaspora nationalism, in the period of Jewish autonomy he refused to subsume his own literary work to either, and he consistently sought the cultural cooperation of those diametrically opposed to his ideology (for example, the Zionist and Hebrew poet Haim Nahman Bialik). The Yiddishists of the Kultur-Lige set out to build an institutional framework that could support a secular, national, Yiddish renaissance. They did so by creating schools, cultural institutions, and publishing houses and by supporting Jewish artists, performers, and writers. The group's leaders sought to break down the barriers between the Yiddish intellectuals and the masses while maintaining the universalist ambition of creating a Yiddish culture on a par with that of other European nations. As summed up in one line below, "To make our masses intellectuals and our intellectuals 'Yiddish,' this is the goal of the Kultur-Lige."

In addition to establishing a presence throughout briefly independent Ukraine, the Kultur-Lige also spread through the new Soviet republics and independent Poland, Lithuania, Latvia, and Romania, though without the same degree of influence. In Kiev, the Kultur-Lige experiment, and Jewish autonomy in general, fell victim to the Bolsheviks' drive for ideological conformity. Following the Red Army's victory in Kiev in January 1920, the Bolsheviks initially allowed the Kultur-Lige to continue operating and even gave it state support, though the government also appointed a special commissar to preside over the whole organization. During 1920 the Kultur-Lige's leaders waged a protracted battle to survive, with their initial resistance to interference yielding to reluctant accommodation to the new realities. The Jewish Section of the Communist Party (Evsektsiia) increasingly gained control of the Kultur-Lige, and in December 1920 the Bolsheviks replaced the Kultur-Lige's Central Committee with an Organizational Committee whose members were either Communists or willing to cooperate with the Communists. Thus, the organization became thoroughly "communized." The Evsektsiia closed or took control of all of the institutions under the Kultur-Lige's control and officially dissolved the group in 1924. The texts below include a statement of the Kultur-Lige's principles, issued at the apex of its organizational freedom, and a summary of its accomplishments in its November 1919 bulletin, issued with an eye to demonstrating its importance to the impending new regime.

The Founding Tasks of the Kultur-Lige

I. THE NEW HEBREW AND YIDDISH CULTURE

The Jewish folk is known as one of the oldest cultural peoples in the world. One of the greatest Jewish attributes is that Jews are a people of the book, a people that loves book culture. In the course of its long and tragic history, the Jewish folk remained consistently true to its Torah, its book, and its ancient culture. The first urge to be awakened in moments of Jewish national renewal, before all else and with a particular force, is the striving toward culture, toward spiritual riches and new moral values.

A variety of historical reasons have caused Jewish culture in the last era to be severed entirely from the Jewish folk masses. The Jewish folk masses could not internalize the religious culture because of its form and essence. The simple working people had no access to it. It remained spiritually estranged from them. The ossified *shulkhn orekh* lay heavy on them, and no spiritual bond was ever created between the masses and the religion.[47] The newly created Hebrew culture has remained with both feet inside the borders of the old, the outdated, and the

47. [The *shulkhn orekh* (literally, the set table) is a code of Jewish law compiled by the Sephardic Rabbi Josef Karo (1488–1575). A manual for all aspects of daily Jewish life, Karo's work—together with the subsequent commentaries on it—remains today one of the most authoritative and comprehensive collections of Jewish law.]

rotten. The old spirit and backward ideology still remained deeply rooted in it. In addition, it was of interest only to small groups of *maskilim*. It could satisfy no more than a handful of semi-intellectuals who strove to create new values from old treasures and to pour new wine into old flasks. This culture was even more distant from the folk masses than religion.

The new Yiddish culture began to grow and develop in tandem with the growth and development of Jewish democracy. This culture carries within it the stamp of democracy and is thoroughly imbued with a new spirit. It is not a culture of the past, nourished only by the past. It is forward-looking and thinks of the future. It is closely tied to the broad masses and is suited to their needs and to their spiritual condition. The more the masses are drawn into the struggle for their human dignity, for their rights, and for their freedom, the more they take an active role in building their own life and create new treasures, new spiritual riches, a new culture.

This new Yiddish culture has two main features that distinguish it from the earlier one. The first feature is language. The new Yiddish culture has its foundation in the Yiddish language, the language of the Jewish folk masses. The second feature is its democratic and secular character. Its roots lie deeply buried in the broad masses and it is very closely tied to them. Drawing its life force from these masses, it sees as its first responsibility the fulfillment of their needs.

Emerging from and nourished by the masses, the new culture is constantly on guard to protect their interests.

The Kultur-Lige has as its goal and responsibility the development and security of this new Yiddish democratic culture.

II. THE HISTORY OF THE KULTUR-LIGE: HOW THE KULTUR-LIGE WAS CREATED

Prior to the Great Russian Revolution, the oppressed nations in Russia had no opportunities to develop their cultures freely. Fearful of every free word, every free expression of the human spirit, the tsarist government brutally harassed the "alien" non-Russian cultures and the languages of all "alien" peoples residing in Russia. The government understood well that this was one of the best methods to keep the masses in darkness and ignorance and, as a result, keep them enslaved and subservient.

The Great Revolution freed all nations and allowed them to freely create their cultures and build their spiritual lives. Disregarding the difficult conditions in which the entire country found itself due to the war and internal unrest, all the previously oppressed nations are beginning to develop their own cultures and their spiritual treasures with great energy and impetus. Like a dammed stream that has been released and begins to rush, the Jewish folk, newly freed, begins to create and build its new culture with tremendous energy and force. Cultural groups, drama circles, literary groups, etc. are sprouting up everywhere. They are seeking to quench their thirst for spiritual nourishment, for pleasures of the soul, and for culture.

As the spiritual culture begins to develop freely, the need to unite these energies, to organize the cultural work, and to introduce a plan to bring together all the initiatives has become clear.

In all parts of the former Russian Empire, institutions with the same goals and objectives have been created among the Jewish democratic elements. In Poland, Lithuania, Great Russia, the Ukraine, and White Russia, cultural leagues have been formed under various names. These are all very successful and are doing important work.

Our Kultur-Lige is still very young and has but a short history. It is a mere nine months since its creation. In its presently constituted form, it is barely half a year old.

Yet it already plays a central role in meeting the most important needs of Jewish spiritual life.

In the early period of its existence, our Kultur-Lige shared its work with the Jewish Ministry. A large part of the cultural work was done through the ministry, which was in the hands of the Jewish democracy. The greatest part of the work tied to education was in the hands of the Department of Folk Education. Since the Jewish Ministry was a state institution, it had the necessary material means and moral weight to establish the various levels of Yiddish schools on a secure foundation. The Kultur-Lige could thus devote itself to other aspects of Yiddish culture.[48]

Upon the liquidation of "national autonomy" and of the Jewish Ministry, the Kultur-Lige had to take over the legacy of the Department of Folk Education and all of its work. This is a large and difficult task requiring a good deal of energy and strength.

48. [Under the various governments of independent Ukraine during the Russian and Ukrainian civil war, the Jewish parties were able to establish a protoparliament, a secretariat, and a Ministry for Jewish Affairs and to conduct a genuine experiment with Jewish autonomy.]

The Kultur-Lige feels confident that it can meet this challenge because it expects to have the necessary moral and material support of the entire Jewish population.

III. CENTRAL WORK OF THE KULTUR-LIGE

- Schools:
The Kultur-Lige cannot take upon itself the task of spreading across the country a network of Yiddish primary and elementary schools, Gymnasia, technical schools, and universities. This should be the work of the democratic state institutions and of the democratic elements in the regions.

We must depend upon municipalities, councils, and *kehiles* to establish a large network of schools, built upon modern foundations. These should meet the educational needs of the entire Jewish population.

The democratic Yiddish Teachers' Union, which in its entirety is part of the Kultur-Lige, is developing the school section. It is expending a great deal of effort to create the new Yiddish school. Through its members in the regions it is changing the old Jewish Talmud Torahs and Crown schools into true primary and elementary schools. The Kultur-Lige has, in addition, a separate responsibility which will have a great impact on the development of the Yiddish schools.

It must create the necessary institutions so that the Yiddish schools can actually exist. It needs to train teachers, prepare teaching materials and resources. It must build model elementary schools, model high schools, and so on.

THE KULTUR LIGE HAS ALEADY BEGUN THIS TASK AND IS ALREADY REALIZING ITS WORK.

- The Yiddish Teachers' Seminary:
The Kultur-Lige supervises and financially supports the Yiddish Teachers' Seminary, which prepares teachers for the Yiddish schools. This is a legacy of the Jewish Ministry, of Jewish national autonomy. The seminary needs to be based on the newest pedagogical foundations, and requires much work and energy. We must ensure that the teachers of the new Yiddish schools are equal to their task.

- The Yiddish Gymnasium:
The Kultur-Lige has opened a Yiddish Gymnasium licensed by the state and

following its program. This is the first attempt at creating a high school in which all subjects will be taught in Yiddish. We have many Jewish Gymnasia, both private and public, but these are essentially Gymnasia for Jews. The Gymnasium that the Kultur-Lige is founding is the first Yiddish Gymnasium. It needs to become a model Gymnasium in the full sense of the word. It needs to follow the latest word in modern pedagogy. This is what the Kultur-Lige is striving for and to which it is turning its attention.

- The Yiddish Folk University:
Democracy is in need of intellectual powers emerging from within, from its own ranks. Specifically, Jewish democracy needs an intelligentsia because, for the most part, the Jewish intelligentsia has until now devoted its energy to the democratic forces of other nations. It is necessary, therefore, for the Jewish folk masses to create their own intelligentsia. This is the mission of the folk universities. They must create intellectual forces that will serve the folk, the masses. They need to prepare Yiddish lecturers on all branches of modern knowledge. In addition, the Yiddish folk university must be a springboard to a full-fledged Yiddish university that will be fully equal to all other state and private universities. It must be able to provide the same high level of education as the others do. It is essential that the full range of education, beginning with elementary school and ending with university, be entirely in Yiddish. The task is certainly difficult. In order to fulfill it one needs profound belief and a strong will. The work requires much energy because everything must be created from the ground up. The entire structure must be built stone by stone. These hardships do not thwart the work of the Kultur-Lige. The enormity of the task imbues this effort with courage and passion. The work has already begun. This past summer there were already courses offered in the Folk University in Kiev. It was a test and a beginning. Now the Folk University in Kiev stands on a firm foundation. The Ministry for Folk Education has approved the charter for the Folk University and has recognized it as an institution of higher learning. Dr. M. Zilberfarb (Bazin) has been chosen as rector.[49] [...]

49. [Moyshe Zilberfarb, one of the more prominent socialist autonomists, or Sejmists, was among the founders of the political group Vozrozhdenie and then of the United Jewish Socialist Workers' Party (Fareynikte). Under different revolutionary governments, Zilberfarb served as first Vice Secretary and then Minister for Jewish Affairs in Ukraine.]

Kultur-Lige

The Kultur-Lige stands on three pillars: on educating the Jewish people, on Yiddish literature, and on Yiddish art and culture. To make our masses intellectuals and our intellectuals "Yiddish," this is the goal of the Kultur-Lige. Support the modern Yiddish school!

Support the cultural fund in the memory of Mendele, Peretz and Sholem Aleichem! Spread the name of the Kultur-Lige!

THE KULTUR-LIGE

Until recently, we have not had a large central group for Yiddish culture. There had been an old society for education, the *mefitse haskole*, a Russian Jewish upper-class society that over the past few decades created, in a philanthropic bureaucratic manner, a sort of Crown school for the Jewish masses.[50] This was to replace the Crown school, or "*shkola*," which at the time Jews found difficult to enter. Later the "Jewish democracy" was able to break into this society and a struggle began, a war between languages, a war over cultural interests. But until the final days of this society, this democratic movement occupied only a small corner. The leadership remained in the hands of the upper classes and the masses could barely hold a few places near the door. Russian and Hebrew remained the mistresses and Yiddish, the servant girl. Yiddish culture would not be built by this society.

Later there arose the Zionist, rabbinic Tarbut, which is thoroughly Hebraist and Israel-oriented.[51] This organization claims a land where Jews do not live as

50. [The authors refer here to the Society for the Promotion of Enlightenment among the Jews of Russia (known by its Russian acronym, OPE). Founded by wealthy Jewish merchants in 1863, the OPE had as its main goal the integration of "ordinary" Jews into Russian society, with the implicit aim of obtaining full rights for Jews as subjects of the empire. In the 1880s and 1890s, younger and more radical Jewish activists sought to "democratize" the group, and by 1905 the OPE had shifted its goals from integration to national Jewish cultural renaissance. The Kultur-Lige dismissed the OPE's supposedly "bourgeois" politics in favor of a more radical Yiddishist agenda (less radically socialist diaspora nationalists in Kiev were indeed more comfortable with the OPE than the Kultur-Lige). Infighting led to the OPE's demise in 1917, although elements of it remained active until the Soviet government shut it down in 1929.]

51. [The Tarbut (literally, culture) was a Zionist-Hebraist cultural organization and network of schools that began in Russia. Between the world wars, the organization spread to Poland, where it was much more active.]

our land, and holds a language that Jews do not speak as our language. Tarbut builds an altar to the old rabbis, the old land, the old language, and is, on this altar, ready to sacrifice the young children of the new era. In the name of this sanctified ancient threesome, Tarbut fanatically and with burning hatred leads the battle against the language of the living Jewish masses, the young and newly emerging Yiddish culture. This Zionist, rabbinic organization is the greatest enemy of the cultural strivings and cultural interest of the Jewish masses.

Yiddish culture had isolated self-sustaining organizations and groups. There was no center to unite all these efforts under one umbrella and to infuse this union with a single plan and one spirit. Our cultural work was scattered and it suffered greatly from that.

The Kultur-Lige is the first large central organization for the new Yiddish culture.

The aim of the Kultur-Lige is to help create a new Yiddish secular culture in the Yiddish language, in Yiddish national forms, infused with the living strengths of the broadest Jewish masses, in the spirit of the Jewish working masses in harmony with their ideal of the future.

The working field of the Kulture-Lige is the entire field of the new secular culture: preschool and elementary children's education, education for the adolescent and adult Jew, Yiddish literature, and Yiddish arts. Our field is broad and new horizons continue to open.

The Kulture-Lige strives to confirm and broaden all avenues that Yiddish culture already possesses. It searches for new paths and seeks to create broad new roads for our culture. It unites the powers of the greatest intellectuals who are doing cultural work in harmony with the Jewish masses. It strives to educate and ready new energies for this work. It seeks to elicit from the depths of the Jewish masses the great creative energies hidden there. It wants to cultivate our masses and make our intellectuals Yiddish: create a Yiddish intellectual mass and a Yiddish mass intellectual. A large goal, yes, and an endlessly broad working field.

The Kultur-Lige has existed a mere one and a half years. These have been the most difficult and painful years. A time of unending upheaval, of the wildest pogroms and slaughters the Jewish people have experienced. A time when cities were isolated for months on end, when death lurked on the roads, and the sword hung over the throat in the city: everyone was in turmoil, hungry, and exhausted.[52]

52. [Jews in Ukraine faced massive anti-Jewish violence and depravation during the

The path of the Kultur-Lige was sown in rocky terrain. Internally, it faced the Zionists, the rabbis, the assimilationists, the enemies of the Yiddish language and of the new Yiddish masses in general. Externally, the Kulture-Lige met with naysayers from all sides. Some looked at us as the bourgeoisie "whom one needed to sweep away with a large broom." Others thought us too revolutionary. From the Left we were viewed as too national; from the Right we were viewed skeptically because we were Yiddish. And every time when the reactionaries had a say they started to constrain the Yiddish word, "impede and not permit" was their slogan, and with that made our work very difficult. In such a bitter time, and under such dire constraints, the Kultur-Lige planted strong roots and grew to be strong, beautiful, and fruitful—a veritable wonder.

Count our institutions. Rest your eye upon them, you will be astonished. There are more than fifty preschools, elementary, and high schools in Kiev and the surrounding provinces; three Yiddish Gymnasia in Kiev, Yekaterinoslav, and Heysin—the first Jewish Gymnasia that are Jewish not because they take Jewish children without a quota but because their entire program and character are Jewish. There are playgrounds and day-care centers, an important Yiddish pedagogical journal, and a publishing house for teaching materials and children's literature, including beautiful art books for children. A pedagogical division in the central library, a special pedagogical museum, a network of evening courses, and three folk universities in Kiev, Odessa, and Yekaterinoslav. A central library housing an archive of important material of the history of the most recent years and a number of local libraries, various courses to train Yiddish teachers and administrators of kindergartens, a Yiddish teachers' seminary founded on the initiative of the Kultur-Lige, a music section with a master choir, several recreational choirs, a theater studio, a studio for the plastic arts, a great book center occupying the most important place in the Yiddish book market in Ukraine and with its own printing house and publishing house that is growing steadily, a historical section, a section for Yiddish literature and philology, a section for Jewish statistics—and all of this in a year and a half!

In all aspects of its work the Kultur-Lige strove to deliver not crass or cheap material but rather fundamental cultural values. The activists around the Kultur-Lige understood that popular does not mean vulgar, that bringing culture to the masses means not bringing what they themselves do not value.

anarchy of the civil war years, from 1918 to 1920. All belligerents had a hand in the violence, but bands loyal to the Ukrainian national governments were responsible for the largest number of pogroms.]

Not only did the Kultur-Lige itself do a lot, but more important, it encouraged others to take action. It brought initiative and direction to what others were doing. The Kultur-Lige sought to remain in touch with all the institutions working in harmony with the forward-looking ideals of the Jewish masses. But the Kultur-Lige remained independent and self-sustaining. It did not join any one stream. It sought to attract and unite the cultural efforts of all movements that agreed with its principles, which were grounded in the Jewish working masses. The power of the Kultur-Lige lay in the unification of these efforts.

There are over 100 divisions of the Kultur-Lige throughout Ukraine. The Kultur-Lige is also widely known in other areas. Based on the model in Ukraine, Kultur-Liges were founded in Petersburg, Moscow, Minsk, and Vilna. Together with the Petersburg and Moscow branches, we are beginning to publish a large encyclopedia in Yiddish. It will be a general encyclopedia with particular attention to everything that has a special connection to Jews. It is an endeavor that will take years and will have meaning for generations to come.

Such, to this point, unheard of and widespread activity demands great financial means and the budget of the Kultur-Lige has truly grown. Suffice it to say that aside from the section for preschool education (OZE) the budget of the Kultur-Lige today is 300,000 rubles a month.[53] Even today with the low value of money this is a large sum. No Jewish cultural organization has ever achieved this.

Special mention must be made of the organizing role of the Kultur-Lige. The Kultur-Lige did not merely attract and centralize the many cultural efforts which would have remained scattered and thus marginal without it; this alone is important enough, but there is something even more important.

Yiddish culture does not yet have a legal public organization recognized and guaranteed by the state, nor is it integrated into the general state organism. We had it for one brief moment in Ukraine, but we soon lost it. At this moment we must build the self-governance of our culture internally, stone by stone. It must first become a fact and then a right. In creating this fact, the Kultur-Lige has a great role to play by organizing the Jewish masses on the basis of their cultural needs. In striving to centralize the cultural work within a unified plan,

53. [The Society for the Protection of the Health of the Jewish Population (known by its Russian acronym, OZE) was founded in 1912 to promote good hygiene and childcare practices and provide healthcare services to Jews. After 1917, when various groups joined together to become subdivisions of the Kultur-Lige's umbrella organization, the OZE and the Union of Jewish Kindergarten Teachers came together to form the Preschool Education Section of the Kultur-Lige.]

the Kultur-Lige has a large role to play in creating the fact of our national cultural self-governance.

The Kultur-Lige is a mere one and a half years old. But in this short time, it has already made itself so necessary that it holds an important place in Jewish life in Ukraine. It is hard to imagine how we got along without it and we cannot begin to imagine any work today without the Kultur-Lige. This is a sign that the Kultur-Lige has a strong foundation and is on the right path.

Our road has just begun. We know the great difficulties that stand before us. But the past one and a half years allow us to face the future with certainty. We believe in the creative forces of the new Yiddish culture. We will overcome all impediments.

The interests of the Jewish masses are with us.

The future is with us.

III | Preservation and Reconstruction in the Republics

9

Democracy Versus the Melting-Pot:
A Study of American Nationality

Horace M. Kallen

Horace M. Kallen, "Democracy Versus the Melting-Pot: A Study of American Nationality," part 2, *Nation*, February 25, 1915, 217–20.

The term "cultural pluralism" is part of the American vernacular today due to Horace Kallen (1882–1974), who coined the phrase in his 1924 essay "Culture and the Ku Klux Klan." Kallen and others had been developing their ideas about cultural pluralism since the very beginning of the twentieth century. Yet the fact that cultural pluralism began with Jewish intellectuals in American universities is often overlooked or unappreciated.

Kallen was born in Berenstadt, Selesia, in Germany and moved to Boston with his family in 1887. He broke with his religious family as a young man and received undergraduate and graduate degrees from Harvard University, where he studied under George Santayana and William James, among others. Kallen taught philosophy at Harvard, Clark College, and the University of Wisconsin before becoming one of the founders of the New School for Social Research, in New York, in 1919. Although Kallen was a secular Jew by his own definition, he took an interest in Jewish culture and issues of Jewish self-definition in his early twenties. In fact, as a student Kallen was among the founders of the influential Harvard Menorah Society, which grew into the Intercollegiate Menorah Association.

The first two decades of the twentieth century saw both mass Jewish migration and considerable debate about the nature of America as a nation. The period between 1905 and the beginning of World War I was the historic high-water mark for Jewish immigration to the United States. It was also a period of growing resistance to unrestrained immigration and concern for the changing demographics in the United States. While most Jewish immigrants agreed on the necessity to "Americanize" themselves, a wide variety of opinions existed about what such a process should entail. This was a time when so-called hyphenated Americans became an object of derision, not least by the American presidents Theodore Roosevelt and Woodrow Wilson. Kallen provided a counterargument against pressure for immigrant conformity, and in "Democracy Versus the Melting-Pot," below, he aimed his argument at two targets in particular. The first was the book *The Old*

World in the New, by a controversial sociologist and colleague of Kallen's at the University of Wisconsin, Edward Alsworth Ross. At the time, Ross was president of the American Sociological Society and a vocal opponent of America's open-door immigration policies. Ross's concern in his book about the double allegiance of immigrants became more inflammatory with the onset of World War I, even before America entered the war. The second target, as the title of Kallen's essay suggests, was the melting pot, a metaphor for the American nation made popular (though not invented) by Israel Zangwill in his play of the same name. In that play, which premiered in the United States in 1908, Jewish immigrants represent the ultimate Americans because their many years of surviving as a minority facilitated their adaptation of American identity. The message of *The Melting Pot*—that Jews will make America more Jewish as they become American—ironically, as David Biale suggests, became the story of Zangwill's play itself. Jewish opponents to Zangwill's play hardly opposed the idea that Jews were the quintessential Americans, or the idea that Jews had something to contribute to the construction of American nationality. But the play established two poles in the debate over Americanization. As Kallen observes in the essay below, the contention centers around difference, and whether it should be eliminated or preserved. For those who opposed hyphenated Americans and favored the melting pot, becoming American meant that immigrants would have to leave behind their Old World nationality. At the other end of the spectrum, intellectuals like Kallen argued that the federal nature of American democracy made the United States uniquely tolerant of difference. Rather than a melting pot, Kallen's preferred metaphor for the American nation was an orchestra. Similar ideas can be seen in the earlier work of Judah Magnes, a vocal proponent of Jewish autonomy in the United States and the president of New York's Jewish Kehillah from its inception in 1909 until its end in 1922. When Magnes spoke out against Zangwill's play in his 1909 "The Melting Pot," he argued that national freedom was a fundamental component of American democracy: "This exalted conception of freedom in America is being extended by the influx of large masses of those very nationalities whose presence here has given rise to the whole problem. They are making Americans realize that the America of the future is to be not a republic of individuals and religions alone, but a republic of nationalities as well. The Melting Pot is not the highest ideal of America. America is rather the refining pot."

Kallen believed that national self-consciousness, which he called *natio*, is if anything strengthened by the immigrant experience in America. Whether America could, in accordance with its traditions, continue to leave its different nationalities to identify and organize as they please he saw as a crucial test of its democratic ideals. Kallen declared in the *Menorah Journal* in 1915 that American nationhood "is in the way of becoming what Swiss nationhood fully is, the liberator and protector of nationality; its democracy is its strength, and its democracy is 'hyphenation.'" Whether or not the United States would become a large Switzerland, the sense that the American nation was still a work in progress left space for Kallen and other pluralists to argue for continued communalism or, in the idea's extreme, ethnic autonomism. Although Kallen recognized the pressure on immigrants to acculturate, he also saw—and no doubt felt personally—that immigrants gravitated back to their culture of origin as they became increasingly comfortable in the United States. Like many other immigrants, Kallen had little desire to return to the religious traditionalism of his childhood, so he crafted a secular cultural nationalism instead. Like Magnes, Kallen considered himself a secular Zionist, but his primary concern was consistently to preserve Jewish *natio* in the diaspora and to create the conditions for Jewish cultural renaissance in the United States. "Democracy Versus the Melting-Pot" was published in the *Nation* in two parts. Part I focuses on the historical evolution of the American nation until Kallen's day. Part II appears in full below.

The array of forces for and against that like-mindedness which is the stuff and essence of nationality aligns itself as follows: For it make [the] social imitation of the upper by the lower classes, the facility of communications, the national pastimes of baseball and motion-picture, the mobility of population, the cheapness of printing, and the public schools. Against it make the primary ethnic differences with which the population starts, its stratification over an enormous extent of country, its industrial and economic stratification. We are an English-speaking country, but in no intimate and inevitable way, as is New Zealand or Australia, or even Canada. English is to us what Latin was to the Roman provinces and to the middle ages—the language of the upper and dominant class, the vehicle and symbol of culture: for the mass of our population it is a sort of Esperanto or Ido, a *lingua franca* necessary less in the spiritual than the economic contacts of the daily life.[1] This mass is composed of elementals, peasants—Mr. Ross speaks of their menacing American life with "peasantism"—the proletarian foundation material of all forms of civilization.[2] Their self-consciousness as groups is

1. [Esperanto and Ido were both invented languages, intended to be universal second languages.]

2. [See Edward Alsworth Ross, *The Old World in the New: The Significance of Past and Present Immigration to the American People* (New York: Century, 1914).]

comparatively weak. This is a factor which favors their "assimilation," for the more cultivated a group is, the more it is aware of its individuality, and the less willing it is to surrender that individuality. One need think only of the Puritans themselves, leaving Holland for fear of absorption into the Dutch population; of the Creoles and Pennsylvania Germans of this country, or of the Jews, anywhere. In his judgment of the assimilability of various stocks Mr. Ross neglects this important point altogether, probably because his attention is fixed on existing contrasts rather than potential similarities. Peasants, however, having nothing much to surrender in taking over a new culture, feel no necessary break, and find the transition easy. It is the shock of confrontation with other ethnic groups and the feeling of aliency that generates in them an intenser self-consciousness, which then militates against Americanization in spirit by reinforcing the two factors to which the spiritual expression of the proletarian has been largely confined. These factors are language and religion. Religion is, of course, no more a "universal" than language. The history of Christianity makes evident enough how religion is modified, even inverted, by race, place, and time. It becomes a principle of separation, often the sole repository of the national spirit, almost always the conservator of the national language and of the tradition that is passed on with the language to succeeding generations. Among immigrants hence, religion and language tend to be coordinate: a single expression of the spontaneous and instinctive mental life of the masses, and the primary inward factors making against assimilation. Mr. Ross, I note, tends to grow shrill over the competition of the parochial school with the public school, at the same time that he belittles the fact "that on Sundays Norwegian is preached in more churches in America than in Norway."

And Mr. Ross's anxiety would, I think be more than justified were it not that religion in these cases always does more than it intends. For it conserves the inward aspect of nationality rather than mere religion, and tends to become the centre of exfoliation of a higher type of personality among the peasants in the natural terms of their own *natio*. This *natio*, reaching consciousness first in a reaction against America, then as an effect of the competition with Americanization, assumes spiritual forms other than religious: the parochial school, to hold its own with the public school, gets secularized while remaining national. *Natio* is what underlies the vehemence of the "Americanized" and the spiritual and political unrest of the Americans. It is the fundamental fact of American life today, and in the light of it Mr. Wilson's resentment of the "hyphenated" American is both righteous and pathetic. But a hyphen attaches, in things of the spirit, also to the "pure" English American. His cultural mastery tends to be retrospective rather than prospective. At the present time there is no dominant American mind. Our spirit is inarticulate, not a voice, but a chorus of many voices each singing a rather different tune. How to get order out of this cacophony is the question for all those who are concerned about those things which alone justify wealth and power, concerned about justice, the arts, literature, philosophy, science. What must, what *shall* this cacophony become—a unison or a harmony?

For decidedly the older America, whose voice and whose spirit was New England, is gone beyond recall. Americans still are the artists and thinkers of the land, but they work, each for himself, without common vision or ideals. The older tradition has passed from a life into a memory, and the newer one, so far as it has an Anglo-Saxon base, is holding its own beside more and more formidable rivals, the expression in appropriate form of the national inheritances of the various populations concentrated in the various States of the Union, populations of whom their national self-consciousness is perhaps the chief spiritual asset. Think of the Creoles in the South and the French-Canadians in the North, clinging to French for so many generations and maintaining, however weakly, spiritual and social contacts with the mother-country; of the Germans, with their *Deutschthum*, their *Männerchore*, *Turnvereine*, and *Schützenfeste*; of the universally separate Jews; of the intensely nationalistic Irish; of the Pennsylvania Germans; of the indomitable Poles, and even more indomitable Bohemians; of the 30,000 Belgians in Wisconsin, with their "Belgian" language, a mixture of Walloon and Flemish welded by reaction to a strange social environment.[3] Except in such cases as the town of Lead, South Dakota, the great ethnic groups of proletarians, thrown upon themselves in a new environment, generate from among themselves the other social classes which Mr. Ross misses so sadly among them: their shopkeepers, their physicians, their attorneys, their journalists, and their national and political leaders, who form the links between them and the greater American society.[4] They develop their own literature, or become conscious of that of the mother-country. As they grow more prosperous and

3. [Kallen refers to the Romantic nationalist idea of *Deutschtum* (spelled *Deutschthum* in Kallen's text), or "Germanness," that was also used to describe the German diaspora. *Männerchore*, *Turnvereine*, and *Schützenfeste* are respectively all-male choirs, gymnastics clubs, and shooting or marksmanship festivals, all of which were brought by immigrants to the United States.]

4. [Lead, South Dakota, was the site of the Homestake gold mine and the heart of the Black Hills gold rush.]

"Americanized," as they become freed from the stigma of "foreigner," they develop group self-respect: the "wop" changes into a proud Italian, the "hunky" into an intensely nationalist Slav. They learn, or they recall, the spiritual heritage of their nationality. Their cultural abjectness gives way to cultural pride and the public schools, the libraries, and the clubs become beset with demands for texts in the national language and literature.

The Poles are an instance worth dwelling upon. Mr. Ross's summary of them is as striking as it is premonitory. There are over a million of them in the country, a backward people, prolific, brutal, priest-ridden—a menace to American institutions. Yet the urge that carries them in such numbers to America is not unlike that which carried the Pilgrim Fathers. Next to the Jews, whom their brethren in their Polish home are hounding to death, the unhappiest people in Europe, exploited by both their own upper classes and the Russian conqueror, they have resisted extinction at a great cost. They have clung to their religion because it was a mark of difference between them and their conquerors; because they love liberty, they have made their language of literary importance in Europe. Their aspiration, impersonal, disinterested, as it must be in America, to free Poland, to conserve the Polish spirit, is the most hopeful and American thing about them—the one thing that stands actually between them and brutalization through complete economic degradation. It lifts them higher than anything that, in fact, America offers them. The same thing is true for the Bohemians, 17,000 of them, workingmen in Chicago, paying a proportion of their wage to maintain schools in the Bohemian tongue and free thought; the same thing is true of many other groups.

How true it is may be observed from a comparison of the vernacular dailies and weeklies with the yellow American press which is concocted expressly for the great American masses. The content of the former, when the local news is deducted, is a mass of information, political, social, scientific; often translations into the vernacular standard English writing, often original work of high literary quality. The latter, when the news is deducted, consists of the sporting page and the editorial page. Both pander rather than awaken, so that it is no wonder that in fact the intellectual and spiritual pabulum of the great masses consists of the vernacular papers in the national tongue. With them go also the vernacular drama, and the thousand and one other phenomena which make a distinctive culture, the outward expression of that fundamental like-mindedness wherein men are truly "free and equal." This, beginning in the dumb peasant masses in language and religion, emerges in the other forms of life and art and tends to make smaller or larger ethnic groups autonomous, self-sufficient, and reacting as spiritual units to the residuum of America.

What is the cultural outcome likely to be, under these conditions? Surely not the melting-pot. Rather something that has become more and more distinct in the changing State and city life of the last two decades, and which is most articulate and apparent among just those peoples whom Mr. Ross praises most—the Scandinavians, the Germans, the Irish, the Jews.

It is in the area where Scandinavians are most concentrated that Norwegian is preached on Sunday in more churches than in Norway. That area is Minnesota, not unlike Scandinavia in climate and character. There, if the newspapers are to be trusted, the "foreign language" taught in an increasingly larger number of high schools is Scandinavian. The Constitution of the State resembles in many respects the famous Norwegian Constitution of 1813. The largest city has been chosen as the "spiritual capital," if I may say so, the seat of the Scandinavian "house of life," which the Scandinavian Society in America is reported to be planning to build as a centre from which there is to spread through the land Scandinavian culture and ideals.

The eastern neighbor of Minnesota is Wisconsin, a region of great concentration of Germans. Is it merely a political accident that the centralization of State authority and control has been possible there to a degree heretofore unknown in this country? That the Socialist organization is the most powerful in the land, able under ordinary conditions to have elected the Mayor of a large city and a Congressman, and kept out of power only by [a] coalition of the other parties? That German is the overwhelmingly predominant "foreign language" in the public schools and the university? Or that the fragrance of *Deutschthum* pervades the life of the whole State? The earliest German immigrants to America were group conscious to a high degree. They brought with them a cultural tradition and political aspiration. They wanted to found a State. If a State is to be regarded as a mode of life of the mind, they have succeeded. Their language is the predominant "foreign" one throughout the Middle West. The teaching of it is required by law in many places, southern Ohio and Indianapolis, for example. Their national institutions, even to cooking, are as widespread as they are. They are organized into a great national society, the German-American Alliance, which is dedicated to the advancement of German culture and ideals. They encourage and make possible a close and more intimate contact with the fatherland. They endow Germanic museums, they encourage and provide for exchange professorships, erect monuments to German heroes, and disseminate translations of the German classics. And there are, of course, the very excellent German vernacular press, the German theater, the German club, the German organization of life.

Similar are the Irish, living in strength in Massachusetts and New York. When they began to come to this country they were far less well off and far more passionately self-conscious than the Germans. For numbers of them America was and has remained just a centre from which to plot for the freedom of Ireland. For most it was an opportunity to escape both exploitation and starvation. The way they made was against both race and religious prejudice: in the course of it they lost much that was attractive as well as much that was unpleasant. But Americanization brought the mass of them also spiritual self-respect, and their growing prosperity both here and in Ireland is what lies behind the more inward phases of Irish Nationalism—the Gaelic movement, the Irish theater, the Irish Art Society. I omit consideration of such organized bodies as the Ancient Order of Hibernians. All these movements alike indicate the conversion of the negative nationalism of the hatred of England to the positive nationalism of the loving care and development of the cultural values of the Celtic spirit. A significant phase of it is the voting of Irish history into the curriculum of the high schools of Boston. In sum, once the Irish body had been fed and erected, the Irish mind demanded and generated its own peculiar form of self-realization and satisfaction.

And, finally, the Jews. Their attitude towards America is different in a fundamental respect from that of other immigrant nationalities. They do not come to the United States from truly native lands, lands of their proper *natio* and culture. They come from lands of sojourn, where they have been for ages treated as foreigners, at most as semi-citizens, subject to disabilities and persecutions. They come with no political aspirations against the peace of other states such as move the Irish, the Poles, the Bohemians. They come with the intention to be completely incorporated into the body-politic of the state. They alone, as Mr. H. G. Wells notes, of all the immigrant peoples have made spontaneously conscious and organized efforts to prepare themselves and their brethren for the responsibilities of American citizenship.[5] There is hardly a considerable municipality in the land, where Jews inhabit, that has not its Hebrew Institute, or its Educational

5. [It is unclear which work by H. G. Wells Kallen refers to here. In *The Future in America: A Search after Realities* (New York: Harper and Brothers, 1906), Wells says almost the opposite, calling the Jews "unassimilated and increasingly unpopular" (185) and listing them among America's "increasing proportion of unassimilable aliens" (120).]

Alliance, or its Young Men's Hebrew Association, or its Community House, especially dedicated to this task. They show the highest percentage of naturalization, according to Mr. Ross's tables, and he concedes that they have benefited politics. Yet of all self-conscious peoples they are the most self-conscious. Of all immigrants they have the oldest civilized tradition, they are the longest accustomed to living under law, and are at the outset the most eager and the most successful in eliminating the external differences between themselves and their social environment. Even their religion is flexible and accommodating, as that of the Christian sectaries is not, for change involves no change in doctrine, only in mode of life.

Yet, once the wolf is driven from the door and the Jewish immigrant takes his place in our society a free man and an American, he tends to become all the more a Jew. The cultural unity of his race, history, and background is only continued by the new life under the new conditions. Mr. H. G. Wells calls the Jewish quarter in New York a city within a city, and with more justice than other quarters because, although it is far more in tune with Americanism than the other quarters, it is also far more autonomous in spirit and self-conscious in culture. It has it sectaries, its radicals, its artists, its literati; its press, its literature, its theater, its Yiddish and its Hebrew, its Talmudical colleges and its Hebrew schools, its charities and its vanities, and its coordinating organization, the Kehilla, all more or less duplicated wherever Jews congregate in mass.[6] Here not religion alone, but the whole world of radical thinking, carries the mother-tongue and the father-tongue, with all that they imply. Unlike the parochial schools, their separate schools, being national, do not displace the public schools; they supplement the public schools. The Jewish ardor for pure learning is notorious. And, again, as was the case with the Scandinavians, the Germans, the Irish, democracy applied to education has given the Jews their will that Hebrew shall be coordinate with French and German in the regent's examination. On a national scale of organization there is the American Jewish Committee, the Jewish Historical Society, the Jewish Publication Society. Rurally, there is the model Association of Jewish Farmers, with their cooperative organization for agriculture and for agricultural education. In sum, the most eagerly American of the immigrant groups are also the most autonomous and self-conscious in spirit and culture.

6. [Between 1908 and 1922, the New York Kehilla functioned as a communal framework to organize, provide assistance, and represent the largest Jewish community in the United States.]

Immigrants appear to pass through four phases in the course of being Americanized. In the first phase they exhibit economic eagerness, the greed of the unfed. Since external differences are a handicap in the economic struggle, they "assimilate," seeking thus to facilitate the attainment of economic independence. Once the proletarian level of such independence is reached, the process of assimilation slows down and tends to come to a stop. The immigrant group is still a national group, modified, sometimes improved, by environmental influences, but otherwise a solitary spiritual unit, which is seeking to find its way out on its own social level. This search brings to light permanent group distinctions, and the immigrant, like the Anglo-Saxon American, is thrown back upon himself and his ancestry. Then a process of dissimilation begins. The arts, life, and ideals of the nationality become central and paramount; ethnic and national differences change in status from disadvantages to distinctions. All the while the immigrant has been using the English language and behaving like an American in matters economic and political, and continues to do so. The institutions of the Republic have become the liberating cause and the background for the rise of the cultural consciousness and social autonomy of the immigrant Irishman, German, Scandinavian, Jew, Pole, or Bohemian. On the whole, Americanization has not repressed nationality. Americanization has liberated nationality.

Hence, what troubles Mr. Ross and so many other Anglo-Saxon Americans is not really inequality; what troubles them is *difference*. Only things that are alike in fact and not abstractly, and only men that are alike in origin and in spirit and not abstractly, can be truly "equal" and maintain that inward unanimity of action and outlook which make a national life. The writers of the Declaration of Independence and of the Constitution were not confronted by the practical fact of ethnic dissimilarity among the whites of the country. Their descendants are confronted by it. Its existence, acceptance, and development provide one of the inevitable consequences of the democratic principle on which our theory of government is based, and the result at the present writing is to many worthies very unpleasant. Democratism and the Federal principle have worked together with economic greed and ethnic snobbishness to people the land with all the nationalities of Europe, and to convert the early American nation into the present American state. For in effect we are in the process of becoming a true federal state, such a state as men hope for as the outcome of the European war, a great republic consisting of a federation or commonwealth of nationalities.

Given, in the economic order, the principle of *laissez-faire* applied to a capitalistic society, in contrast with the manorial and guild systems of the past and the Socialist utopias of the future, the economic consequences are the same, whether in America, full of all Europe, or in England, full of the English, Scotch, and Welsh. Given, in the political order, the principle that all men are equal and that each, consequently, under the law at least, shall have the opportunity to make the most of himself, the control of the machinery of government by the plutocracy is a foregone conclusion. *Laissez-faire* and unprecedentedly bountiful natural resources have turned the mind of the state to wealth alone, and in the haste to accumulate wealth considerations of human quality have been neglected and forgotten, the action of government has been remedial rather than constructive, and Mr. Ross's "peasantism," *i.e.*, the growth of an expropriated, degraded industrial class, dependent on the factory rather than on land, has been rapid and vexatious.

The problems which these conditions give rise to are important, but not primarily important. Although they have occupied the minds of all our political theorists, they are problems of means, of instruments, not of ends. They concern the conditions of life, not the *kind of life*, and there appears to have been a general assumption that only one kind of human life is possible in America. But the same democracy which underlies the evils of the economic order underlies also the evils—and the promise—of the ethnic order. Because no individual is merely an individual, the political autonomy of the individual has meant and is beginning to realize in these United States the spiritual autonomy of his group. The process is as yet far from fruition. We are, in fact, at the parting of the ways. A genuine social alternative is before us, either of which parts we may realize if we will. In social construction the will is father to the fact, for the fact is nothing more than the concord or conflict of wills. What do we *will* to make of the United States—a unison, singing the old Anglo-Saxon theme "America," the America of the New England school, or a harmony, in which that theme shall be dominant, perhaps, among others, but one among many, not the only one?

The mind reverts helplessly to the historic attempts at unison in Europe—the heroic failure of the pan-Hellenists, of the Romans, the disintegration and the diversification of the Christian Church, for a time the most successful unison in history; the present-day failures of Germany and of Russia.[7] Here, however, the whole social situation is favorable, as it has never been at any time elsewhere—everything is favorable but the basic law of America itself, and the spirit of American institutions. To achieve unison—it can be achieved—would be to

---

7. [World War I was raging when Kallen wrote this essay.]

violate these. For the end determines the means, and this end would involve no other means than those used by Germany in Poland, in Schleswig-Holstein, and Alsace-Lorraine; by Russia in the Pale, in Poland, in Finland. Fundamentally it would require the complete nationalization of education, the abolition of every form of parochial and private school, the abolition of instruction in other tongues than English, and the concentration of the teaching of history and literature upon the English tradition. The other institutions of society would require treatment analogous to that administered by Germany to her European acquisitions. And all of this, even if meeting with no resistance, would not completely guarantee the survival as a unison of the older Americanism. For the programme would be applied to diverse ethnic types, and the reconstruction that, with the best will, they might spontaneously make of the tradition would more likely than not be a far cry from the original. It is, already.

The notion that the programme might be realized by radical and even enforced miscegenation, by the creation of the melting-pot by law, and thus by the development of the new "American race," is, as Mr. Ross points out, as mystically optimistic as it is ignorant. In historic times, so far as we know, no new ethic types have originated, and what we know of breeding gives us no assurance of the disappearance of the old types in favor of the new, only the addition of a new type, if it succeeds in surviving, to the already existing older ones. Biologically, life does not unify; biologically, life diversifies; and it is sheer ignorance to apply social analogies to biological processes. In any event, we know what the qualities and capacities of existing types are; we know how by education to do something towards the repression of what is evil in them and the conservation of what is good. The "American race" is a totally unknown thing; to presume that it will be better because (if we like to persist in the illusion that it is coming) it will be later, is no different from imagining that, because contemporary, Russia is better than ancient Greece. There is nothing more to be said to the pious stupidity that identifies recency with goodness. The unison to be achieved cannot be a unison of ethnic types. It must be, if it is to be at all, a unison of social and historic interests, established by the complete cutting off of the ancestral memories of our populations, the enforced, exclusive use of the English language and English and American history in the schools and in the daily life.

The attainment of the other alternative, a harmony, also requires concerted public action. But the action would do no violence to our fundamental law and the spirit of our institutions, nor to the qualities of men. It would seek simply to eliminate the waste and the stupidity of our social organization, by way of freeing and strengthening the strong forces actually in operation. Starting with our existing ethnic and cultural groups, it would seek to provide conditions under which each may attain the perfection that is proper to its kind. The provision of such conditions is the primary intent of our fundamental law and the function of our institutions. And the various nationalities which compose our commonwealth must learn first of all this fact, which is perhaps, to most minds, the outstanding ideal content of "Americanism"—that democracy means self-realization through self-control, self-government, and that one is impossible without the other. For the application of this principle, which is realized in a harmony of societies, there are European analogies also. I omit Austria and Turkey, for the union of nationalities is there based more on inadequate force than on consent, and the form of their organization is alien to ours. I think of England and of Switzerland. England is a state of four nationalities—the English, Welsh, Scotch, and Irish (if one considers the [British] Empire, of many more), and while English history is not unmarred by attempts at unison, both the home policy and the imperial policy have, since the Boer War, been realized more and more in the application of the principle of harmony: the strength of the kingdom and the empire have been posited more and more upon the voluntary and autonomous cooperation of the component nationalities. Switzerland is a state of three nationalities, a republic as the United States is, far more democratically governed, concentrated in an area not much different in size, I suspect, from New York city, with a population not far from it in total. Yet Switzerland has the most loyal citizens in Europe. Their language, literary and spiritual traditions are on the one side German, on another Italian, on a third side French. And in terms of social organization, of economic prosperity, of public education, of the general level of culture, Switzerland is the most successful democracy in the world. It conserves and encourages individuality.

The reason lies, I think, in the fact that in Switzerland the conception of "natural rights" operates, consciously or unconsciously, as a generalization from the unalterable data of human nature. What is inalienable in the life of mankind is its intrinsic positive quality—its psychophysical inheritance. Men may change their clothes, their politics, their wives, their religions, their philosophies, to a greater or lesser extent: they cannot change their grandfathers. Jews or Poles or Anglo-Saxons, would have to cease to be. The selfhood which is inalienable in them, and for the realization of which they require "inalienable" liberty, is ancestrally determined, and the happiness which they pursue has its form implied in ancestral endowment. This is what, actually, democracy in operation assumes.

There are human capacities which it is the function of the state to liberate and to protect; and the failure of the state as a government means its abolition. Government, the state, under the democratic conception, is merely an instrument, not an end. That it is often an abused instrument, that it is often seized by the powers that prey, that it makes frequent mistakes and considers only secondary ends, surface needs, which vary from moment to moment, is, of course, obvious: hence our social and political chaos. But that it is an instrument, flexibly adjustable to changing life, changing opinion, and needs, our whole electoral organization and party system declare. And as intelligence and wisdom prevail over "politics" and special interests, as the steady and continuous pressure of the inalienable qualities and purposes of human groups more and more dominate the confusion of our common life, the outlines of a possible great and truly democratic commonwealth become discernible.

Its form is that of the Federal republic; its substance a democracy of nationalities, cooperating voluntarily and autonomously in the enterprise of self-realization through the perfection of men according to their kind. The common language of the commonwealth, the language of its great political tradition, is English, but each nationality expresses its emotional and voluntary life in its own language, in its own inevitable aesthetic and intellectual forms. The common life of the commonwealth is politico-economic, and serves as the foundation and background for the realization of the distinctive individuality of each *natio* that composes it. Thus "American civilization" may come to mean the perfection of the cooperative harmonies of "European civilization," the waste, the squalor, and the distress of Europe being eliminated—a multiplicity in a unity, an orchestration of mankind. As in an orchestra, every type of instrument has its specific timbre and tonality, founded in its substance and form; as every type has its appropriate theme and melody in the whole symphony, so in society each ethnic group is the natural instrument, its spirit and culture are its theme and melody, and the harmony and dissonances and discords of them all make the symphony of civilization, with this difference: a musical symphony is written before it is played; in the symphony of civilization the playing is the writing, so that there is nothing so fixed and inevitable about its progressions as in music, so that within the limits set by nature they may vary at will, and the range and variety of the harmonies may become wider and richer and more beautiful.

But the question is, do the dominant classes in America want such a society?

10

The Future of Judaism
Mordecai M. Kaplan

Mordecai M. Kaplan, "The Future of Judaism," *Menorah Journal*, June 1916, 160–72.

In the first half of the twentieth century, few individuals did more to reconstruct Jewish thought, practice, and ritual in the United States than Mordecai Kaplan (1881–1983). Though Kaplan is best known as the founder of Reconstructionist Judaism, his intellectual influence can be seen across the American Jewish denominations. Kaplan was born in Svencian, Lithuania, in the Russian Empire, and immigrated to New York at the age of eight. Both Kaplan's father, who was a rabbi, and Kaplan himself were influenced by Yitshak Yaakov (Isaac Jacob) Reines (1839–1915). An important rabbinic figure in Lithuania, and late imperial Russia as a whole, Reines was one of the founders and first leaders of the Orthodox Zionist *Mizrahi* movement, as well as the head of an Orthodox yeshiva that combined secular studies and rabbinic religious training. Kaplan received a yeshiva education but went on to earn degrees from the City College of New York, the Jewish Theological Seminary (where he received his ordination in 1902), and Columbia University. Kaplan worked at the Orthodox synagogue Kehilath Jeshurun in New York until 1909, when he became principal of the Jewish Theological Seminary's newly established Teachers Institute.

Kaplan believed in the necessity of adapting Jewish thought and practice to the challenges of modern science and society, and despite considerable opposition in his own day (he was formally excommunicated by the Union of Orthodox Rabbis in 1945), he conceived of or initiated many of the radical changes in Jewish ritual and communal life that have been broadly adopted by American Jewish denominations. For example, he believed that Judaism should reflect the equality of the sexes, and, in 1922, his oldest daughter was the first woman to celebrate a bat mitzvah. Perhaps most important, Kaplan believed that the synagogue should stand at the center of American Jewish life, preserving Jewish difference by serving as the focus of Jewish communal, cultural, and religious activities. Throughout his long career, Kaplan published prolifically on Jewish philosophy, the meaning of Judaism, and the challenges of preserving Jewish life in the United States.

Beginning with his early articles in the *Menorah Journal*, Kaplan struggled to define Judaism in a way that would preserve Jewish autonomy and be compatible to America's democratic ethos. He eventually synthesized these ideas in his work *Judaism as a Civilization: Toward a Reconstruction of American-Jewish Life*, published in 1934. Kaplan contributed frequently to the *Menorah Journal*, a publication of the Intercollegiate Menorah Association that became the major English-language venue for intellectual debate on Jewish culture and society in America before World War II. In fact, Kaplan was one of a group of Jewish intellectuals to write in the *Menorah Journal* on questions of American pluralism and Jewish nationalism.

In 1915–16, the *Menorah Journal*'s first years, Kaplan published a five-part series called "The Meaning of Judaism," about the nature of Judaism and how to preserve Jewish nationality in American society. In these articles, Kaplan first articulated the key concepts he would develop and return to over many years—in particular, that the Jews are a distinct people, and that what defines Judaism is a collective Jewish consciousness. In "How May Judaism Be Saved?"—the third article in the series—Kaplan discusses both the promise and the danger that American freedom posed to Jewish national identity. According to Kaplan, American democracy's far-reaching individual rights create pressure for Jews to shed their separate collective identity, but at the same time, those rights' legal protections also afford Jews an opportunity to construct communal institutions capable of sustaining a separate Jewish nationality. In the final article, "The Future of Judaism," from which the selection below is taken, Kaplan more explicitly explores the possible diverging paths that American Jews face. Kaplan believed the United States, like European countries, to be developing a "New Nationalism" that, in combining nationality and state religion, required the conformity of its citizenry (though this was not at all what Theodore Roosevelt meant when he coined the term "New Nationalism" in 1910). The fact that America's state religion is (or will be) "the Religion of Democracy" is particularly threatening to Jewish collective identity because of its inclusivity. Thus, for Kaplan, the only way to preempt the end of Jewish nationality in America is to construct institutional and theological (or, perhaps, metaphysical) defenses. Kaplan's resulting call for intellectuals to become involved in communal institutions echoes the sentiments expressed by the Jewish autonomists in Eastern Europe and demonstrates the truly transnational nature of Jewish societal dilemmas during the period. Although Kaplan was a devoted Zionist, it is clear that—at least at this point in his life—he interpreted Zionism strictly as preserving the messianic impulse in Judaism, and therefore the eternality of Jewish collective consciousness.

Kaplan wrote these early articles in the midst of a war that many blamed on nationalism, and in an environment of growing nativism in the United States. Furthermore, he wrote at a time of contentious, ongoing debates in the United States about what it means to be American, and the nature of the United States as a nation. Kaplan had no knowledge of what path American nationalism, or "Americanism," would take, and he worried that Jews might lose everything in the process. Instead, he proposed that Jews use spiritual nationalism and Jewish autonomy to ensure that the Jewish people—Israel—preserve their collective consciousness and, in the process, ensure that the United States remains a pluralistic society.

The Jewish Emancipation has entangled Judaism in nearly all of the perplexing world problems of the day. No wonder, then, that it has rendered the fate of Judaism dependent upon the final outcome of the struggle between the Church and the State for the possession of man's soul. Though the State-Church question has now been pending for several centuries, it still remains one of the loose ends of political thought. Very few political thinkers have had the courage to push their theories to their logical conclusions. Hobbes, who is one of the few, went so far as to advise his sovereign to determine what religious dogmas should be taught by the clergy; but who knows whether he really meant what he said?[8] On the other hand, the hope that the Gordian knot would be cut once for all by separating State from Church has proved illusory. The avowed purpose of granting everyone freedom of conscience and giving to each religious sect the right to work out its destiny is turning out to be a mere stalking horse. The State has become ambitious to develop its own soul and its own religion. The inwardness of the events in a country like ours confirms the truth of the *third thesis* enunciated in the course of these articles, *that in the collective consciousness of any stable group we have the making of a religion.*[9] The severance of the State from the Church is the preparation and ground-clearing for the advent of a new era in the inner life

8. [In *Leviathan*, his most famous work, Thomas Hobbes (1588–1679) argues for the necessity of a sovereign authority—based on the consent of the people—over nations in order to avoid civil war. As Kaplan mentions here, Hobbes believed that to maintain peace in a society, the sovereign leader must govern ecclesiastical powers.]

9. [The four articles preceding "The Future of Judaism" in Kaplan's series in the *Menorah Journal* were "What Judaism Is Not," (October 1915), "What Is Judaism?" (December 1915), "How May Judaism Be Saved?" (February 1916), and "Judaism and Christianity" (April 1916).]

of peoples, an era in which the unity of State and Church will be replaced by that of Nationality and Religion.

The day will come when the Church will be disestablished in other countries besides America and France. But in each case disestablishment will constitute only an intermediate stage leading to a more natural and intimate union between a people and its faith. It is this interregnum in the spiritual life of the American people that has brought about a new and unprecedented condition in Judaism, and that calls for thought and action along different lines from those pursued hitherto. The manner in which American Jewry utilizes the period of spiritual interregnum in which it finds itself will constitute a precedent to be followed by Jewry the world over. If we rest content with the unanalyzed jargon of conventional ideas on Judaism, and waste our energies in aimless organization and spiritless philanthropies, the opportunity for making provision for the perpetuation of Judaism will be wasted. A time is coming when it will be not only difficult to live a Jewish life in America, but almost impossible. That will be when Americanism, in the sense of an American Religion, or the Religion of Democracy, will have come into being. It will probably take three or four generations to evolve; but since the certainty of its coming is apparent, Judaism should not fritter away the precious hours either in self-complacent day-dreaming or in ill-considered and sporadic enterprises.

THE CHANGE IN THE CONCEPTION OF GOVERNMENT

The merging of Nationality and Religion can be traced in a large measure to a change in ideas as to the province of government, the meaning of nationality, and the function of religion. The last fifty years have witnessed a decided departure from the principles that governed political life during the greater part of the century following the American and French Revolutions. The axiom accepted by those who were responsible for the liberal movements during the eighteenth and nineteenth centuries was that a State should govern as little as possible. The principle of laissez faire was appealed to against every measure that threatened individual liberty, however beneficent it might prove both to the individual and to the community. The doctrine of non-interference which was advocated by John Stuart Mill led Herbert Spencer to the startling conclusion that the State had no other function than to protect the life, liberty and property of its citizens.[10]

10. [John Stuart Mill (1806–73) suggested that a government's power must be limited

Even compulsory education he looked upon as an act of aggression. But while he was protesting against State interference his own State was extending its power. It assumed the right to compel parents to educate their children; it provided and paid for their education; it intervened in matters that concerned the public health; it subsidized works for public convenience; it regulated labor and issued factory laws; it organized the professions and censored the morals of the people. Instead of being regarded as a necessary evil the State is now esteemed as an indispensable good. How completely public opinion has veered round is reflected in the change that has taken place in the use of the term "progressive," which, after having been associated with the curtailing and retrenching of the powers of the State, has come to connote the extension of its sphere of control to the point of collectivism and paternalism.

A second factor that makes for the development of that self-conscious group life which we term Religion is the New Nationalism.[11] The enlargement of the sphere of government is itself a corollary of the deeper meaning which nationality has acquired within the last fifty years. Love of nation, of mother country or fatherland, is no new thing; but it remained for a long time merely instinctive. As previously indicated, the break with the Roman Church which took place in England and Germany represents the first intimation of self-conscious nationalism. Even those who refused adherence to the Protestant cause developed a zeal for their nation greater than for their Church. The story has come down from the reign of Elizabeth that a number of English Catholic youth, who were sent to study at the College of Rome, cheered the news of the defeat of the Armada, although they were aware that halters were ready for their necks whenever they should return to England.

---

in order to protect the liberties of the individual. Individuals must be free to do as they wish so long as they do not harm others; this is what Kaplan refers to as "the doctrine of non-interference." Like Mill, Herbert Spencer (1820–1903) was a utilitarian, who believed, as Kaplan writes, that the state's only function was to protect individual liberties, in order to promote the greatest happiness for the greatest number of people.]

11. [In a 1910 campaign speech, President Theodore Roosevelt made a call for a "New Nationalism." This political theory demanded a large federal government that could oversee and protect individual liberties and property rights and guarantee social justice. Like the utilitarians, Roosevelt believed that the government's top priority should be ensuring the welfare of the people.]

THE RELIGIOUS SIGNIFICANCE
OF THE NEW NATIONALISM

The New Nationalism, from which the historic religions have most to apprehend, is based on the conviction that a nation is more than a physical fact. Nationality is assuming a sacrosanct meaning, because it is recognized as being more than the result of living together in one country or part of a country. The economic and social interest as well as the political strivings of a people give rise to a common history and to common purposes, which convert it into an organism whose every part strengthens and is strengthened by the others. A people is a moral and spiritual entity, a magnified person. The various ways in which the State expresses its solicitude for the physical and moral well-being of the individual have the effect of translating love of country into a manifold of practical checks and duties, and of making patriotism an active sentiment not only in time of war but also in time of peace.

Though Mazzini himself was a good Christian, yet when he said, "Italy is itself a religion," he was paving the way for the more vital religions of the future.[12] A diplomatist writing on the war in the near East, who has had an opportunity to acquire first-hand knowledge of the inner life of the Balkan peoples, speaks of national consciousness as a moral force that possesses subliminal qualities in every way identical with those we have been in the habit of associating with religion. Of the Greeks he says, "The Megali Idea, the consciousness of their individuality, is to the Greeks what monotheism is to the Jews." He certainly displays a far truer appreciation of what Jewish monotheism denotes than most of those who allude to it as an evidence of philosophical insight in our people.

To be sure, untold crimes have been committed in the name of nationality. We should learn, however, to separate patriotism from the base alloys of vanity and pugnacity. Those of us who ascribe the present European cataclysm to nationalism run riot will recoil with horror at the suggestion that nationalism is to become dominant. But calmer reflection will teach us to discern the true cause in unbridled imperialistic ambitions and not in the sentiment of nationalism. That patriotism has been a torch which has set on fire the passions of people against people cannot be denied. Yet the great religions of the world have also imbrued man's hands in blood. The religions of love were no less adept in the

12. [Giuseppe Mazzini (1805–72) contributed to bringing about an independent and unified Italy.]

use of fire and sword than those which openly claimed the right to employ them as a means of spreading the true doctrine. That a State could do no wrong is certainly a dangerous theory; yet it is no less dangerous than the doctrine that still prevails in the greater part of the world that the Church or its head is the infallible guide to salvation and truth. If our better reason tells us that it is not the use but the abuse of religion that has led to bloodshed, why not believe the same of patriotism? There is no doubt as to its future sway over men's minds and hearts. The very sacrifices which each of the warring countries has demanded of its population will endear it to its citizens with a love never known before. If any good is to come of this war it will not be the weakening of national consciousness but the sobering of men's minds from the madness of imperialism. We have reason to believe that if men learn to conceive a sense of loyalty and duty that transcends the boundaries of country, it will be through so construing and interpreting the meaning of the lesser loyalties as to render them an indispensable means to the higher loyalties.

GENUINE RELIGION MUST BE ROOTED IN EVERYDAY LIFE

The third idea which is religionizing national life is the conviction that religion is genuine and vital only when it is rooted in the actual and immediate interest of everyday life. To the extent that it helps to raise to a higher plane of values the actual relations between men and women, between the individual and society, and only in so far as it can inject ideal interest into our buying and selling, into our labor and leisure, into all that we do, say and think, can a religion escape degenerating into a mummery. Men could not have invented a more mischief-breeding arrangement than the artificial division between the spiritual and the temporal. When churchmen, in their eagerness to justify the existence of the Church by the side of the State, assign to each distinct jurisdictions, they deprive the spiritual of content and intrinsic interest, and abandon the temporal to its own blind impulses. When Nelson said to his sailors, "Boys, love your enemies but hate a Frenchman like poison," he exhibited the result of a contentless spirituality.[13] Sentiments that are not based on interest are hollow, and interests not enlightened by sentiments become selfish and brutal. A religion which has not the courage to claim the whole man does not deserve to possess even a part

13. [Horatio Nelson (1758–1805), a British naval hero.]

of him. If it has nothing but general maxims to offer to the work-a-day life it is sure to forfeit even the attention that is paid to it at week-ends.

A striking illustration of how important it is for religious doctrines to be rooted in the actual life of the people that profess them is given by A. Mitchell Innes, who served the English Government in Egypt in an administrative capacity.[14] He points out that only in a system of jurisprudence as conducted in the Orient can the teaching of divine reciprocity, "Condemn not and ye shall not be condemned; forgive and ye shall be forgiven," have any meaning or application. The Mohammedans take that teaching seriously and practice it in their courts, whereas it would entirely upset the whole system of criminal jurisprudence as practiced in Christian States. "Christian dogmas," he says, "have the disadvantage of being exotic in our country, while in theirs it is native to the soil; and it is a curious and instructive sight to see our parents trying to implant Christian precepts in their blue-eyed children's minds, while we vainly strive to uproot them from the minds of our Eastern subjects." The growing coldness in this country to organized religions, in contrast with the gradual deepening of faith in the spiritual possibilities of the civic community, verifies the wisdom of his observation.

The opinion is gaining ground that a Church which can be separated from a State should never have been united with it. Christianity with its one hundred and eighty-six denominations in the United States, besides a large number of individual churches, can never expect to develop into the religion that will be synonymous with the soul of America. On the one hand, the percentage of the population identified with the Church is constantly decreasing, 30 percent being the present estimate; on the other, the State is superseding the Church in its hold on the popular imagination and preempting all the love, loyalty and self-surrender of which the human being is capable. We cannot avoid the inference, therefore, that the center of gravity of American spiritual life has shifted away from the Church.

THE COMING RELIGION OF DEMOCRACY

The Religion of Democracy will not be heralded into the world with miracles of catastrophic nature. It is insinuating itself so gradually as hardly to be per-

14. [A British diplomat who served in Egypt, Siam, the United States, and Uruguay, Alfred Mitchell-Innes (1864–1950), favored national systems like the one he observed in Egypt, which combined law, religion, and custom.]

ceptible. It is going on as a process of metabolism, the new replacing the old cell by cell and atom by atom. The domestic, the industrial, the social and the political life are being so transformed as to contribute to an organized American consciousness, from which will arise the faith in America and in her people, a development much akin to that which took place in Israel.[15] In a literary production from the pen of a Christian minister we read the following:

For a God of our own
We cry, and we groan
In secret, and search
The whole earth! But in church
"Keep still," they tell us,
"Or the Old may be jealous
And lay waste our age
In a fatherly rage!"

For the first time in Occidental civilization there is evolving a collective self-consciousness. America will probably lead the way among the Western nations in the substitution of a home religion for an imperial one.

Under such circumstances it is ill-fitting to adopt the attitude of most of the religious standpatters, who, after having been driven from one position after another, come out with the announcement that they retreated for strategic reasons. To refuse to succumb to defeat is heroic, but to describe it as a victory is despicable. The habit of finding texts to explain away the inevitable is particularly odious in men who should look the truth in the face. Christianity hardly gains in respect when its spokesmen wriggle out of all difficulties with their "Render unto Caesar the things which are Caesar's."[16] Nor is Judaism's reputation enhanced when its representatives misapply the motto, "The law of the land is supreme."[17] Most Jews will repudiate as unctuous sophistry Morris Joseph's

15. [Kaplan refers here to ancient Israel.]

16. [Matthew 22:21 was put to various purposes in Europe and the United States, as an argument for the separation of church and state and as an argument both for and against the incorporation of moral and religious judgment into government.]

17. [Kaplan alludes here to *dina de-malhuta dina* (the law of the kingdom is the law), a doctrine from third-century Babylonia arguing that Jews in the diaspora should defer to non-Jewish authorities on issues of financial jurisdiction. Although the premise of this doctrine was the quid pro quo recognition by non-Jewish authorities of Jewish autonomy in all other aspects of Jewish life, by the nineteenth century Jewish reformers

teaching that "No Jew has the right to excuse himself on religious grounds from serving on a jury or from voting at an election on the Sabbath . . . Let the Jewish citizen break the sabbatical law so that he may keep inviolate the greater duty—that which he owes to the State."[18] The truth of the matter is that Judaism is being crowded out by the claims and prerogatives of the State. Those to whom Judaism is more than a medley of colorless platitudes, those who experience it as a living consciousness, will meet the situation bravely and make the establishment of a home where Judaism shall be free to live and develop in its own way their main aspirations as Jews. [. . .]

THE PROSPECTS OF JUDAISM IN AMERICA

Let us hope that the shattering impact of the social and intellectual forces that have been let loose against Judaism will shock it into a newer self-realization. No need is more urgent than to think clearly and deeply. A people as well as an individual may reason *Cogito ergo sum*. What Judaism requires at the present time is not subtle reasoning, but the fearless facing of facts, together with a keen sense of reality. The main principle that we should keep in mind is that beliefs and practices are the expressions and manifestations, but not the thing-in-itself of religion. They are to the latter what language is to thought. While they might at one time have rendered its essence articulate and transferable, they neither create it, constitute it, nor enable it to meet difficulties. For a religion is essentially the invisible and psychic force which holds together a heterogeneous mass of human beings and makes of them an organically constituted whole, a genuine organism and not a mere legal fiction.

The main practical inference that we should draw from this conception of Judaism is that it is unthinkable apart from Jewish group life. The Jews are not a voluntary organization pledged to certain abstract principles. They are not an "invisible church." They constitute a social organism with a self-conscious soul. The integrity of this social organism is the primary condition of the existence of Judaism. Hence, for Judaism to be at all possible, the Jews must live in aggregates that can exercise some form of autonomy. Group life is to the collective mind

---

had reinterpreted the doctrine as an argument against Jewish autonomy and for the legal integration of the Jews into the state.]

18. [Morris Joseph (1848–1930) was a well-known, and sometimes controversial, English Reform rabbi who published widely on Jewish issues in both books and in the Anglo-Jewish press.]

what the body is to the soul. Were social autonomy absolutely impossible in America we would not hesitate to say that Judaism is impossible in America. On the other hand, if we were able to look forward to social autonomy as a permanent factor in American life, on the assumption that the American nation will prove to be a federation of nationalities, we would affirm that Judaism may have a permanent home in America.

In our estimate, however, Americanism will not tolerate the continuance of other than geographical groups. It will have states but not churches; it will ultimately develop a religion of its own. But that will not take place in our days. America has still history to make; for to a religion which means a collective soul, history is indispensable. As long as Church and State are separate, and Religion and Nationality have not yet come together, Judaism would be in entire conformity with the best American ideals thus far formulated if it were to foster that autonomy without which it must forthwith perish, and provide for that immortality without which it would not have the heart to go on living. To anticipate the Americanism of the future is to make twelve o'clock at eleven—a procedure of questionable morality.

THE TRUE FUNCTIONS OF THE SYNAGOGUE

In order that there shall be no mistakes as to the spirit and motive of the social autonomy which Jews should cultivate, and that there shall not be the slightest reason to suspect it of un-Americanism, it must center about the Synagogue. America rightly resents all social autonomy that is not lifted to the plane of religion. Thus the function of the Synagogue will appear in a new light. A far heavier responsibility rests upon it than that of providing a vestried Sunday School for the young, and divine services for the elders. It should become a social center where the Jews of the neighborhood may find every possible opportunity to give expression to their social and play instincts. It must become the Jew's second home. It must be his club, his theatre and his forum. It should be even his courtroom to which he might take all arbitrable disputes so as to avoid figuring as a litigious citizen.

The adoption of this point of view would put a new spirit into all our social, philanthropic and educational endeavors. Jews would not have to be shamed into them. Hospitals, homes for the aged, Young Men's Hebrew Associations, would be utilized as a means of fostering Jewish consciousness. As it is, they are for the most part in the hands of social workers who look upon Judaism as a misfortune, and who would manifest their love for the beneficiaries by easing them of what to them appears an unnecessary burden.

The recognition of the true essence of Judaism would put new life into Jewish education. It would give to it aim and content. It would rescue it from the inefficient girl teachers who volunteer their services or want to earn their pin-money. The Hebrew language would be cultivated not only for Synagogue responses but as the medium of expression for a regenerated Israel, and as the most tangible evidence in the Diaspora of the collective mind of the Jewish people. A new spirit would pervade our ceremonial observances. Being animated by the definite purpose of fostering the Jewish consciousness, they would cease to be mere mechanical routine. Wherever revision is necessary, it would be affected not through attrition and individual whim, but as the result of careful deliberation on the part of an authoritative body representing Universal Israel. Some solution would be found for the Sabbath question. All our efforts to regenerate Jewish life can be of no avail if we are deprived of the very power of assembly, as is the case if we are unable to keep our Sabbaths and Festivals. We would realize the need of a Jewish world-congress to consider the problems of Judaism, a congress that would afford guidance and inspiration to the millions in the Diaspora.

"THE PASSION OF JUDAISM FOR IMMORTALITY"

In the meantime the life of the nations will proceed in its onward course, heedless of what we Jews may or may not do. Nationality and religion will ultimately amalgamate. Judaism will, therefore, be possible in the Diaspora only as long as the Church remains dominant. With such a prospect before us, Judaism would appear to be a forlorn hope if we were to surrender our faith in Israel's return to Zion. As a collective consciousness, Judaism has a passion for immortality which it must satisfy. Hence the irresistible urge to seek for itself a home where it shall be assured of enduring unto the end of days. This is what Zionism means from the standpoint of Judaism. For the majority of Jews the world over, Zion is the pledge that Judaism is eternal: The real Zionist platform is not the one formulated in the Basle program, but the prayer in our ritual which reads, "Let our eyes behold Thy return to Zion."

Judaism is neither racial pride nor individual illumination but the mind of the Jewish people or the soul of Israel. He to whom Israel's past is a personal memory and Israel's future a personal task is a religious Jew. This conception of Judaism calls for a program big enough and heroic enough to appeal to the imagination. It is a conception that will save us from intellectual lassitude and contentious sterility. It has action, affirmation and distance to it. It suggests far-reaching measures for the possibilities of the long roll of years.

11

A Basis for Jewish Consciousness
René Hirschler

René Hirschler, "Un fondement de la conscience Juive," *Revue Litteraire Juive* 3 nos. 1–2 (1929): 6–14.

Though René Hirschler (1905–45) rose rapidly to become a figure of prominence in French Jewish religious and communal life, his murder in the Holocaust at a young age probably prevented him from becoming a better known intellectual figure. Most of what has been written about Hirschler concerns his resistance and communal aid activities during the war. Hirschler was born in Marseille and graduated from the Rabbinical School of Paris in 1928, and from there he became rabbi of Mulhouse, in Alsace. At the age of thirty-four, just before the Germans occupied France, Hirschler was appointed chief rabbi of Strasbourg and the Bas-Rhin Department. Though he wrote few essays, Hirschler was a prolific public orator and letter writer, and he published collections of his speeches and letters.

When Hirschler wrote the essay below, he was only twenty-four years old and a recently ordained rabbi. The *Revue Litteraire Juive*, edited by Pierre Paraf (1893–1989), served as a venue for intellectual debate about Zionism, Jewish nationalism, religion, acculturation, and — most explicitly — the creation of a Jewish renaissance. Hirschler's (limited) place in these debates appears to be as a figure whose nationalism was influenced by contemporary French Zionists such as Paraf and Edmond Fleg (1874–1963), whose national concerns focused primarily on fostering Jewish unity and Jewish cultural and intellectual renaissance. Hirschler chose not to center his own nationalism geographically or ideologically, and he called for a reinvigorated Jewish consciousness to unify all of the people of Israel, both religious and secular. The essay below is a meditation on the unifying nature of the collective Jewish consciousness (in an almost Jungian sense), and though he couches his argument in religious terms, it is clear that the feeling of Jewish consciousness is rooted in the very minimal belief in the eternality of Israel. If the feeling of Jewish consciousness — rather than religion, ideology, or even nationalism — formed the basis for a Jewish renaissance, people who had otherwise turned away from Judaism could be pulled back into the people of Israel.

In the essay, it is not clear whether Hirschler is calling for an organizational "Union" for world Jewry or rather is speaking generally of a united Jewish consciousness, but in either case his unified Israel transcended politics, religion, and national borders. Furthermore, Hirschler did his utmost to put his ideals into practice in his own life. As chief rabbi of Strasbourg before the German occupation, he assisted the American Joint Distribution Committee in unifying all Jewish aid organizations in France (those for natives and those for refugees) in a single new organization, the Commission Centrale des Organisations Juives d'Assistance, and he became its secretary. Throughout the war, until his death, Hirschler worked on behalf of foreign-born Jewish prisoners and, in 1942, became chaplain general for foreign Jews in the Free Zone internment camps. Hirschler was arrested in December 1943 with his wife, Simone, and most likely died in 1945 in the Austrian camp Ebensee.

Along with the rest of humanity, the Judaism of today has its concerns. It would be futile to deny it. Here is not the place to study the reasons for this rupture in the equilibrium—reasons that more often than not lie outside of us—it will suffice to note and observe that a new Jewish problem has come into existence, for the Jews themselves.

The questions that divided Judaism until now were above all of a religious nature, yet the social question today increasingly mixes in, and the problem grows as political elements far from simplify it. Each formulation has its partisans—fierce ones—who treat as adversaries those who in good conscience cannot accept it as a dogma. We tear each other apart and we sometimes forget in the polemics that which should dominate the debate: the supreme interest of Judaism.

Without doubt, these struggles are a demonstration of the intense vitality of our community and this may be a consolation for us. As for the men who live by them, they try to reason with their Judaism, and it would be neither just nor generous to doubt their good intentions. There is thus here a latent force consuming itself and spreading without great benefit to the common good.

Indeed, each day we encounter a considerable number of Jews who are justly disgusted by this spectacle; and this is no way to reel in the indifferent and assimilated. Such is the first outcome of our divisions. And above all, in acting this way, we forget that adversaries lurk around us, all the more dangerous the better they hide themselves. We must not ignore that there are victims, and that the zeal of those seeking converts grows greater and greater.

We must defend ourselves; we must win back those who, most often out of ignorance, were lost. It is not that we fear for the future of Judaism, but we must not allow ourselves to be injured and weakened.

It is not for us to recreate this Judaism, but to understand it, to perpetuate it, and to participate in its life. And as proof I call upon a feeling that each of us finds at the back of his conscience and that he rarely thinks through.

The Jew—almost as an act of faith—believes in the permanence of Israel. I would like to analyze this intimate feeling here: to prove that it is not in vain, that it cannot be in vain. I would like to show that each of us, whatever our position within Judaism, can justify it with worthy arguments. And in order to remain effective, we will perhaps thereby see our necessary role and action within Israel.[19]

For the Jewish believer, the permanence of Israel is obvious. Can an absolute truth have an end? An eternal God presupposes an eternal religion. As early as the first pages of the Bible, these two affirmations are intimately linked. This is God blessing Abraham and showing him a glimpse of the future of his descendants. These are our Patriarchs, our prophets crying out their faith in the destiny of their people. God made a vow; He will keep His promise. For His choice, according to the word of Isaiah, God placed Israel "in an eternal excellence and joy that will last from generation to generation."[20]

Many among us are satisfied by these reasons and apply ourselves to following the path traced by our ancestors, in order to participate in this eternity. But today's man often demands more proof to form that certainty and the following lines are addressed especially to him. With him, therefore, we shall examine some points specific to Judaism and discover their permanent value.

The Jew believes that God is One ... It is useless to show after so many others how this dogma of God's Unity, the source of all humanity, satisfies our reason. One need only refer to the valuable little book by Mr. Fleg, *Why I Am a Jew*, and we can see everything that this dogma still contains for people educated at school during a scientific century.[21] Already, this singular idea should assure Israel its immortality.

---

19. [Here, Israel means the Jewish people or nation (in Hebrew, *Am Yisrael*) rather than a Jewish state. From the early nineteenth century onward, French Jews generally preferred the term *israélite* to *juif*, a term that was often used pejoratively. The reference to Israel here may also have reminded readers of the Alliance Israélite Universelle, a Jewish philanthropic organization founded in 1860. The organization's Talmudic slogan, "Kol yisrael arevim ze ba-ze"—"All of Israel are responsible for one another" (Shavuot 39a)—may have been the most familiar use of the word "Israel" for French Jews.]

20. [Isaiah 60:15.]

21. [Edmond Fleg (1874–1963) was a French essayist, playwright, and poet whose most

It is also in unity that the Jew looked for his social ideal. For him, all men are brothers, sons of the same father; equals before one and the same God. As a guardian of what he believes is the truth, he does not feel superior to others, but different. This is his profound doctrine.

In its laws, it did not forget the stranger who has the right to justice and to liberty. "Remember that you were a stranger in Egypt" repeats the sacred code. Now, these generous ideas have conquered the civilized world and our century has conceived of some noble thoughts, that some freely imagine to have invented but which the Jew has already long cherished. We often speak about the League of Nations and we all want to trust its efforts: but the Jew especially will recognize there his most ardent aspirations.[22] The voice of the prophet known in our hearts still echoes in the Judean Hills, "Make haste and come, all of you, surrounding nations. Unite ... the spears will one day turn into plowshares, the swords into pruning hooks."[23]

A community that gives life to such an ideal for centuries must serve as a link between peoples. In subsisting, it will always be a ferment of happiness and peace that fate has cast outward. For the good of humanity, Israel must therefore live. Here, we are assured as much by our reason as our feelings.

Though the greatness in such ideas is undeniable, the greatness of Israel may be recognized by yet other hallmarks. The example of its history is sublime. And if it is true that pain and thought are what give value to a man, who will measure that of Israel? For centuries, he dragged across the world the heavy privilege of being the poor and miserable Jew. Nothing that could cause suffering of either soul or body was spared him. For centuries, he was a puppet in the hands of princes and peoples, and cast away after having been used roughly. He suffered, they laughed; he consumed himself, a human torch, with the divine name on his lips and they applauded.

And regardless of how others laughed and applauded at his misery, Israel turned inward and studied. What astonishment for he who glances through the story of our ancestors to discover the intense life of these unfortunate people!

---

famous work is *Pourquoi je suis Juif* (Why I am a Jew), an essay he wrote in 1928. In this work Fleg traces his journey from ambivalent agnostic toward Judaism and Zionism.]

22. [The League of Nations (1919–46) was formed after World War I in order to promote a peaceful and secure community of nations. Hirschler admires the League, seeing in it not a twentieth-century "noble thought" but an ancient Jewish ideal with origins in the Hebrew Bible.]

23. [Isaiah 2:3–4.]

And it was a great French historian from the last century who pitted the intellectual inertia of the Middle Ages in all its splendor against the spiritual activity of the Jew in his infamous Jewish quarter [*juiverie*].[24] Flourishing Talmudic academies blossomed in France, in Germany, in England. Grammarians, poets, theologians competed with one another in scientific reason and genius. Jewish philosophers imparted Greek and Muslim wisdom to Christian Europe. Jewish doctors founded modern medicine, curing popes and kings to the great indignation of their peoples.

And before this picture how could we not have faith in the destinies of a people who can boast such a past? How can it be conceived that such greatness may ever be exhausted or disappear? Others were larger, more powerful than Israel, but in a different way. The power of weapons is short-lived: victors today might be vanquished tomorrow. Does not the history of peoples demonstrate that when two civilizations find themselves in conflict, the greater triumphs, sooner or later, even if it is the weaker party? It was so for Greece, so for Israel.

Israel was enslaved, she suffered as much as one can suffer, but she remained herself. Persecutions passed, the pyres were extinguished, Israel remains. Others have aged, she still feels young. How profound now the divine word seems to me: "The definitive victory comes neither from strength, nor violence, but from My spirit."[25] How, Jew, my brother, how could you not believe this?

Abandonment itself does not permit us to doubt it. A strange phenomenon, in effect: the Jews who are ignorant of their religion and their past, the Jews who repudiated from their lives everything that could distinguish them from the rest of humanity, conserve in the depths of their consciousness the feeling that they are still different from "others." They assimilated, or rather, they tried, but there remains in them a sense of Jewish worth that is far from disappearing. Most of them, incidentally, do not want it to disappear. They feel more or less vaguely that this particular thing within them is something great. And in certain circumstances, their consciousness participates in the consciousness of Israel, of which it is a fragment: a vestige that remains so vivid that the most incredulous never dwell in the indifference that their total negation would imply. It will shake all our secret foundations, those of our most distant, most intimate heritage that we

24. [Hirschler is probably referring here to the work of the philosopher and historian Ernest Renan.]

25. [Zechariah 4:6.]

ourselves quite often ignore. We hear a call, awakening in us a thousand latent and foolhardy atavisms, this unquenchable voice of the "speaking dead" as one modern writer strongly asserted.[26] Whether we yield to this voice or we resist, it arouses in us a new person with sympathies, repulsions, desires, where we often no longer recognize ourselves. It is not with impunity that we are the sons of a people who thought, cried, and hoped for such a long time!

How could the conscious Jew then doubt the reality of this Jewish worth, of this Jewish consciousness that he feels living within him? From whatever point of view he studies Judaism he cannot believe that this Judaism, one day, will no longer be.

If it is so, if we think, if we affirm that Israel will overcome these times, can we reasonably abandon participating in this eternity? Let us remember that each of us is like a moment in the life of Israel. Between the past and the future we have our place and our responsibility. An act is never isolated in a man's life, and so it is with us: we are what yesterday made of us, as our *oeuvre* will be tomorrow.

It is therefore not a matter of believing, of affirming, and of speaking . . . or of writing. We must act. Act, as our ancestors acted so that we could be who we are proud and happy to be: Jews. Act, so that our sons do not cease to be Jews. Now, can he who is disinterested in the common good maintain that all does not stop with him? He feels, maybe he knows, what he is, but what will his children be? The link that attaches him to the Jewish community is loosening more and more, to the point of one day disappearing, imperceptibly. And Israel will continue to live out its sublime destiny without him. Is this here not a sort of moral suicide?[27] Often, moreover, the one falling away catches sight of this fact, and when at the end of his life he thinks of returning to his fathers, he sometimes regrets his choices. Have you ever heard the moaning of someone who feels himself to be the last of his race and who looks at his grandchildren as if they were strangers?

From this humble study of a feeling that we consider to be, potentially, a foundation for universal Jewish consciousness, it becomes clear that our indifference is as dangerous as it is illogical, on the one hand, and on the other hand, that our

26. [Eugène-Melchior, vicomte de Vogüé, *Les morts qui parlent* (Paris: Plon, 1901). Melchior de Vogüé was known for his travel writing as well as his romantic colonial fiction, of which this book is an example.]

27. [National and moral suicide were common metaphors for assimilation during this period; see my introductory essay to this volume.]

activity must be directed in a very determined way. In order for our action to be effective, it seems to me to call first for a uniting of all those who are animated and inflamed by Jewishness [*la chose juive*], and all those who have not yet forgotten their origins. I fear that this Union might be, at least for the moment, slightly chimerical. But this is not a reason not to work on it. And there are many of us who desire it, without abandoning it for our own ideas. We have enough of these vain struggles that benefit no one and only discredit those who support them. Impossible, you say? What of it! Does not Israel know plenty about unity, she who taught it to the world? Impossible, no!

Judaism has already known so many crises, wherein logically, humanly, it should have perished and out of which it has always come stronger, always more robust; Judaism takes power in the infinite vitality of its resources, such that it seems unreasonable to him who studies it and knows it that it should yet again have the energy necessary for its salvation, as confused as the conditions of its renaissance may be.

If we believe the lessons of history, this renaissance will spring from its bosom. And our generation, provided that it becomes conscious of itself, can serve this divine cause. This must be the first goal of our efforts: a renaissance through the union of good wills, Union through renaissance. But it must be remembered that an action is only viable in Judaism provided it moves within the framework established by fifty centuries of thought and history in the mold that is cast by its genius and is its tradition. This here will be the subject for other studies, the value of which the author of these lines will not exaggerate, but whose necessity he affirms.

Some twenty centuries ago, a scholar whose memory the Talmud has conserved, grappling with difficulties of a similar order to ours, and enflamed by an ardent indignation, borrowed from the psalmist this heart-rending cry: "It is time to act for you O Lord, they have broken your law!"[28] In turn, we his grandchildren exclaim: "It is time to act for you, O Judaism, they are tearing you apart!"

---

28. [Psalm 119:126. The psalm is about acting correctly in accordance to the Torah. But in the Talmudic context, the psalm is cited in a discussion about whether or not it is legally permissible to read publicly from separate Torah scrolls (presumably in the case of a missing flap or error). Generally, reading from a Torah with an error would be prohibited; however, the rabbis conclude that since the public reading of the Torah is indispensable (citing the psalm as evidence), when it is time to work or act for the Lord, they break the Law. In other words, sometimes fulfilling one Jewish law requires breaking another.]

12

What Is Jewish Tradition?
Avrom Golomb

A. Golomb, "Vos iz yidishe traditsiye," *Oyfn sheydveg* 2 (August 1939): 37–58.

Many Jews in 1939 were pessimistic about the long-term prospects of European Jewry, but few could have been more disillusioned than the diaspora nationalists who fled Eastern Europe. It had been more than twenty years since the passing of the hope that the Russian Empire might transform itself into a constitutional or revolutionary state where Jews would have equal national and civic rights. The Soviet Union provided virtually no space for an autonomous Jewish life; Jews in the successor states in the Baltics and Poland had lost many of the rights they had enjoyed in the 1920s; and Germany, Austria, Hungary, and Romania all had fascist governments. Furthermore, war looked possible, and few opportunities for emigration remained open. It is in the context of deep disillusionment and pessimism that a small group of émigré diaspora nationalists in Paris founded the journal *Oyfn sheydveg* (At the crossroads) in 1939. The journal's founders and participants had all been influenced by the theories of Dubnov and Zhitlowsky and had been involved in Jewish political and communal life as Yiddishists, diaspora nationalists, and socialists to varying degrees. A variety of views are represented in the two published and one unpublished volumes of *Oyfn sheydveg*, but on a whole the publication represented a decided turn inward, away from ideologies that, one way or another, sought Jewish integration into the European body politic.

Unlike the editors and most of the other contributors to *Oyfn sheydveg*, Avrom Golomb (1888–1982) lived far away from Europe in 1939, in Winnipeg, Canada. Golomb was born in Stravenik, in the Russian Empire, and was given a religious education in Lithuanian yeshivas. He became an active Yiddishist and diaspora nationalist, was particularly well known as a pedagogue, and was among those who moved to Kiev to participate in building the Kultur-Lige. With the end of Jewish autonomy in Ukraine, Golomb moved to Vilna, where, from 1921 to 1932, he headed the new Yiddish Teachers' Seminary under the auspices of the Central Yiddish School Organization (commonly known by its Yiddish acronym TsYSHO). A well-known Yiddish educator, Golomb wrote Yiddish pedagogical materials for teachers, including the only known guide for science teachers in Yiddish, *Praktishe arbet af natur-limed* (Practical work in the natural sciences). After a short stay in

Palestine, Golomb moved to Winnipeg to become director of the I. L. Peretz School (he moved to Mexico City after the war). Despite his being in Winnipeg, *Oyfn sheydveg*'s editors invited Golomb to become a regular contributor to the Paris-based journal.

Golomb was the only contributor to *Oyfn sheydveg* whose concerns had always been more pedagogical than political. The TsYSHO schools, especially in eastern Poland, were a haven for educators from what David Fishman calls the "national-romantic" wing of Yiddishism, those who sought to cast modern Yiddish literature as a continuation of the folk spirit. Golomb and others like him saw themselves as heirs to the religious leaders of old, responsible for endowing subsequent generations with the essence of Judaism and tradition as they perceived them. This was a conception of the Jewish nation deeply influenced by I. L. Peretz: simultaneously secular and rooted in religious texts, preserved in the folkways of the people and yet constantly evolving. In "What Is Jewish Tradition?," Golomb interprets *yidishe traditsiye* as an evolving set of rituals and texts and a way of life preserved in the Jewish people both socially and biologically (shaped as people are by their environment). Golomb credits the Pharisees for ensuring that nothing in Judaism is ever permanently fixed. Jewish texts and all aspects of the Jewish way of life can be reinterpreted by the folk and given new meaning, and leading intellectuals can add new works to the Jewish *oeuvre*. In this model of national life, Jewish tradition is built from the works of Peretz or Sholem Asch as much as from the biblical books of the Prophets (an idea whose origins can be found in Peretz's own work). To Golomb, the fact that such tradition ultimately rests with the people themselves rather than in a single place or text had preserved the Jewish people throughout history, but the modernizer's hostility to and misinterpretation of the tradition undermines the possibility of Judaism's continued existence.

Even in 1939 Golomb remained a diaspora nationalist, albeit a pessimistic one (as evidenced in his article "The Decline of Yiddishism," written for the third, and never published, volume of *Oyfn sheydveg*). The essay "What Is Jewish Tradition?" is composed of "fragments" from a larger work, *Yidn un yidishkayt*, which Golomb never published. Selections from the essay (approximately its first and last thirds) appear below.

There is no "eternal Jewish people" and there never was one. The concept, "eternal Jews," refers only to smaller or larger segments, tribes, branches of Jews—who in every generation create the Jewish folk. And even this creation is constantly losing withered leaves and branches. These fallen parts can sometimes be as large as the main trunk itself or even larger. Often, only small segments of the "numerous Jewish people" manage to emerge from the labyrinth of Jewish joys and troubles. Only these can, together with the poet, recite:

"Endured
and tempest tossed till here . . ."

There are only a few Jews who manage to overcome the obstacles and the destructions. They are the only ones who

"penetrated
slipped through
through every break and breach."[29]

And every such kernel of truly eternal Judaism [*yidishkayt*] is in its time small and barely visible.[30] Only later, through the aberration of history, does the reverse occur. The tiny and once weak currents now appear to us as strong and powerful. The others, which were great in their time, have been totally obliterated by history and now appear to us as foolish and insignificant. So it was with the Prophets and their opponents, the Pharisees and theirs, and so forth. If we examine closely the bearers of Jewish eternity in every generation we see that the secret lies not in heroism, nor in material or spiritual riches, rather in something we call—*tradition*.

This word is often used to describe that which remains stable and unchanged through the generations. In truth, it is actually the opposite. *Conservatism* means to preserve old traditions in their unaltered form—to conserve them. *Tradition* however means to *receive* and *transmit* in a dynamic and constantly evolving manner. It is no coincidence that in ancient Judaism this concept was expressed by two separate terms, *kabbala* and *mesora*—receiving and transmitting. If conservation is a stagnant pool, then tradition is a flowing stream. If conservatism is a spice box handed down as an heirloom through the generations, then tradition is the product carried by the conveyor belt from one workshop to another. And every workshop, each generation, and its environment places its own stamp, its

29. [In the last line (in Yiddish, *durkh ale brukhn un brokhn*), the poet makes a play on words: Both words can mean breach, and *brokhn* can also mean catastrophe.]

30. [Throughout the essay, Golomb seems to use *yidishkayt* in the religious sense, as Judaism, and it has been translated as such.]

own image, onto this received material. Neither the pious Jews of Frankfurt nor the *shtrayml*-wearing Jews of Krakow are the only carriers of tradition.[31] No— these are the carriers of conserved Judaism, which bears absolutely no relation to the living tradition. Traditional Judaism is and must be able to be changed, *to take on different forms.*[32]

Every individual carries in him something forged by his biological and social inheritance which shapes his character, his path in life, and how he responds to his environment. This may be called the "spiritual face," the ego, or the "I"—it is all the same. This is not the cultural treasure, the amassed wisdom and the like—it is man himself, in his environment, his actions and reactions that mat- ter. Taken collectively—this is *tradition.*

If we truly delve into exploring the essence of the concept "tradition," the only true transmitter of Jewish eternity, we have no difficulty seeing that it is, in fact, a synonym for *folkstimlekhkayt.*[33] This is a relatively new concept for us, one which I believe was introduced by Peretz (in *Folkstimlekhe geshikhten*[34]), but whose meaning is not at all new. This term, "folk character," describes that part of us and our conduct which is not dependent on our ideological consciousness, but rather on the collective subconscious—collective habits. Folk character does not lie in learned or studied behaviors but is rather found in our very essence. It is found in temperament, socially acquired habits, tendencies and opinions—all this, which happens by itself, from within itself, and most importantly, the man- ner in which it happens from within itself. Folk character and tradition are in every respect closely related concepts. In Jewish history, there is only one basis for eternity—that is the *tradition of the folk* in life. Every generation and every society in which such a tradition exists lives with Judaism and passes it on to the next generation. Where this tradition is absent there lurks demise, regardless of whether it comes in the form of assimilation or of petrified conservatism. In either case, these two negative forces coexist in Jewish communities bereft of tradition.

And this life-tradition of ours is truly very modest. It does not create any great theories, has no parties, no followers. It conducts its own history, keeps its own accounts, and measures movements and events according to its own

31. [A *shtrayml* is a fur-trimmed hat worn mainly by some groups of Hasidic males after marriage, especially on Sabbath and holidays.]

32. [The italicized phrase is written in Hebrew: *poshet tsura ve-lovesh tsura.*]

33. [Popular or "folk" character.]

34. [This literary genre created by Peretz is often translated as "stories in a folk manner."]

"historiosophy."[35] It does not allow itself to be led by our intelligent and educated "enhancers" of Judaism or preachers of morality. Tradition always follows its own course, separate from our culture makers and history writers. Until now, it has always been right and its judgments correct. The folk tradition is, in truth, the silent, nameless holy tailor from *Kidush ha-Shem* who accompanies the simple Jew to the *beys medresh* or to the court of the nobleman and provides the Jew, in the worst of times, with a drop of faith.[36] He allows the study houses to be burned—because Judaism does not reside in their wood and stone. And he accompanies the Jews to the cemetery to their martyrdom.

So what is this tradition? What are its ways, where do they lead, and who forged these paths?

Where to begin is a problem, because it is truly "without body and without bodily form." It has always avoided being bound to a defined content, to specific forms; it has always stubbornly opposed and fought any effort to confine Judaism and fix it. There can be no embodiment of holiness: "Thou shall not make for yourself an idol," and "to this day, no one knows his grave."[37] No one knows—because we did not want to know. No holy grave sites are needed. The later cult of grave sites in the Land of Israel and elsewhere was a foreign element which never connected organically to Judaism. When the *kabbala* tried, very crudely, to create an embodiment of God, tradition fought against it, and to the degree that the *kabbala* did succeed in insinuating itself into Judaism, its sensuous symbolism led to the rise of the Sabbatian movement.[38] There is no cult of personality in the tradition. There is nothing that must be accepted as fixed or final. This is true even for the Torah itself, which is believed to be fixed and cannot go further. The Talmudists, the early creators of the tradition of Judaism, understood that it is the oral Torah not the canonized written one which

35. [Theological history, or making history do the work of theology.]

36. [Golomb refers here to the novel and play by Sholem Asch (1880–1957), set during the Khmielnitski uprisings of 1648–49.]

37. [According to Deut. 34:6, Moses is buried in an unspecified location in the valley of Moab. Later rabbinic thinkers interpreted this as God's way of preventing idolatry (see Mishna Sotah 14a).]

38. [The Sabbatian movement centered on the kabbalist and messianic pretender Sabetai Tsevi (1626–76), who garnered a vast number of disciples across Europe, North Africa, and the Middle East. His arrest and subsequent conversion to Islam devastated many of his followers.]

separates the Jews from the other nations of the world.[39] Judaism is not a fixed formula. God himself, the old, traditional, Jewish God, is not embodied in something material, he doesn't even have a name, his essence cannot be formulated and must not be formulated. There can be no material objects. Judaism must be a process of constantly becoming—but without holy objects, without fetishes. It is not the Torah that is holy, but the *learning* of Torah: *"The study of Torah above all."*[40] If it becomes absolutely necessary, *"To serve God, learn his Torah."*[41] The Jews have endured not because they have the Torah, but because they study it: *"As long as the voice is the voice of Jacob,"* and as long as *"the children are at the rabbi's house,"* then the *"hands of Esau"* will be powerless.[42] This means that as long as the Torah continues to be studied, the survival of Judaism is not in danger.

Peretz's "sick boy" asks why the synagogue is not as beautiful as the church.[43] But according to Jewish tradition, this is the way it should be; walls can decay, be burnt, destroyed—they are not Judaism. Tradition succeeded *in wresting Judaism from the stony embodiment of the Temple.* These were the first steps of Judaism into eternal life.

Furthermore, the first and most important principle in the Jewish tradition is a negative one:

(A) *"Do not make for yourself an idol."*[44] Do not bind the essence of Judaism to any permanent form. Everything in Judaism must remain fluid, moving, and changeable in the course of history. Everything in Judaism must stay with its people and accompany it into exile.[45] No temples or holy places, no mountains and valleys, no holy prophets, ancestors, graves, no saintly persons or martyrs could go. Not even the holy scrolls of the Torah, the parchment, or the letters of the words could go if they could not produce fresh dewdrops of new Torah. Even God himself, in his greatness, had to pick himself up and go into exile with his

---

39. See *Sefer ha-agada*, chapter 3, 165. [The oral Torah, also known as the oral law and oral tradition, distinguishes rabbinic interpretation from the canonized biblical text, known as the written law.]

40. [The italicized phrase is written in Hebrew: *ve-talmud tora k'neged kulam.*]

41. [The italicized phrase is written in Hebrew: *et la'asot la-adonay—hafru toratekha.*]

42. [The italicized phrases are written in Hebrew: *Kol zman she'ha'kol kol Ya'akov, tinokot shel beit-raban,* and *yadayim yaday Esav.*]

43. ["The Sick Boy" (1914) was a short story by I. L. Peretz.]

44. [The italicized phrase is written in Hebrew: *Lo ta'ase l'kha pesel.*]

45. [In Yiddish, *golus.*]

people.[46] He was compelled to accommodate himself to the continuing changes in being transmitted from generation to generation and place to place. He had to and must continue, from time to time, to alter his character, his appearance, and his nature.

The old "God of Vengeance" sat down with his people at midnight prayers to mourn the exile of the *shkhine*.[47] King David, one of the few Jewish kings not relegated to the waste heap of historical memory, was forced to don his Sabbath caftan and sit down in every Jewish city and town to recite Psalms. King Solomon was forced to do penance for the vanity and transgressions of his majestic reign.[48] The fiery Prophet Elijah, the first ancestor of the Pharisees, readily and willingly transformed himself into the wandering folk creation, Elijah the Wanderer.[49] Had they not done this, they too would have been left behind and forgotten. Because *whatever cannot move forward with the tradition will inevitably be obliterated in popular memory.*

This *ahistorical* approach, maintaining the malleability of the entire cultural inheritance and all the cultural heroes, ready to take on new and different forms and duties, is one of the foundations and secrets of Jewish "eternity." There is no history and no "historic truth." A people's entire past is neither a museum artifact nor is it the preservation of graves—holy, precious, yes, but graves nevertheless. What could the Jewish people, constantly burning yet not consumed, have given these holy, ancient, graves—those old heroes, ancestors, prophets? It would have been even more difficult for the "Eternal Jew" to have to march through lands and history bearing this sacred and historic burden.[50] And so, Jewish tradition never made a monument of the past but rather constantly endeavored

---

46. [See my introductory essay to this volume.]

47. [*Shkhine* (commonly written *shekhinah*) refers to God's presence. For more details, see note 74 in the chapter "Paths That Lead Away from *Yidishkayt*."]

48. [According to the Talmud (Sanhedrin 20b), King Solomon's extravagant lifestyle led to his reign gradually weakening until he ruled over only his staff—this was his penance.]

49. [Due to his simple dress, mysterious origins, and miraculous ascension to heaven in a chariot of fire (see Kings 1 and 2), Elijah took on the persona of "Elijah the Wanderer" in rabbinic and medieval Jewish folklore and became an especially popular figure in Jewish folklore in Eastern Europe (as Eliyohu hanovi). Elijah the Wanderer is a miracle worker and positive figure in Jewish folklore, not to be confused with the "wandering Jew" of Christian folklore.]

50. [Or wandering Jew, also known as Ahasuerus. See note 30 in the chapter "Jews as a Spiritual (Cultural-Historical) Nation among Political Nations."]

to make it a partner in the present. What sustenance could the exquisitely and artistically created looming figure of the biblical Elijah the Prophet offer the Jews, to help them endure generation after generation? But Elijah from the *tradition*, the "blessed memory," the warm and kind-hearted constant companion of the Jew from circumcision to the grave, the "holy tailor," the "old beggar" (from Leivik's "The Golem")—he became the psychological and moral force in their lives.[51] Such an Elijah is after all much more than a "historic hero."[52] The Jew did not have to bear his history, but rather the transformed history continued to carry the Jew forward and help him live, survive fire and sufferings throughout the ages. A chapter of Psalms, without commentary, full of errors, was itself a life force. The entire Tanakh, studied rationally through biblical criticism, is merely a burden which provides the Jew with nothing more than material to forget.

The *maskilim* taught us to disdain any rabbi who, however accomplished in Talmud and the commentaries, could think that Yohanan Ben Zakkai, Rabbi Akiva, and Yehuda Hanasi were contemporaries.[53] Moreover, for that person, they are not real people; they are *Tanaim*, no more than opinions expressed in the Talmud.[54] This is not simply a question of ignorance. If any schoolboy can learn by heart the chronologies of all sorts of kings and rulers, then they could easily teach such a thing in the yeshiva. They could, but they have no *desire*, no *need*. Judaism is absolutely not about preserving the memory of great people or holy grave sites. It is not holy stones or holy bones. Thus, the folk tradition as initiated by the Pharisees eradicated any form of idolatry in Judaism, in order to ensure its continued existence.

This was the first and foundational principle of Pharisaic Judaism: "*Do not make any idols for yourself*" and "*do not look upon a vessel*" even if that "*vessel*" be Moses himself.

The second principle is a positive one:

(B) *Judaism is the constant pouring and reshaping of yesterday's content into the mold of today.* Every "today" weaves its threads into the fabric. Every generation receives

---

51. [The "holy tailor," the *heylike shnayderl*, is another reference to the poor tailor in Sholem Asch's *Kidush ha-Shem*. The "old beggar" (*alter betler*) refers to the Elijah character in the Yiddish poem "The Golem," by Leivik Halpern, also known as H. Leivik (1886–1962).]

52. Very characteristic: why did Jewish tradition select specifically Elijah and Jeremiah to accompany Judaism? Because these two prophets led Judaism in this very direction. They were the first creators of tradition among Jews, of traditional Judaism.

53. [These three rabbinic figures represent the most famous Talmudic personalities.]

54. [The *Tanaim* are rabbinic sages for the first two centuries C.E.]

the oral Torah from the previous, transforms it into written law, continues to build further on this, and so on and so forth. This continual "*transformation of a melody*"[55] of the written law into the oral, and back into the written—this is the way of traditional Judaism. And the oral Torah must, in each case remain oral, "*for it is forbidden to express in writing*," meaning it may not be made fixed.[56] The following legend fills one with true awe for the healthy approach of traditional Judaism's creators: "Master of the Universe, says Moses, give them the Mishna in writing," and he receives the following response: "What then will distinguish the Jews from the other nations of the earth?" This is to say that had the oral law been a priori permanently fixed, there would be no Judaism. When may an oral law be written down? When there is a new one beginning to emerge in the life of the folk. This is how the Men of the Great Assembly canonized the Torah,[57] the same with the Mishna, then the Talmud and so on and on. An old study house may be torn down only when a new one already exists. The Torah is holy, not by itself alone, but with all the "*innovations*" and with the "*overlapping layers*" that grew around it, as "any innovation discovered by a faithful student was already given to Moses at Sinai."[58]

The accepted belief that the oral law grew out of the written law is false, absolutely false. Oral law is created in each generation from within life itself, but it must be bound to the written law, as it is written "*if not from the Torah, from where?*"[59] How does one conclude this from the Torah? It is found in "*minhag mevatel halakha*," "*custom supersedes the Law*," though the new must be able to connect with the old.[60] If not, it means that there is something foreign, inorganic, and harmful in the new; it becomes unacceptable. The source of the Torah is always life itself: the marketplace, the home, celebrating together, the foods, traditions, joy and sorrow, conduct and lifestyle. This is, so to speak, the "living Torah,"

55. [In Yiddish, "*gilgl fun a nign*," is the title of a famous short story by I. L. Peretz.]

56. [The italicized phrase is written in Hebrew: *i ata rashay le'omram bikhtav.*]

57. [Much has been attributed to the so-called Men of the Great Assembly (also known as the Great Synagogue), including canonization, though little is known about it historically. Tradition most commonly associates the Great Assembly with the events described in Nehemiah 8–10.]

58. [The italicized phrases are written in Hebrew: *Khidushay tora; tilay tilim;* and *Kol ma she'talmid vatik atid le-Khadesh netana le-Moshe mi-sinay.* For the last, Golomb gave the Yiddish translation in a note (not included here).]

59. [The italicized phrase is written in Hebrew: *min ha-Tora minayin.*]

60. [Golomb provides both the original Hebrew and his translation into Yiddish, translated here into English.]

the oral Torah. The written Torah comes last. The shapers and molders of tradition Judaism were very focused on maintaining the specific character of the "living Torah." There was a special term created for this, "*halakha*" (initially also "*Mistorin*"[61]), from the word "*halakh*," in the sense of "*hilkhot ha-khayim*," meaning the way of life, customs, or lifestyle as we refer to it today. With time, as these life norms and forms became fixed, they became petrified as laws and rules. As the oral law became written law, "*halakha*" also lost its original meaning and instead came to mean "*khok*," a rule or law. But "*halakha*" grew out of our way of life, and the people's Judaism [*folkstimlekher yidishkayt*] was its first meaning. And, "With each *halakha* where there is a doubt and the court does not know what to do then go to the people—and do that." Or, "Leave it to them, Israel, for if they are themselves not prophets, they are the children of prophets."[62]

This very *halakha*, this regard for the folkways as the source of the Torah, culture, and eternal survival—this is the achievement of the Pharisees. They set Judaism on the double rails of "*halakha*" and "*agada*" (way of life and literature), and only onto those rails. These two foundations have sustained Judaism more than kingdoms, dynasties, political heroes, holy books and so on. *Halakha* deserves the primary credit. From it grew *agada*, from its earliest beginnings to our very own "Tevye the Dairyman."[63] And here lies also the meaning of the Talmudic expression: "*Since the destruction of the Temple God's world is restricted by the four walls of* halakha."[64] Bialik was wrong to call this world shrunken.[65] Because

61. [Unrevealed.]

62. [The italicized phrases are written in Hebrew: *Kol halakha she'hi rofefet be-bet din ve-en ata yodeya ma tiva, tse u're heikh ha-tsibur noheg—u'nehag*, and *Hanakh lahem le-Yisrael, im ein nevi'im hem, b'ne nevi'im hem*. Golomb provides the Yiddish translation in a note (not included here).]

63. [Though difficult to define, and sometimes translated as legends, *agada* most commonly refers to the nonlegalistic texts in the classic rabbinic canon. These texts tend to be more literary than the legal discussions and include a strong folkloric element. The project of Hayim Nahman Bialik (1873–1934) and Yehoshua Hana Ravnitski (1859–1944) to compile the folklore in the Talmud in a multivolume collection, called *Sefer ha-agada* (referred to above by Golomb), was influential in focusing on the Talmud as literature. Golomb's broad definition of *agada* as "literature" ties the rabbinic texts to modern Jewish literature like Sholem Aleichem's nineteenth-century Yiddish stories featuring the character Tevye.]

64. [The italicized phrase is written in Hebrew: *me-yom shekharav bet ha-mikdash en lo le-hakadosh barukh hu ela daled amot shel halakha*. Golomb provides the Yiddish translation in a note (not included here).]

65. *Dvarim she'be'al-pe*, chapter 1, 130.

that would mean that the Jewish God, Judaism, is found in stone, and not in the written law.

This *halakha*—in its constant evolving *in statu nascendi*—has kept Judaism alive, and in the end that is the achievement of the Pharisaic Torah. It is no wonder that all our enemies since then hold pre-Pharisaic Judaism in esteem, and hate us, the living Jews. They are correct: from the Pharisees we get not "today's Jew," just the "eternal Jew," and what they know this became—a pity. Those who hate us are also joined by a good number of Jewish antisemites (found even among the nationalists and some cultural activists), who can, to this very day, not forgive the Pharisees for their work. They did, after all, and without any hesitation, ruthlessly eliminate from the literature of their day everything that did not fit into their interpretation of Judaism. "*Everyone who brings home more than the twenty-four books brings confusion into his home.*"[66] Everything must adapt itself to the folk tradition—this was the teaching of the Pharisees. They were the ones who established the normal cycle of culture upon which the cultural life of every community is built. The soil and foundation of cultural life are the folkways, the conscious and unconscious life of the masses and all that is personal in that life—customs, morals, traditions,—in one word, *halakha*.

However, if the soil is not worked, not cultivated—it grows wild. It needs to be worked and weeded of the foreign and wild grasses that are constantly ready to overtake it. Optimal conditions for healthy growth must constantly be sought. These are the social obligations of cultural life. The task of the cultural and artistic elements of society is to cultivate and raise the cultural fruits from out of the raw earth, the *cultural values*—art, literature, science, law. The second stage of cultural progress is to replant the cultural soil with carefully chosen seeds, cleansed, and freed of everything that is foreign, inferior. This is the task of the organs that spread culture—publishing houses, schools, libraries, theaters, and so forth.

And thus closes the cycle of cultural life, from one custom into another. The schematic for this natural circle is as follows: folkways, arts and sciences, folk educational institutions, folkways. If the circle is internally intact and all the parts are organically whole—then the future of the people is assured. Nothing can threaten it. That is why the creators of traditional Judaism expended so much energy in shaping and establishing a way of life and in setting the *halakha*—on

66. [The italicized phrase is written in Hebrew: *Kol ha-makhnis le-tokh beto yoter mi-kaf daled sfarim- mehuma hu makhnis le-veto.* Golomb provides the Yiddish translation in a note (not included here).]

the "*tinokot shel bet raban*,"[67] children and learning, these, the most important elements of the cultural cycle.

The movements, trends, and theories that failed in the course of Jewish history did so because they sought to interrupt the natural cycle of cultural life. They tried to introduce foreign cultural elements into the life of the folk. And what was foreign, remained foreign. They all, without exception, led to degeneration, death, and assimilation. The eternal tragedy over which the Prophet continues to mourn, "*For he hoped it would yield grapes, instead it yielded wild grapes*" (Isaiah, chapter 5).[68] They all began with the best of intentions, thinking they were planting a vineyard, but instead ended up with wild grapes. *Every turn from tradition leads to wild growth*. [...]

Other nations had two centers the individual needed to serve. One was religious, the church. In this realm it was not only faith, religious practice, and ritual that mattered, there was great importance also attached to the sociopolitical aspect —the power of organized religion over the individual. Then there was the question of the secular power—the state, the ruler, the king, etc. The competition between these two loci of power compelled the individual to divide his life in two. "Render unto Caesar what is Caesar's and to God what is God's."[69] Two different views of society coexisted, for better or for worse. For the individual, life was thus divided into living for one's home, for God (really, for the Church), and for the king.

For Jews, the war between religion and state, between religious and secular power, ended long, long ago. There is no longer a secular power. Only one center has existed for thousands of years, religion. It therefore colored all aspects of life and it would be difficult to find anything in traditional Jewish life free of religious sanction. This is not because Jews are a nation of religious servants, but because as the only center, religion naturally cloaked everyone and everything in its mantle. And another thing: the Jewish religion was not taken from someone else. It grew with the folk through the generations. Such was not the case with other nations who, despite having fully developed rich cultures of their own, took on a new belief. The old cultures rooted in the nation submitted to

67. [Literally, "children of the rabbi's house."]
68. [The italicized phrase is written in Hebrew: *Va'yikav la'asot anavim, va'ya'as be-ushim*.]
69. [Matthew 22:21. See also note 16 in the chapter "The Future of Judaism."]

the new and foreign one. We are not interested in how these new arrangements succeeded; the pairing of the principle "might makes right" with that of "might from right" or how the beliefs of the Nazarenes of the Galilee resonated with the Nordic Vikings. What is of the essence for us is to underscore that the European nations have two sociopsychological centers of culture: the indigenous and "barbaric" one, and the acquired one. The Jewish religion, on the other hand, grew organically with the people and from the people. Everything that the folk created over the generations became sanctified. Religion did not appear and take over the life of the nation, just the opposite. The life of the nation proclaimed itself to be for religion and thus sanctified everything it had created throughout the generations. The tradition of life became the religion.

Jewish religion had the authority of a generations-long tradition to sublimate instincts, customs, and lifestyles. For the rest of the world their indigenous culture, literature, and art were viewed as treasures worth preserving and guarding so as to be passed on to future generations. But these had no real meaning for the essence of life. Like a piece of jewelry, they can certainly enhance and beautify life, but cannot shape it. Culture and life come from separate wellsprings and each follows its own logic and course. Jews who lived like the other nations disappeared in ancient times. Those who remained within Judaism were the ones who carried forward the tradition of the Prophets, but there were no treasuries, idols, or any objects to guard. The only thing worth keeping was the Torah—in order to learn how to live. If not, there is no need for it. Torah and life must exist together; without life, the Torah is meaningless. "Whoever knows the Torah and doesn't live according to it, it is as if he has no God at all." That is why the Torah cannot remain pristine, bejeweled and under lock and key like a treasure in heavily guarded cellars of life. Torah must constantly be kneaded, permitted to rise, and then reshaped to suit life. It must be kneaded into life. If they are separated—there is no Judaism. Jeroboam Ben-Navot tried this in reforming the old Jewish "national" cult; the Sadducees tried in their time, as did the Karaites later[70]; and the *maskilim* in our day tend towards this. The result was always the same—conversion and ruin. [...]

70. [According to the biblical narrative and later rabbinic exegesis, Jeroboam led the northern Israelite kingdom to idolatry. The Sadducees were a sect in the Second Temple period who rejected the teachings of the Pharisees. Similarly, the Karaite movement emerged as a response against rabbinic authorities and rejected postbiblical law.]

Only in this way did the Pharisees succeed in shaping a Judaism that has endured and through which the Jewish people endured (only those parts of it which were faithful to the tradition). Only in this way could they shape this specific people with its specific identity and self-awareness. The "normal" nations continue to have their material nationalism; soundly built, tangible, embodied in land, country, graves, architecture, and literature. This very nationalism, piled high to the stratosphere with all of these elements, stands now at the ready to destroy the world in a flood of blood and fire . . .

If you speak to one of our modern, worldly Jews—whether they be national or nationalist—utter the words "tradition," "*halakha*," and he will immediately be struck by fear and stare at you in wonderment or with pity. He immediately sees for himself a rabbi in a *shtrayml* and all the negative associations of the Middle Ages. The modern Jew is frightened: *"The Philistines are upon you, Israel!"*[71] "This one is a reactionary. His Judaism is cloaked in clerical garb" . . . From everything I have said in this "*mamer*"[72] it should by now be clear that to say this is blatantly false! One must understand the difference between tradition and conservatism. If one doesn't understand, it is because one chooses not to. The leaders themselves, the Jewish nationalists, the cultural activists, the builders of the new forms of Jewish identity and consciousness, are not organic Jews. They are lost sheep, forced into their Jewish identity. Their frightened response has nothing to do with the essence of Jewish tradition and its path through eternal generations.

71. [The italicized phrase is written in Hebrew: *Plishtim alekha, Yisrael!*]
72. [Usually used in reference to a religious essay or commentary.]

13

Is America Exile or Home? We Must Begin to Build for Permanence
Israel Knox

Israel Knox, "Is America Exile or Home? We Must Begin to Build for Permanence," *Commentary*, November 1946, 401–8.

Although Israel Knox (1904 or 1907–1986) lectured widely in the United States on Jewish communal issues and published prolifically on Jewish issues in the important Jewish periodicals of his day, he is not well known today, as either a Jewish communal or intellectual figure. Knox was born in Russia (the precise location is unknown) and came to the United States as a boy, in 1912. After earning a doctorate in philosophy from Columbia University in 1936, Knox directed the English-speaking division of the Workmen's Circle in New York for ten years (1937–47). After that he taught philosophy, first at Ohio University and then at New York University, where he taught from 1951 until his retirement in the late 1970s.

In November 1946, Knox's article "Is America Exile or Home?" set off a lively, yearlong debate in the fledgling *Commentary* magazine about the nature of the Jewish community and Jewish nationalism in the United States. *Commentary* was founded in 1945, a moment when American Jewry—and, for that matter the world—was, in Knox's words, "at the crossroads." The destruction of European Jewry made even more crucial questions, already debated for many years, about America's place in shaping the Jewish future. In the tradition of the *Menorah Journal*, *Commentary* sought to provide a venue for Jewish scholars, intellectuals, and public figures to debate Jewish politics and culture in the United States. In his controversial article, Knox presses American Jews to view the current moment through a Dubnovian lens: if Jewish history follows a pattern of shifting hegemonic centers, then the United States is surely poised to conclusively inherit Europe's mantle. But American Jewry's leadership, according to Knox, had not yet gained the necessary self-confidence to create the institutional framework for the next phase of Jewish civilization, instead deferring to the remnant leadership of the Jewish community in Europe and focusing on the political objectives of Zionism. It is the latter factor that troubles Knox most because that focus, he believes, is out of sync with how American Jews as a whole view the Zionist project. If American Jewish institutions do not focus their educational efforts on building a cultural and permanent foundation for Jewish life in the United States, then being Jewish will become decreasingly meaningful to American Jews.

Responses to Knox's essay largely discussed where and how to focus American Jewish energy during the Jewish cultural revival. Some argued for the promotion of Jewish high culture; others focused on accepting English as the new Jewish language; and still others argued against an institutional approach to cultural revival. Some also dismissed the idea of building Jewish culture in America at all, arguing instead that Jews should embrace American culture and its spirit of universalism. Interestingly, only Knox's arguments about how to "build for permanence"—not his premise that America was home, rather than exile—provoked controversy. Knox's claim that Zionism mistakenly equates peoplehood and statehood and his insistence that "the United States is neither Galut nor *hutz la-aretz*" met with no response or challenge from the American Jewish figures who wrote in *Commentary*. Instead, in the forums that followed on topics such as "Jewish Culture for America?" and "Jewish Culture in This Time and Place," the contributors presumed the leading role of the American community in what remained of world Jewry in 1946 and 1947.

Because of the war and the extermination camps, America's Jewish community has today become the largest and strongest in the world. This statement has been dinned into the ears of American Jews from the pulpit, press, and platform, and above all by the spokesmen of fund-raising campaigns. Though in the process of repetition it has become almost a cliché, it still remains a fact. It is the most significant thing that has happened to American Jews, changing their outlook and their attitude toward the remaining Jews overseas as well as towards themselves. Traveling around the country and talking to Jews of various shades of opinion and of various degrees of Jewishness, one becomes inescapably aware of this.

Last year's Roper poll on Zionism among American Jews corroborates this, and no less in its negative than its affirmative answers. The 10 percent who expressed opposition to Zionism took pains to explain that their opposition implied no lack of interest in the welfare of non-American Jews. And one found, in discussion with young and old, men and women, "nationalist" and "anti-nationalists," over the length and breadth of the United States, that the 80 percent approving Zionism were usually not thinking of Zionism at all. They confusedly identified a Jewish state, which is a political concept, with a homeland-refuge, which is a social-cultural, and in many cases a quasi-philanthropic, concept. Their pro-Palestinism was primarily an expression of a heightened sense of responsibility, as members of the largest community in the world, for the Jews left in devastated Europe.

It is regrettable that American Jewry's new status and new self-consciousness have been left unexplored and unexamined, are indeed mentioned only when hearts are to be touched and money is to be gathered. For the fact carries profound implications. It was Dubnow who pointed out that the history of the Jews, while a dispersed global history, is essentially a history of centers—Palestine, Babylonia, Spain, France, and Western Germany, Poland, Russia.[73] Always, amid the multiplicity of their environments, the Jews possessed one or more centers of gravity, thus rendering them cohesive, however scattered. Through this pattern, they were enabled to lift themselves above the two lower levels of nationhood, racial and territorial, to the third level, the cultural or spiritual. If Dubnow is right, the American Jewish community is now on the threshold of history. It is confronted by the fateful opportunity to shape here, in an atmosphere of tolerance and freedom, the good Jewish life on the highest level.

Now this opportunity demands more than stereotypes and an eagerness to gather funds, vital as this last may be. It requires an understanding of the American Jew in terms of the American scene, as well as in relation to Jews abroad, an analysis of his institutional and communal experience as a Jew, and a redefinition of values, an appraisal of the content of Jewishness. Unfortunately, there is little evidence of any deep changes in organized Jewish life in America; all is as it was. By and large, thinking and leadership move down the same time-honored and time-worn paths. Of course, there can be no quarrel as to the urgent need and the imperative duty to bind up the wounds of Jews in Europe, to help them find places of safety or to reconstruct their lives in their pre-war homes, and to continue to aid toward the upbuilding of Palestine. But one can quarrel with American Jewry for its passive acceptance of a purely secondary role. For all its power and its promise, our community seems still content to remain an auxiliary and submissive means to Jewish ends elsewhere, conceived of as somehow more real and more worthy. Is America, after all, just another center, an inferior one at that, without too bright a future, or is its destiny— as all facts seem clearly to indicate—that of *the* center for our day and our generation?

73. [See the editorial introduction to Simon Dubnov (spelled Dubnow by Knox) and his essay "Jews as a Spiritual (Cultural-Historical) Nation among Political Nations."]

In the eyes of ardent Zionists, the survival of the Jews as a people and a culture is impossible without Jewish statehood. Europe must be emptied of its remaining Jews. In America, Jews may linger on, but without real hope. Shlomo Katz's article in the April issue of *Commentary*, "No Hope Except Exodus," is not exceptional; it is representative.[74]

Jacob Lestchinsky has dealt with this theme repeatedly in *Der Yiddisher Kemfer*, organ of the Labor Zionists, and has given it its most extreme formulation in his book *Vohin Gehen Mir?* (Where Are We Going?"—reviewed in the November issue of *Commentary*).[75] In this book he does not hesitate to predict, in Cassandra-like accents, the darkest future for American Jewry.

Not many weeks ago, this writer heard with amazement a noted Hebrew poet declare that the hundred thousand Jews in the camps in Germany should be sent at once to Palestine, not only because they must have a chance to live like normal human beings, but because in Palestine they would become the repositories of *our* future too. The irony is that this statement was made in the auditorium of one of the most prosperous synagogues in America, under the chairmanship of a Jewish leader, a very prominent rabbi, whose indorsement [sic] is sought even in presidential elections.[76] It was warmly applauded by men and women who almost without exception will stay in America, as will their children. They were conceding that they should not—hence need not—search their own souls, clarify Jewish experience in America, and turn their minds to the task of making the Jewish community here not only substantial but creative.

It is therefore not surprising that the traveler through America meets innumerable Jews, particularly in smaller cities, whose burning Zionist nationalism

74. [On the unfeasibility of the diaspora and the inevitability of a Jewish return to Palestine, Shlomo Katz writes: "The sole long-range solution remains territorial concentration—in a word, Zionism . . . Zionism does not presuppose an exodus from a region where one is not called for. It only predicates, on the basis of two thousand years' experience, that sooner or later any Jewish community will feel this need" ("No Hope Except Exodus," *Commentary*, April 1946,17).]

75. [Due to his experiences in Europe in the 1930s, Lestchinsky (spelled here Lestchinsky) became very pessimistic about the Jewish future in the diaspora. Later, he was one of the first people to attempt a reckoning of the Holocaust's demographic impact on world Jewry.]

76. [The rabbi referred to here is probably Stephen S. Wise, a Reform rabbi and Zionist leader. The poet may be the political activist and Israeli poet Natan Alterman or any number of lesser-known Zionist Hebrew-language poets who were prominent in this period.]

goes hand in hand with a cold indifference to Jewish education, to the cultural enrichment of America's own Jewish community.

Of course, some Zionists do attempt to integrate their nationalism with a serious interest in the Jewish community in America—not only as auxiliary to the upbuilding of the Palestine Commonwealth, but as important for its own present and future. But here, too, the effort bears curious fruits. In the final balance, the integration turns out to be a frail affair, with the interest of the American Jewish community receding into the background.

It is the professed belief in an American integration that supposedly marks the margin of difference between the American Jewish Congress and the American Zionist Organization.[77] Thus this year's pre-convention issue of *Congress Weekly* contains, in its leading editorial, the following statements among other similar ones—"Out of its deliberations [those of the Congress][78] should come leadership and guidance for a Jewish way of life in the American community"; and again, "we cannot make our life as totally Jewish as Palestine's Jews do, we must strive to make it as thoroughly Jewish within the framework of the American democracy as will express our historic awareness and will to survive."

In the same issue, however, there is an article, "Congress Ideology Redefined," in which America is graciously placed in an intermediary class between Land of Israel and Exile. The writer, Max Nussbaum, speaks of America as *hutz la-aretz*— "outside the land." But even at that, the writer feels he may be doing an injustice to Palestine, and hastens to add apologetically, "Palestine will always reign supreme in Jewish thought, and even the reintroduction of *hutz la-aretz* will not detract from its paramount importance."

Little wonder that the initial paragraph in the editorial has this to offer by way of "leadership and guidance": "The violent anti-Semitism rampant in defeated Germany and in the so-called new European democracies will have repercussions on Jewish life in America, for germs of Nazism are being carried to these shores by American soldiers returning from Germany"! This accords with the ultra-nationalist tendency to disparage the American Jewish community, to cast shadows on its long-range security, even when summoning it to service and to

---

77. [The American Jewish Congress was founded in 1918, primarily by East European Jews, to provide an organizational alternative to the American Jewish Committee's dominance of Jewish communal and diplomatic affairs. The American Jewish Congress was consistently pro-Zionist and evolved into a membership-based Jewish advocacy organization.]

78. [The square brackets in the text here are Knox's.]

action. To achieve this, it habitually exaggerates, as here, some isolated phase of the multi-form relations between Jews and the rest of the people in America. (Incidentally, this distortion also colors a good deal of our anti-defamation activity.)

This "integration" loses much of its cogency in yet another manner. There is a disposition, even among some of the sincerest adherents of Jewish cultural creativity, to render the task easier by the simple device of some kind of purge. Thus, Menachem Boraisha,[79] an outstanding Yiddish poet, tells us in *Congress Weekly* (April 12) that "if the truth is to be recognized without fear or reservation, it must be realized that it is foolhardy to build a Jewish future on the strength of all five million American Jews," and that "a million men and women ready to bear the burdens and privileges of full Judaism will be greater safeguards for Jewish continuity than five million Jews to whom their future is either a curse or an accident."

There is, of course, an element of truth in the indictment. President Louis Finkelstein of the Jewish Theological Seminary has been calling attention to the failures of Jewish education, to the threat of extensive intermarriage, and to the disregard of Jewishness as a heritage and as a set of contemporary values among many of our Jewish youth.[80] There is also historical evidence to confirm the notion that a self-conscious and devoted core may save Israel as a people today just as it has done in preceding centuries. But Mr. Boraisha's words are nevertheless a counsel of despair and the bitter fruit of a "failure of nerve," of a refusal to deal soberly and constructively with Jewish realities in America. And recent history should make us cautious about all schemes to build national futures on self-appointed "élites."

Mr. Boraisha may be right in saying that "the 25 percent who give their children a Jewish education are the Jews who count." But one is equally right in adding that education cannot be cut off from the main stream of social experience, that it cannot be an "island by itself." His concept would mean isolating the Jewish child twice—once, from American society as a whole; and again, from the majority of American Jews. The healthier plan would be to develop the kind of program that would enable 80 or 90 percent of American Jews to give

79. [Menachem Boraisha (1888–1949) was a well-known Yiddish poet and essayist who wrote for a number of Yiddish newspapers and journals in the United States.]

80. [Louis Finkelstein (1895–1991), in addition to being a prominent scholar, was one of the most influential Jewish religious and communal leaders of the mid-twentieth century.]

their children a Jewish education. That would provide a rounded rather than a truncated expression of cultural variety within the framework of American democracy.

This is a hard goal to reach. But nothing less will do. Now that we have lost one-third of our people and the European citadels of Jewish culture, it is with a sick heart that one reads of a "purge" of American Jews that would cast off four million, no less.

It is seldom realized to what extent the Jewish education movement in the United States—both in ideology and practice—proceeds under the twin signs of defeatism about America and the priority of Palestine. But for evidence one need only look at the official literature of the Jewish education movement. Need one wonder at its limited appeal, the weakness of its creative impulse in American terms? (But Jewish education requires an article in itself).

Even if, in view of the magnitude of the emergency, concentration of our community's efforts upon Europe and Palestine was completely understandable, it is not so easy to condone the almost total disregard in these "years of destiny" of the legitimate diversity of Jewish life in America, and the almost purely exploitative attitude of Jewish organizations to the American Jewish community.

Their interest in the community has been confined to using it for their own ends. And each organization has presumed to speak, without modesty and without reservation, for all American Jews, as well as in the hallowed name of those millions who perished in Europe.

At one of the Washington sessions of the Anglo-American Commission of Inquiry on Palestine, a prominent Jewish figure interrupted a speaker in fiery protest, insisting that he did so on behalf of five million American Jews. The sheer comedy of his pretension was revealed in the same session by the variety of outlooks that were presented, in keeping with the diverse character—social and political—of the Jewish community in America.

"Unity" was the catchword of Jewish organizations. There were times, as in the months preceding the sessions of the American Jewish Conference, when it was impossible—almost heretical—to discuss anything else.

The "sound and fury" of the national Jewish organizations resound more violently in the closer confines of the smaller localities. But the amazing thing about it, whether in New York or in the provinces, is that the agitation is limited to the small minority of the "organized" Jews. It does not reach—it is not interested in—the "plain" Jews, the unorganized and unaffiliated, who happen to be in the vast majority, and whose interest in Jewish political programs is at best nominal, and in most cases nil. Somewhat less than 50 percent of this vast majority can even claim membership in synagogues. Behind the slogan of unity, there is, of course, a real need. It is reasonable that Jews—as they look at the problems of Central and Eastern Europe, of Palestine, and of their own community in America—should want to achieve a measure of coherence, the elimination of organizational duplication and conflict and the wise conservation of energy and imagination and idealism for the things that must be done both here and abroad.

But, as one observes the mechanism of Jewish "unity" in America, it becomes clear that the organizations most loudly clamoring for it are more interested in a show of total unity for their own programs than in the substance of working agreements for aims on which there is genuine accord. Some of the constituent members of the American Jewish Conference, which was presumably the vehicle of "unity," bear names that are far more ostentatious and deceptive than that of the Conference itself.[81] This is no harmless "semantic" misdemeanor, but a serious source of public confusion. To those interested in "unity" as a political tool, the creation of the American Jewish Conference represented a triumph. But today, even its most enthusiastic supporters would be constrained to confess that in the end it proved a hollow victory. Complete political or ideological unity of American Jews is impossible—and undesirable. It would involve uniformity of spiritual and political attitude and belief—it would exclude variety and diversity. Such unity is achievable, in the sense that the American Jewish Conference sought it, only under totalitarianism, which is in turn possible only through a police state. No free democratic society can achieve such unity without losing its freedom and its democracy. It means enforcing the violent ascendancy of one set of dogmas—and the eradication of all dissent. It means the reduction of cultural content to the lowest common denominator and the bartering away of principles for expedience.

The American Jewish Conference was doomed to failure because its sponsors selected one particular program—that of political Zionism—as the program

81. [The American Jewish Conference was an organization composed of delegates from various other national Jewish organizations. Its main purpose was to determine the American Jewish community's role in representing Jewish demands and helping to further the Zionist cause. The conference first met in 1943 with participants ranging from moderate to right-leaning or "maximalist" Zionist organizations. Jewish leaders would later bemoan the difficulty in coming to a consensus on an American Jewish agenda.]

of the Conference, and made dissent from it a treasonable heresy. Thus, from the beginning, the Conference undermined its ostensible purpose, which was to bring every possible recognized Jewish group and organization, and even "unaffiliated" Jews, into a single representative body. However, had it started out with a recognition of the difference and variety in American Jewish life and thought, it could have easily achieved, not a regimented unity, but a functional unity, a unity of action on specific undertakings and definite aims agreed upon. One feels confident that such agreement for unified action could have been found for a fight against the White Paper,[82] for the liberalizing of American immigration laws, for relief and "rehabilitation," and for broader Jewish education. But the Conference chose to espouse the maximum program of Zionism, to devote itself to the ecstatic consideration of abstract political matters, and to brush aside, quite heedlessly, the hard and immediate realities of Jewish experience. As a result, it organized only those it had already organized, and its unity included in the end only those who were from the start its loyal rank-and-file.

Is it far-fetched to see the source of this contemptuous effort to manipulate American Jewry in the almost pathological insistence by the "nationalist" organizations upon a sort of "self-effacement" for the American Jewish community, in their ardent desire to tie the future of our people to the chariot wheels of Palestine and Palestine only, to deprecate the rest of the world, including America, as Galut, or with kinder condescension as *hutz la-aretz*, a kind of limbo?

Yet America's Jewish community remains the largest and the most fortunate in the world. But it can succor and safeguard less fortunate Jewish communities, in the long view, only if it maintains its own self-respect. It must look upon itself too—in Ahad Ha'am's classic description of the new Palestine—as a "spiritual center," as a home of Jewish living and learning and doing.[83]

The Jerusalems of Lithuania and Poland and other European lands lie in ruins for the present—although even there Jewish life may yet be restored. The

82. [The White Papers were a series of British governmental policy statements issued between 1922 and 1939 to guide the country's policies in Mandatory Palestine. Many Jews considered the White Papers' restrictions on Jewish immigration to be a betrayal of the British promise in the 1917 Balfour Declaration for "a national home for the Jewish people."]

83. [Ahad Ha'am (Asher Zvi Hirsch Ginsberg, 1856–1927) argued that Zionism's purpose must be spiritual—to build in Israel a spiritual and cultural center for world Jewry—rather than material.]

communities in South America and Africa are relatively small. There are more than two million Jews in the Soviet Union, but there is a curtain between them and us; to be sure Yiddish is an official language, yet there is not a single Yiddish daily newspaper in the whole of Russia, and not a single Russian periodical in any language, devoted to Jewish affairs. In a sense, this may not be strange at all, since cultural autonomy in the Soviet Union is merely linguistic, according to the formula—"socialist in content and nationalist in form." As to Biro-Bidjan, proclaimed as an autonomous Jewish region, we have no information—and it is pathetic to watch the American sponsors of Biro-Bidjan try to establish by mere conjecture the number of Jews in Biro-Bidjan.[84]

America, the Soviet Union, and Palestine today contain the largest Jewish communities, and Palestine is unquestionably a shining star in our sky. It has developed rapidly and has provided a home against all odds for hundreds of thousands of Jews in the recent dark years. And especially gratifying to the humanist, Jew and non-Jew alike, is the fact that it has produced in the *kvutzot* and *moshavim*[85] not only a new type of Jew, but a new type of human being—one who can live the cooperative and the good life without regimentation, without sacrificing his individuality.

But the passion of Zionism remains political, and Zionism continues to cling to an antiquated notion that equates peoplehood with statehood. And so it regards Palestine not only as one bright star in our sky but as the sky itself, with all else shadow.

But the United States is neither Galut nor *hutz la-aretz*. It is the home of five million Jews. And it is, in the final consideration, our freest home. It is folly, and almost a kind of blackmail, to hold over us the threat of the imminent destruction of that freedom. Granted, there are forces at work in America for the curtailment of that freedom; but there are forces at work for its expansion, too. And we ourselves can help tip the scale, we too are involved in the "destiny" of America. Moreover, the world is small and hatred travels fast. Should America's

84. [Birobidzhan (or Biro-Bidjan), a region in the Soviet far east, was dedicated a "Jewish homeland" in 1928 and officially named the Jewish Autonomous Region in 1934. Many American Jewish socialists took to the cause and raised money for agricultural settlement and cultural work in Birobidzhan. The Soviet government, however, quickly lost enthusiasm for the project, purging many of its leaders between 1936 and 1939. In the period immediately following World War II, when Knox writes, Birobidzhan was experiencing a short-lived revival.]

85. [Agricultural settlements.]

democracy wither away, what Jews anywhere could live in safety and security, even in Palestine?

There is hope, although no guarantee, in the historic fact that not a single country that has gone through the period of expanding political democracy, beginning with the English, French, and American revolutions, has succumbed to totalitarianism. By the same token, all the countries that embraced totalitarianism are, without exception, countries that had little, if any, democratic tradition, and where the transition from feudalism to capitalism was sharp and sudden, or belated and incomplete.

America in crisis is an America that must link together intelligent social control and technological advances within the framework of its democratic heritage. That way lies hope for America and for the Jews in America. The distinctive trait of the Jewish ethos has always been its universalism and the effort to translate its ethos into the just action. By committing ourselves intimately to the democratic destiny of America, by aligning ourselves with the forces for its preservation and its deepening, we not only build firm foundations for our own survival—we act out the spirit and the implication of the Jewish ethos.

If America's Jewish community is to come of age, it must acknowledge itself, in Dubnow's terms, as a Jewish center. But there are two preconditions. First, Jewish organizations must not, in any circumstances, demote America to a lowered status; they must not regard our own community as inferior in Jewish worth, as incapable of cultural creativity. Second, "American-minded" Jewish organizations, although theoretically opposed to this view, must not unwittingly sustain it by pursuing a negative and "defensive" policy, directed largely against anti-Semitism, rather than a positive and fruitful policy for a "tolerant and abundant" America.

Happily, there are manifest the beginnings of an earnest, self-sustaining Jewish life in America. As one observes not only New York, but numerous smaller localities, one carries away the impression of a growing and self-respecting "feeling for Jewishness" among American Jews. Often, it is vague and inarticulate, expressing itself in almost trivial ways. It is amusing but also touching to hear "assimilated" young parents with little Jewish knowledge say that they have named their child Ilane rather than Elaine because of reverence for their grandfather who was called Isaac. One is taken aback when "secular-minded" young parents ask whether they would be committing a grave "sin" if they were to affiliate themselves, for the sake of their children, with a synagogue or temple.

One recalls a modern young mother lighting Sabbath candles long after the sun had set (when it is no longer permissible to do so) simply because of her "feeling for Jewishness." One hears another young mother planning to have her child taught Yiddish so that her child may speak the language of the common folk, because "it holds the tears and laughter, alas, mostly the tears, of the millions who died *al kiddush hashem* in Europe."[86]

Of course, one sees also the drabness, the vulgarity, and above all, the indifference, rampant everywhere. But the drabness reflects, in part, the cultural poverty of the general environment; the vulgarity is, in measure, the product of our commercial civilization; and the indifference flows from sheer ignorance of things Jewish, both in their historic meaning and the contemporary values.

On the organizational level, the traveler, as he visits town after town, learns to appreciate the magnitude and sweep of Jewish philanthropy. Doubtless it is not always marked by the finest moral perceptions, and social pressures play their part. But philanthropy among American Jews is more than charity. It is the sole non-partisan, non-political means available for Jews to identify themselves with their people, to express their sense of solidarity and Jewishness. It is precisely in the sphere of philanthropy that American Jews have exhibited their greatest tolerance for difference and variety, and have contrived to sit together, though often with opposing views, on behalf of large and agreed-upon purposes. Here, unity in Jewish life achieves decent and useful expression. This pattern is being followed to good effect in many cities in connection with Jewish education.

One finds a growing interest in books on Jewish subjects. The Yiddish newspaper is still ubiquitous in America, and its influence, confined to the older generation, impinges to some extent, through casual discussion at home, upon their children as well. It reaches approximately three hundred thousand homes and is read by over half a million Jews. Although there are no Hebrew daily newspapers, copies of current Hebrew periodicals can be found in every town. And though the Anglo-Jewish press in the smaller localities is provincial and often insipid, some national publications in English are coming to the fore and beginning to play a role in the shaping of Jewish public opinion.

One hears with gratification of the increased interest of a number of national organizations in cultural activities and in programs aimed at encouraging

86. [*Al kiddush hashem* is Hebrew for "in sanctifying the name" (of God) and is used to describe those perceived to have died as martyrs, in this case in the Holocaust.]

creativity in American Jewish life. The sponsoring of this very magazine by a national organization as an organ of free cultural expression, hospitable to diverse views and unhampered by propagandistic or political aims, may stand as a symbol of this new and most hopeful development.[87]

However, these harbingers of a better future are still the exception, not the rule. The "feeling for Jewishness" among younger people and the cultural allegiances of the older folk are still used primarily by Jewish organizations for political ends. The paramount concern is always to win adherents for some Jewish political cause rather than to build a knowledge of Jewish values and culture. Today the knowledge of things Jewish among young people who belong to the "nationalist" organizations is little superior to that of the "unaffiliated"; where there is some knowledge, it is fragmentary, indoctrinated, and shallow. The rich cultural activity of the Zionist organizations in American is a thing of the past.

Now if American Jews are to constitute a community, they must have shared experiences, and such experiences cannot be merely "political" nor can they always be imported from the outside. They must be cultural, "spiritual" if you will. And they must grow out of one's "native soil," that is to say, they must be authentic and organic. Above all, we must have a plan and program of Jewish education that, in an atmosphere of freedom and breadth of understanding, will give substance to our "feeling for Jewishness."

This education must neither be "tribal," on the one hand, nor so general, on the other, as to lose all Jewish distinctiveness. It must be at once unique and universal. The roots of religious liberty in America are deep and strong, and it is possible, within the framework of religious education broadened by our concept of cultural democracy, to include many elements of "secular" Jewish culture together with our full heritage of social and ethical idealism. That heritage reaches from Micah's deathless pronouncement—"It hath been told thee, O man, what is good and what the Lord doth require of thee; only to do justly, and to love mercy, and to walk humbly with thy God"[88]—to the poems of indignation and compassion just come to us from the ghettos and concentration camps of eastern and central Europe. In all likelihood, the instrument of this education will not be to any great extent the parochial school, supplanting the

87. [*Commentary* was founded in 1945 by the American Jewish Committee.]
88. [See Micah 6:8.]

democratic public school where children of all religions and ethnic groups meet together, but Jewish schools that supplement the public schools.

America's Jewish community is at the crossroads. The way ahead is surely not straight and smooth, but it is visible. The question is irrepressible: Will Jewish organizations in America give up the delusion that this is Galut—exile, and settle down to the task of building here, in freedom and security, the good and creative Jewish life? In sum, will they recognize *as organizations* what Jews *as individuals* have long ago acknowledged: that we—and our children and our children's children—are here to stay, that *this* is home!

Epilogue

14

Jerusalem and Babylon
Simon Rawidowicz

Simon Rawidowicz, "Jerusalem and Babylon," in *Judaism* 18 (1969): 131–42, a condensed translation and paraphrase by Frank Talmage of *Bavel ve-Yerushalayim* (Waltham, MA: Ararat, 1957), 506–26. Republished in Simon Rawidowicz, *State of Israel, Diaspora, and Jewish Continuity: Essays on the "Ever-Dying People,"* ed. Benjamin Ravid (Waltham, MA: Brandeis University Press, 1998), 229–39.

With the European community in fragments or behind the Iron Curtain (with some exceptions, such as Great Britain) and the Zionists' success in establishing a refuge for world Jewry, after 1948 Israel became the focus of national identity for Jews in the diaspora as much as for those in the new state. Israel, together with modern Hebrew, became the political and cultural locus for world Jewry. The creation of a Jewish nation-state changed permanently how Jews, from the most secular to the most religious, perceived the meaning of Jewish peoplehood by creating a new category of Jews: Israelis, who were citizens of the Jewish state. For most Zionists living in the diaspora, the change reflected merely the Jews' "normalization," the marker of Zionism's greatest success. For Simon Rawidowicz (1896–1957), however, the separation of Jews into Israelis and others marked a troubling division in the people of Israel (*am Yisrael*).

Rawidowicz was born in the town of Graevo, in the Russian Empire, to a family that emphasized both Jewish religious scholarship and modern Hebrew literature. Rawidowicz attended a *heder*, studied Talmud with his father, and at fourteen went off to the Lida Yeshiva (though he spent only a year there). Rawidowicz's father, Chaim, read the Hebrew literature of the Haskala and was involved from the early 1890s in organizations fostering Jewish settlement in Palestine, such as Hoveve Zion (Lovers of Zion). Thus, although Yiddish was for the Rawidowicz family, as for most Jews in the Russian Empire, the *mameloshn* (mother tongue), the family was unusually devoted to the development of Hebrew culture, and even to a Hebrew vernacular. The father's love of Hebrew would have a lifelong impact on the son, as Rawidowicz promoted Hebrew's cultivation by Jews beginning in his teenage years in Graevo, in Bialystok (where he founded a Hebrew school and theater), through his time in Berlin studying philosophy (where he founded the Brit Ivrit Olamit, or World Hebrew Union), and until his death (when he was chair of the Department of Near Eastern and Judaic Studies at Brandeis University). Rawidowicz published prolifically in Hebrew, Yiddish, and German — writing especially on Ludwig Feuerbachs, Nachman Krochmal, and Moses Mendelssohn — and over the years he edited a number of Hebrew periodicals. Of particular concern to Rawidowicz was the goal of making Jewish thought available to Jewish scholars in the unabridged original Hebrew, and toward that end he founded the Ayanot Publishing Company in Berlin, in 1922, and then the Ararat Publishing Company in England, in 1942.

Like many Hebraists, Rawidowicz was also a Zionist who expressed a strong desire to settle in the Land of Israel. Yet he was at the same time disturbed by the seeming success of those who sought to orient Zionism toward the negation of the *galut*, whether interpreted as diaspora or exile. Like Dubnov, to whom he considered himself intellectually indebted, Rawidowicz saw efforts to push Jewish cultural life from the diaspora to Israel as based upon a fundamental misunderstanding of the nature of Jewish existence and what made the Jews unique as a nation. To counter the spiritual Zionists who sought to put Israel alone in the center of the Jewish renaissance, Rawidowicz wrote several articles and speeches devoted to contemplating the nature of Jewish existence in the diaspora. He repeatedly pointed out that while Zionism could exist as a political and cultural movement, and even bring forth a state, attempting to negate the diaspora — in spirit or content — was a destructive form of messianism. Most problematic, to Rawidowicz, is how the "negators" could discourage Jewish cultural creativity in the diaspora, and in Israel erode the principle that all Jews worldwide share a spiritual and national bond. Thus, negating the diaspora is strangely denationalizing, as it frees Israelis (or, before the founding of the State of Israel, "Hebrews") from seeing themselves as Jews, and Jews remaining in the diaspora from participating in Jewish national culture. Hence Rawidowicz's anger over the state's name: to use the name Israel, rather than *Eretz Yisrael* (the Land of Israel), or something else, implied that membership in *am Yisrael*, the people of Israel, required citizenship in the state.

The essay "Jerusalem and Babylon" comes from a larger work, *Bavel ve-Yerushalayim* (*Babylon and Jerusalem*), which Rawidowicz completed between 1951 and his death in 1957. This work, when published posthumously, received little attention. It included searing criticism of both Zionism and American Judaism and was published in a Hebrew that was dense with Talmudic references. In it Rawidowicz crystallized and expanded many of his earlier ideas about the problem of messianism in Zionism and the necessity of developing Hebrew culture in the diaspora. He also developed a set of symbols through which Jewish sovereignty and continuity should be interpreted. Rawidowicz no doubt felt that the problems he had worried about earlier in his life had become more acute with the creation of Israel. He failed, however, to fully absorb the cataclysmic toll on Jewish life wrought by the previous fifty years. Still, the following essay serves as a fitting epilogue to our volume.

1

Is 1948 to mark a new era in Jewish history? From our present vantage point, it does not appear likely that this question can be answered in the affirmative. The year 1948 did less to inaugurate a new order by providing solutions to old problems than it did to engender a host of new ones. Among these are: the relationship between the communities of the Land of Israel and the Diaspora; the feasibility of *kibbutz galuyot*, the ingathering policy of the State of Israel; a reconsideration of the place and function of the Zionist movement; a reassessment of the traditional concept of redemption; the danger that the Diaspora communities will ignore their own responsibilities and look to the new State alone for leadership. Indeed, the very meaning of the age-old name "Israel" has been rendered problematic.[1] Yet despite all this, many a valuable lesson may be derived from the experiences of 1948. Surely not the least of these is that of *Jerusalem-and-Babylon*.

2

In 1933, when Hitler came to power and the Third Reich began to reckon its new era, the end of the Jewish community in the Diaspora was quite generally predicted—even by those who most wished to see it flourish. This did not happen.

1. [Rawidowicz strongly opposed using "Israel" for the state's name, arguing that to do so effectively ascribed a strict geopolitical meaning to a term that historically had included all Jewish people, thereby undermining Jewish unity. On this issue, Rawidowicz had an extended correspondence with Israel's first prime minister, David Ben-Gurion (1886–1973). Rawidowicz also opposed the Law of Return, passed in 1950 to guarantee automatic "nationality" to all Jewish immigrants to the state. Rawidowicz believed that, just as diaspora Jews deserved rights as a minority around the world, so did Muslim and Christian minorities warrant equal treatment in, and access to, the Land of Israel.]

I claim, rather, that the events of 1933 taught us the secret of survival of Diaspora Jewry. This consisted of both a driving inertia and a tenacious will for survival that manifest themselves in every community whose survival is threatened. We learned that no Diaspora community completely and deliberately disbands itself unless forced to do so by expulsion. I saw this fundamental law of the existence of the Diaspora—"the law of survival and continuity"—stamped in fire and blood in the events of 1933. I saw it operative in the Holocaust years after 1933, just as I see it operative today. Thus what many would call the destruction of the Diaspora, I call the survival of the Diaspora. Even after the Holocaust, I maintain: survival of the Diaspora. In short, what the wretched years that followed 1933 could not achieve, the happier circumstances of 1948 are not to achieve either. As it was before 1948, so shall it be afterwards: *Jerusalem-and-Babylon*.

The face of Israel has two profiles—Babylon and Jerusalem. This is the way it has been for more than two and a half millennia; this is the way it is in the twentieth century; this is the way it shall be for some time to come. He who denies either denies all, for Israel is not Jerusalem nor is it Babylon; it is Jerusalem-and-Babylon, Babylon-and-Jerusalem. Every Jew worthy of the name is rooted in both—in a Jerusalem that is rooted in Babylon and in a Babylon rooted in Jerusalem.

By Jerusalem, we mean Jerusalem as a symbol of the Land of Israel in its entirety. By Babylon, we mean not only that territory that lies on the banks of the Tigris and Euphrates, but every place that is not Jerusalem. Babylon has appeared in many guises: as the Babylon of Ezra and Nehemiah, of Hillel and Rav Hiyya, and of all the Babylonian sages down to R. Hai, the last of the *geonim*, in the eleventh century; as the Egypt of the Temple of Onias and of Philo; as the Spain of R. Hasdai ibn Shaprut, R. Solomon ibn Gabirol, and R. Judah Halevi; as the Africa of R. Isaac Alfasi; as the Spain and Egypt of Maimonides; as the Franco-Germany of Rashi and the tosaphists and, in a later age, of Moses Mendelssohn and Moses Hess, Theodor Herzl and Hermann Cohen; as the Poland and Ukraine of R. Israel Baal Shem Tov and his disciples; as the Lithuania of the *gaon* of Vilna and the Haskala; as all the modern European communities with their strivings and concerns, spiritual and material.[2] Yet Babylon appears in the

2. [The individuals listed here represent almost 2,500 years of Jewish thought outside the Land of Israel, or "Jerusalem." Rawidowicz is pointing to the diversity of Jewish experience by including a sampling of intellectual creativity in "Babylon" since the creation of the diaspora.]

guise of these scholars and leaders only insofar as they themselves are the symbol of a people—the men, women, and children of Israel.

Babylon, in the guise of Egypt and the wilderness, was prior to Jerusalem in time. Babylon, too, was the theater of two-thirds of Jewish history, while the remaining third itself was not totally devoid of the presence of Babylon. On the other hand, Jerusalem gained priority in sanctity and in esteem in the hearts of the nation. Yet, in the end, such priorities prove to be illusory, for there is only Babylon-and-Jerusalem, Jerusalem-and-Babylon—one entity, one Israel.

There are those who see only Jerusalem. For them, Babylon was merely an interlude, a way station, a chimera. Others see only Babylon; Jerusalem was but is no more, and any attempt to restore it is doomed to failure. Indeed, to their minds, Babylon has become Jerusalem, and the waters of the Jordan flow in those of the Rhine, the Thames, and the Hudson. Finally, there are those who effect a "technical" compromise: "Let the odds be in favor of Jerusalem, but place a small wager now and then on Babylon."

None of these approaches is mine. I am as far from those who have said that Jerusalem could be built only on the ashes of Babylon as I am from those who have said it could never be rebuilt at all. Our Rabbis asked: "What is engraved on the coinage of Jerusalem? David and Solomon on one side; Jerusalem, the Holy City, on the other" (*Baba Kamma* 97b). Should the rebuilt Jerusalem come forth and claim: "In 1948 the fate of Babylon was sealed; its end is imminent"—Babylon shall answer: "Look at the world, and look at history; look at the coinage of Israel." What is engraved on the coinage of Israel? Jerusalem on one side, Babylon on the other.

3

Jerusalem is the point of destination, the end of the journey; Babylon is transition, the journey itself. Babylon is the agent of fomentation, the gadfly that ferrets out the permanent that lies concealed within the ephemeral, the regeneration that lies concealed within destruction. Babylon represents not complacency and satisfaction with the status quo but an inner struggle against the status quo. In Babylon there is no room for incompetence, ineptitude, or slovenliness. Babylon represents only unlimited unconditional, single-minded commitment.

Babylon-and-Jerusalem signifies the unflinching and unbending battle of Israel for her survival, a dauntless struggle for her life and ideals. Many are the garbs in which Israel in Babylon has appeared since the end of the First Commonwealth.[3] It is our duty to ensure that every garb in which Babylon clothes itself—now and in the future—be woven into the texture of Israel, of Babylon-and-Jerusalem, that it fit the very soul of Israel and not be a mere cloak on a mannequin.

Shabby and threadbare is the cloak in which our Westernized "theologians" and European and American assimilationists have dressed themselves, rejecting any genuine Jewish existence and declaring that Judaism is a "religion—only a religion." This emaciated and emasculated "religion" of theirs, feeding as it does on fear and insecurity and acceptable only to the apathetic and uncommitted, is merely a subterfuge for denying Israel as a living and vital people. Conceived to be a "religion like any other religion," it demands neither obligation nor allegiance. To its adherents, Judaism and Christianity are one at the core. They live in a "Judeo-Christian civilization" and delude themselves into thinking that European and American Christians also live in that Judeo-Christian civilization. Theirs is a religion that is all compromise and shortcut, with little real content to offer. It is a simple matter, then, for its devotees to dabble in one of the modern "theologies"—be it "liberal" or "dialectical" or "existential"—and to vaunt themselves before their flocks in their pseudomystical "religion." All they need have is faith, a great leap of faith that brings fulfillment to the "leaper" and a murmur of adulation from his reading and listening audience. Unfortunately, none of these leapfrogging theologians has learned that the religion of Israel, built as it is upon centuries of thought and practice, is not to be attained by leaps and bounds. It is evident that the Judaism of many of these *baale teshuvah* who are preaching and teaching their "theologies" in Israel is only a façade.[4] Their lack of desire or ability to reveal themselves as *Jews* and their contempt for traditional Jewish values are repulsive to anyone sincerely concerned with Jewish survival. If they were only to express themselves in the language of Abraham, Isaac, and Jacob, their sham Judaism would immediately give itself away. They do speak in the language of the gentiles, and in that language their simulated Judaism looks authentic enough to their naïve and ignorant audiences.

3. [The First Commonwealth refers to Jerusalem, or the entire Kingdom of Judah, before the siege of Jerusalem by the Babylonians. According to the Hebrew Bible, Solomon's temple in Jerusalem was destroyed, and the Jews were forced into exile in Babylonia. They were permitted to return and rebuild the temple (the Second Temple) when the Persians defeated the Babylonians.]

4. [*Baal teshuva* (literally, one who answers) is the term used to describe a lapsed or nonpracticing Jew who becomes religious.]

This religionism only, this degenerate sacerdotalism *sans culte*, is but one of the approaches antagonistic to the concept of Israel's wholeness. Yet another is characterized by the attempt to place Judaism in a straitjacket—either by interpreting its past or by drawing blueprints for its future. I refer to the modern penchant for "extracting" the "essence" of Judaism by attempting to pin it down to one or the other of its manifold aspects. In this there is little profit. More important than the determination of an essence is the effort to preserve Judaism's catholicity, to encourage its striving for breadth, to nurture its impulse to creativity. Over against all the mummifying and stultifying typologizing to which Judaism has been subjected in recent years, I should advocate a different sort of approach. I should suggest that this is no time to canonize Torah but to reopen it in the light of the experiences we have acquired in our peregrinations from country to country, nation to nation, era to era. I should urge Israel to treat its sclerosis of generations and to pump fresh blood into its veins, to place new emphasis upon the *process* of the development of Judaism and the evolution of a living community meeting the challenges it has faced in its historic struggles.

Worthy of praise is that pharisaic scholar who refused to acknowledge canonization and finalization even in the realm of revelation. Penetrating that greatest of mysteries, the revelation of God to man in the Torah of Israel, he maintained that the words of the Torah were not given in an absolutely clear-cut way but that in each word of God there are "forty-nine aspects of *tahor* (clean)" and "forty-nine aspects of *tame* (unclean)" (*Midrash Tehillim*, 12:5). We must pay careful attention to these words of R. Yannai.[5] Therein lies a unique and decisive conception of revelation—one that is open, nondefinite, nonabsolute: the Torah that God gave on Mount Sinai through His prophet Moses to His people Israel is an open Torah. The same sage placed a question in the mouth of Moses: "Lord, how long are we to wait for a decision?" God answers: "It is up to the majority to decide." Study, interpret, delve into every aspect of the Torah—it is your decision. May we not, indeed must we not, understand this answer as an imperative for all time? Open up the Torah! Let it be open to you! Let your hearts be open to it!

The "opening" we seek will not be without its perils. There will always be those who would carry such a process to extremes in the belief that there are no holds barred at all. Such a free-for-all is not what I have in mind. This "opening"

5. [Rabbi Yannai was the third-century head and namesake of a religious academy in the Upper Galilee that is frequently cited in the Talmud.]

must be carried out with the greatest circumspection. For this reason I set down the following ground rule: our "opening" must come from within and not from without. It must accrue to the advantage of Israel and not be used to promote her assimilation. Such an opening must come from an inner necessity and compulsion; if its object is truly the renewal of the House of Israel, it will seek a submission to the yoke, and will not comprise an effort to shake it off. This is to be an opening, not a breach; a rooting, not an uprooting.

Every attempt at reform in Israel in the nineteenth and twentieth centuries that sought to determine the essence of Judaism ended in seeing only one tree of the forest, one part of the whole: the part labeled "religion" (to the extent that this might be acceptable to the "enlightened" Jew of twentieth-century Europe or America), or the part labeled "nationality" (to the extent that this might be acceptable to the Jewish citizen of Europe and America). This is the result of an attempt to create an abridged, part-time Judaism, the product of a coming to terms with the transformation of Judaism from a life-embracing reality to an activity limited to an hour a week or a few days a year. Yet, some more than came to terms with this transformation; they embraced it, and encouraged it, and envisioned it as the very redemption of Israel. They "devote" their one hour to Judaism, but not a speck of it appears in their activities the remainder of the week. Such are the apostles of a new age, who are totally unaware that the gospel they preach is long outmoded.

Over against this, a true opening means a heart-and-soul struggle for the wholeness of Judaism in its catholicity in form and content. It must stem from a grave concern, the kind of concern one feels for oneself and especially for one's household. It comes from one's very being and cannot be imposed from without. If this opening is to be truly achieved in accord with the spirit of Israel, then they who initiate it must be members of the household, of the House of Israel. They must be Jews in the "original," and not Jews in "translation"—Jews who have translated themselves so far from Judaism that they have no clear notion of what Judaism is or is not. A breakthrough cannot be achieved by those who have never come to grips with the tradition but only by those steeped in it. Just as no true reformation comes about unless it proceeds out of its own "hoary" and "antiquated" antecedents, so no revolution of the spirit can yield any blessing unless it imbibes the very tradition against which it has reacted.

In sum: Israel has need of those who would *disclose*, not those who would *close*; of those who would make a *breakthrough*, and not those who would make a *break*. Mar, the son of Rabina, who composed the petition that concludes the "Eighteen

Benedictions," prayed for an opening: "Open my heart in Your Torah."[6] If I were among the liturgists, I should venture to add: "Open Your Torah in my heart, in our hearts." Israel both now and in the future must study a Torah that both opens and is open. The "modern world" is closed and shut. Its "Torah" is closed and shut. The world has need of a spiritual and moral reopening, and it is this that Babylon-in-Jerusalem demands. Her prayer is for an open Israel, an open mankind, an open world.

4

When Moses Mendelssohn said "*Jerusalem*" in the early 1780s, he meant the idealized Jerusalem, the symbol of perfect harmony between state and religion, morality and authority, will and power.[7] Eighty years later, Moses Hess said "*Rome and Jerusalem*"—Jerusalem and the agent of her destruction side by side. He juxtaposed the two adversaries in his hope that the liberation of the one would result in the liberation of the other.[8] The new Jerusalem that began to rise from the ashes at the end of the last century and returned to her former estate in 1948 is not the Jerusalem of Mendelssohn and his disciples. It was Hess's vision of Jerusalem that was realized in 1948. Ironically, this happened at a time when Rome no longer occupied the position of eminence she held when Hess wrote, while France, upon whom Hess pinned his hopes, was in bad straits.

I do not espouse the approach of Mendelssohn, nor do I, like Hess, look at Jerusalem through Roman glasses. My eyes are focused not on Rome but on the House of Israel, and in that House I see Babylon-and-Jerusalem.

I am making no predictions concerning the longevity of Babylon. I say only that Babylon has existed, does exist, and will continue to exist for some time to

6. [The Amidah ("standing" prayer) or *Shmone esre* ("eighteen," for the number of blessings) is the central prayer of Jewish liturgy, often referred to in the Talmud simply as *tefila* ("prayer"). The final meditation to which Rawidowicz refers here (Talmud Berachot 17a) includes the phrase "open my heart in Your Torah."]

7. [Moses Mendelssohn (1729–86) published *Jerusalem* in 1783. In this work, he argued for the separation of religion from the state, a system wherein the state could not interfere with the practices of Jews. The book's title, *Jerusalem*, refers to a utopic, tolerant, democratic state, one that Mendelssohn believed Mosaic law describes.]

8. [Moses Hess (1812–75), one of the first theorists of what would come to be known as communism and Zionism, published *Rome and Jerusalem* in 1862. The book calls for Jews to return to the Land of Israel to form an agrarian society and achieve self-determination as a state. See my introductory essay to this volume.]

come, and that as long as it does so, it must continue to retain its character as an integral part of Israel. Every obstacle in the path of this goal must be eliminated; every attitude and point of view antagonistic to it must be suppressed. As for prophecy, I shall leave that to the prophets. The prophets of doom in Israel, the "negators of the Diaspora" within Zionism or the negators of Israel outside Zionism, have underestimated Israel's powers of regeneration. We do not know what lies in store for Babylon in the future, whether it be tranquility or tribulation. There are those who feel that suffering is necessary for the survival of the Jewish people. I say that persecution as such was never beneficial to any society, and never will be. If I were one of those who think that our national identity can be maintained only with a knife at our throats and not in a free and open society, I should not be preoccupied with its preservation. It may be that persecution has served as a stimulus to some (woe to the children of Abraham, Isaac, and Jacob who need this sort of "encouragement"!), but it was never of decisive influence. I pray neither for it nor for its "encouragement." It must not be made a sine qua non for survival, as if the absence of anti-Semitism would spell the end of Israel. Babylon is no more a hell than it is a heaven. It is a fact—no more than this, and no less.

There are some for whom Babylon can only be America, which to their minds is to attain (if it has not already done so) the stature of Babylon of old. Others are skeptical of America and claim that it can never reach that status: only one Babylon is possible, they claim, the Babylon of antiquity; upon it every Diaspora community must be modeled.

The fact is that the Babylon of the Judean exiles, of the *amoraim*, the *saboraim*, and the *geonim*, was unlike any of the other Babylons of our history.[9] Yet they are all Babylon. Indeed, is the Jerusalem of the twentieth century the Jerusalem of the Prophets and the early rabbinic teachers? Yet twentieth-century Jerusalem, without priest or prophet, king or Temple, Mishna or Gemara, is still Jerusalem.[10]

Babylon has no prescribed garb incumbent upon its communities for all time. Its garb of yore cannot be reimposed today as the style for us, who may, indeed

9. [These are terms for the rabbinic scholars from the different periods of religious creativity in Babylonia.]

10. [The Mishna is a compilation of oral traditions from early Judaism, redacted in the third century. Rabbinic commentaries on the Mishna, called the Gemara, were composed over the course of the next three centuries in Babylonia and the Land of Israel. The Mishna and Gemara together form the Talmud, of which there are two compilations: the Babylonian Talmud and the Jerusalem (also known as Palestinian) Talmud.]

must, fashion a garb appropriate to our physical and spiritual circumstances. Israel's ever-growing wardrobe includes many such garbs—one for every Babylon that has striven creatively to express its identity as Israel. Babylon ultimately represents an act of opening—of the spirit and of the mind, on the threshold of life and the threshold of hope. As long as Babylon remains open, neither she nor Israel shall perish. Babylon dare have nothing of the stultifying or the stultified, the petrifying or the petrified. She must be characterized by a perpetual motion, the motion of Israel in the world. This is the way of Israel in her wholeness, of man in his wholeness, of the world in its wholeness.

5

Titus, who destroyed Jerusalem 1,884 years ago, saw the destruction of Jerusalem as the destruction of Israel—"Your city, your people, and you yourselves are doomed to perish" (Josephus, *Wars*, 6.6.2). Babylon laughed in the face of the destroyer. The sacred capital was burned to the ground, but the seed of Abraham, Isaac, and Jacob lived on. They recognized the difference between being struck a heavy blow and being struck a *mortal* blow. From this the entire world learned how to recover after a defeat, to distinguish between one battle on the field and the perennial battle for survival. After the destruction of both the First and the Second Temples, there were those who expressed their shock, as it were, at the words of Asaph: "'A hymn of Asaph. O God, the nations have invaded Your domain.' They complained: 'The text should have used a phrase like "weeping of Asaph, lament of Asaph, dirge of Asaph." Why does it say "hymn of Asaph?" The Holy One blessed be He, has caused Temple and Sanctuary to be destroyed, and yet you sit singing a hymn.' He replied: 'I sing a hymn because the Holy One, blessed be He, has poured out His wrath on the wood and stone, and not upon Israel'" (*Lamentations Rabbah*, 4:15).[11] This distinction between Israel and her "wood and stone" was a message of liberation and redemption to man (and not to Israel alone) from his "wood and stone."

David made his faith in God contingent on his paternal inheritance, on "Jerusalem." "If men have incited you against me," he cried to Saul, "may they be

11. [*Lamentations Rabbah* is one of the great works of rabbinic literature that falls outside the scope of the Talmud. It forms a part of a collection of *midrashic*, or exegetical, works. The selection quoted here comes from the *midrash* on the biblical Book of Lamentations, which mourns the destruction of the First Temple.]

cursed before God, for they have cast me out and kept me from sharing in the inheritance of the Lord, and have said, 'Go, serve other gods'" (1 Samuel 26:19). Since the end of the First Commonwealth, Babylon has continued to reject this Davidic concept. To be sure, there were those in the Second Commonwealth who tried to revive it, albeit in a new formulation. Later, in the Middle Ages, Judah Halevi, that poet-philosopher, whose heart ever yearned for Jerusalem, tried in his way, too, to reestablish it.[12] Are not his *Kuzari* and poetry a paean to Jerusalem, a campaign to infuse Israel with devotion to its land? Babylon heard, but could not fully accept the words of this man of Jerusalem who appeared in the "Babylon" of Spain, seeking to turn the clock backwards and erase Babylon from history. Yet this denial of Israel's ability to exist outside the borders of the Land of Israel continued to resound throughout the centuries. It was heard from the time of David who expanded the borders of the First Commonwealth to that of Titus who destroyed the Second; from the time of the heretic who said, "Since the day you were exiled from your land, the Law of Moses has been suspended," to that of the many heretics who were to follow; from the time of Saul of Tarsus and his disciples to that of Benedict Spinoza; from the time of Karl Marx and his followers, who turned their backs on Israel-and-Babylon, to that of the "negators of the Diaspora" within Zionism.[13] Despite the variations, one basic theme preoccupied all of these; because the Temple was destroyed and prophecy has ceased, because there was no king in Jeshurun and no *Shekhinah* outside the Land, the exile has placed the Torah in abeyance, and the new covenant has replaced the old. In other words, it is both impossible and pointless to preserve Israel or Judaism in a "free humanistic-democratic-liberal" world or in a "socialist-communist" world. All of these, within Israel and without, denied Babylon. Yet Babylon would not be denied, for Babylon would not deny herself. Babylon prevailed over every one of these nonbelievers and skeptics, who, more

12. [Judah Halevi was a twelfth-century Spanish poet, philosopher, and physician. He is known for his Hebrew poetry and his philosophical work, the *Kuzari*. The essays in this work take the form of a dialogue between the pagan king of the Khazars and four men: a philosopher, a Christian, a Muslim, and a Jew. The work aims to demonstrate the superiority of Judaism and concludes with the king's conversion. Halevi ultimately decided to settle in Jerusalem, where he is believed to have died shortly after arriving.]

13. [Rawidowicz argues here that Zionists who negate the diaspora had precursors in Saul of Tarsus (Jesus's apostle Paul), Spinoza in the seventeenth century, and Marx in the nineteenth century—all of whom argued that the end of Jewish sovereignty in Israel should mark the end of Jewish particularism in the diaspora.]

than any persecution, would put the very soul of the nation in jeopardy. Babylon gave them a rude awakening and proved that their postulates were all false. Babylon gave the lie to all those in the past three thousand years who would have "negated" her. So may she continue to do in time to come.

It is quite apparent from all this that the problem of Babylon-and-Jerusalem is not a problem for our time alone. Those who have debated the status of the Diaspora did not invent it, not in 1882, not in 1897, and not in 1948.[14] It is, moreover, a question that is like no ordinary question, for it contains within itself its own answer. Babylon and Jerusalem? Yes, Babylon *and* Jerusalem!

In Israel's conception, Jerusalem represents both a land and a state. Babylon is neither land nor state, but a "household." The strength of Babylon lies in the fact that it "houses" Israel wherever they may be. Whether Israel appears as a nation or a religious communion, a land, a state, or the communities of the Diaspora, it is above all a household—the House of Israel. Babylon represents for us those who are members of the household and not those who are strangers to it.

Jerusalem has been seen and still is seen as the quick and "final" solution, the total redemption of Israel. "Jerusalem" has been considered a synonym for "panacea" or "universal antidote" and a symbol of ease and normalcy with all that these imply. It is as if, once Jerusalem is established, Israel will know no more sorrow or anguish. To this I reply: "Babylon-and-Jerusalem." The Babylon in Babylon-and-Jerusalem neither denies the possibility of redemption nor posits it as a sine qua non for the existence of Israel. Babylon represents the unceasing yoke of Israel, of Torah, and of learning. The purpose of Babylon is the imposition of this yoke, for he who imposes the yoke in Israel supports the soul, the spirit, the life, the creativity of Israel.

Jerusalem-and-Babylon represents a coincidence of opposites, of the redeemed and the unredeemable, of stabilization and upheaval. Babylon is merely another word for that great paradox that has been Israel in the world from the end of the First Commonwealth to the beginning of the Third: the paradox of a stateless nation longing for redemption but surviving without it; marked for upheaval but able to stand firm; waiting for a miracle but defying all miracles and all laws of nature together. The pairing of Jerusalem and Babylon—before 1948 and after—complicates this paradoxical fact of Israel all the more, this fact

14. [These are the dates of three events considered significant in the history of Zionism: widespread anti-Jewish violence in Russia (1882); the first World Zionist Congress in Basle, Switzerland (1897); and the founding of the State of Israel (1948).]

full of frustrating yet fruitful perplexity and anguish for every son of Babylon-and-Jerusalem in every generation.

The eternal union of Babylon-and-Jerusalem shuns the deception that the redemption has come; it proclaims not: "Yours is the task of completion." Babylon-and-Jerusalem largely implies a "quiet revolution," a "dynamic conservatism," a guiding wisdom and prudence drawn from the fount of the thought and deeds of generations.

6

Jerusalem-and-Babylon does not promise that all will be sweetness and light. It spells danger, but a danger tempered with the words "fear not, My servant Jacob."[15]

There is no guarantee of Jerusalem's permanent security, even if she be blessed with political independence. All who see Jerusalem as a first and last resort, as an impregnable fortress "far removed from anti-Semitism," are living in delusion. Jerusalem remains forever isolated, surrounded by enemies on all sides who are ready to pounce upon her at every opportunity. Babylon, for her part, is insecurity incarnate. Her abode is "open country," exposed to any and every passerby in the arena of history. She has neither will nor power to alter this fact, for it is, indeed, unalterable. As long as man breathes on this earth, there will be a "Jerusalem" and there will be a "Babylon."

Israel had no need for the exhortation uttered by that distinguished Briton when he undertook his battle to the death against Adolf Hitler.[16] Since its earliest beginnings, Israel's way has been that of blood, sweat, and tears. Her children were to be strangers throughout the world; oppression was to precede every redemption, and the birth pangs of the Messiah were to increase to the point that those who prayed for him every day would cry, "May he come, and may I not see him!" Israel has known no other way than this, this way of Babylon-and-Jerusalem, and she is destined to know no other.

If there is such a thing as a "royal road"—for Israel or any man—the way of Babylon-and-Jerusalem is not it. The way of Jerusalem has been the way of all

15. [This is spoken by God in the books of Isaiah and Jeremiah.]

16. [The "Briton" referred to here is Winston Churchill, who, when he became prime minister of the United Kingdom in 1940, promised "victory at all costs" against the Nazis in a famous speech before Parliament.]

those seers of Zion from the days of the destruction of the First Temple through the twentieth century when Jerusalem rose again from the ashes. Those who walk this road say: "The way of Israel is the way of Jerusalem—a royal road for a royal people." The way of Babylon is the way of all those—from the time of Ezra and Nehemiah to the present—who would deny Zion's right of existence. The way of Jerusalem-and-Babylon is the way of Israel in its wholeness. It is the master highway that connects all those routes we have traveled from the time that Abraham went forth from the land of his birth to the days of his descendants who are returning to the land.

The Jewish thinker in our time must help pave the way of Babylon-and-Jerusalem for our generation and for generations to come. This is the only way of those who have ever been engaged in that great enterprise known as Israel. In the light of Babylon-and-Jerusalem, we shall study, ponder, and live that unique and fantastic "spectacle" known as the history of Israel, the history of Jerusalem-and-Babylon. It is on this path that we must proceed—the path of an Israel that is whole in a world that is whole.

7

The mountains of the spirit are craggy and steep, whether they be firmly implanted in the earth or dangling by a thread. Whenever I ponder the question of Israel through the generations and in our generation, I feel as if I were climbing one of those mountains. The mountain of Israel is steeper and craggier than most. As I near the peak, I feel that with one more step I shall stumble into the abyss that lies in wait for such mountaineers as I. A feeling of solitude and depression overcomes me. There pass before my mind's eye other thinkers in Israel, who have walked with great trepidation at the brink of that abyss, thinking the thoughts that would lead to the top of the mountain. The more steep and treacherous the mountain, the more profound their thoughts. Is not every act of thought that ventures to probe beneath the surface one that points to the top of the mountain? Does not any thinker, any time and anywhere, who seeks to weld the old to the new, the past to the present, to blaze a trail for himself through the mountains of history and find a highway that would connect all such trails—does not that thinker walk the brink of the abyss? "Fortunate" is he who has not scaled those mountains and has not tottered at the edge of the abyss. Of such fortune I want no part.

The world has stood at the brink of the abyss—not only in our time, not only in the atomic age, but from the dawn of history. It is as if man were born into the world carrying his abyss with him, bearing it on his back, bearing it in his heart. Israel meets the world at the brink of the abyss. There Israel meets herself, and there she walks her way—the way of Babylon-and-Jerusalem.

Suggestions for Further Reading

GENERAL
The following readings are helpful for understanding a number of the central concepts and movements associated with diaspora nationalism.

Bartal, Israel. "Autonomie, autonomisme, diasporisme." In *Les juifs et le XXe siècle: dictionnaire critique*, edited by Élie Barnavi and Saul Friedländer, 36–46. Paris: Calmann-Lévy, 2000.
———. "From Corporation to Nation: Jewish Autonomy in Eastern Europe. 1772–1881." *Jahrbuch des Simon-Dubnow-Instituts/Simon Dubnow Institute Yearbook* 5 (2006): 17–31.
Fishman, David E. *The Rise of Modern Yiddish Culture*. Pittsburgh: University of Pittsburgh Press, 2005.
Frankel, Jonathan. *Prophecy and Politics: Socialism, Nationalism, and the Russian Jews, 1862–1917*. Cambridge: Cambridge University Press, 1981.
Goldsmith, Emanuel S. *Architects of Yiddishism at the Beginning of the Twentieth Century: A Study in Jewish Cultural History*. Rutherford, NJ: Fairleigh Dickinson University Press, 1976.
Goren, Arthur A. *The Politics and Public Culture of American Jews*. Bloomington: Indiana University Press, 1999.
Janowsky, Oscar Isaiah. *The Jews and Minority Rights (1898–1919)*. New York: AMS, 1966.
Moss, Kenneth B. *Jewish Renaissance in the Russian Revolution*. Cambridge: Harvard University Press, 2009.
Pianko, Noam. *Zionism and the Roads Not Taken: Rawidowicz, Kaplan, Kohn*. Bloomington: Indiana University Press, 2010.
Smith, Anthony. "Zionism and Diaspora Nationalism." *Israel Affairs* 2, no. 2 (1995): 1–19.
Veidlinger, Jeffrey. *Jewish Public Culture in the Late Russian Empire*. Bloomington: Indiana University Press, 2009.
Wistrich, Robert S. *The Jews of Vienna in the Age of Franz Joseph*. Oxford: Oxford University Press for the Littman Library, 1989.

PART I. FROM HASKALA TO NATIONAL RENAISSANCE

Perets Smolenskin
Barzilay, Isaac E. "Smolenskin's Polemic against Mendelssohn in Historical Perspective." *Proceedings of the American Academy for Jewish Research* 53 (January 1986): 11–48.
Feiner, Shmuel. *Haskalah and History: The Emergence of a Modern Jewish Historical Consciousness*. Oxford: Littman Library of Jewish Civilization, 2002.
Freundlich, Charles H. *Peretz Smolenskin, His Life and Thought: A Study of the Renascence of Jewish Nationalism*. New York: Bloch, 1965.
Meyer, Michael A. *Response to Modernity: A History of the Reform Movement in Judaism*. New York: Oxford University Press, 1988.

Smolenskin, Perets Ben Moshe. *Ma'amarim*. 4 vols. Jerusalem: Hotsa'at Keren Smolenskin, 1925–26. This collection of Smolenskin's key essays includes introductory essays by Joseph Klausner and Ben Zion Dinur (Dinaburg).

See also, in the general section above: Frankel, *Prophecy and Politics*; Wistrich, *The Jews of Vienna in the Age of Franz Joseph*.

Simon Dubnov

Doubnov [Dubnov], Simon. *Lettres sur le judaïsme ancien et nouveau*. Translated and edited by Renée Poznanski. Paris: Cerf, 1989. See especially Poznanski's introduction, "S. Doubnov, l'homme et son époque," 11–70.

Dubnov, S. M. *The Demands of the Jews*. Philadelphia: Jewish Publication Society, 1917. This is a translation made for American audiences of Dubnov's Russian pamphlet, *Chego khotiat evrei* (Petrograd: Muravei, 1917), written after the tsar's abdication.

Dubnow [Dubnov], Simon. *Nationalism and History: Essays on Old and New Judaism*. Edited by Koppel S. Pinson. Philadelphia: Jewish Publication Society of America, 1958. This English translation of Dubnov's "Letters" was made from the abbreviated and considerably edited Hebrew edition of 1937. Nevertheless, it provides the best guide in English to Dubnov's political philosophy.

Hilbrenner, Anke. *Diaspora-Nationalismus: Zur Geschichtskonstruktion Simon Dubnows*. Göttingen, Germany: Vandenhoeck and Ruprecht, 2007.

Kel'ner, Viktor Efimovich. *Missioner Istorii: Zhizn' i trudy Semena Markovicha Dubnova*. St. Petersburg: Mir, 2008.

Kochan, Lionel. *The Jew and His History*. New York: Schocken, 1977.

Nathans, Benjamin. "On Russian-Jewish Historiography." In *Historiography of Imperial Russia: The Profession and Writing of History in a Multinational State*, edited by Thomas Sanders, 397–432. Armonk, NY: M. E. Sharpe, 1999.

See also, in the general section above: Fishman, *The Rise of Modern Yiddish Culture*; Janowsky, *The Jews and Minority Rights*; Veidlinger, *Jewish Public Culture in the Late Russian Empire*.

Nathan Birnbaum

Fishman, Joshua A. *Ideology, Society and Language: The Odyssey of Nathan Birnbaum*. Ann Arbor, MI: Karoma, 1987. The appendix to this volume includes translations of fifteen essays by Birnbaum.

Olson, Jess. "The Late Zionism of Nathan Birnbaum: The Herzl Controversy Reconsidered." *AJS Review* 31, no. 2 (2007): 241–76.

———. *Nathan Birnbaum and Jewish Modernity: Architect of Zionism, Yiddishism, and Orthodoxy*. Stanford: Stanford University Press, forthcoming 2012.

Rechter, David. "A Nationalism of Small Things: Jewish Autonomy in Late Habsburg Austria." *Leo Baeck Institute Yearbook* 52 (2007): 87–109.

Rozenblit, Marsha L. *The Jews of Vienna, 1867–1914: Assimilation and Identity*. Albany: State University of New York Press, 1983.

See also, in the general section above: Goldsmith, *Architects of Yiddishism at the Beginning of the Twentieth Century*; Wistrich, *The Jews of Vienna in the Age of Franz Joseph*.

I. L. Peretz

Peretz, Isaac Leib. *Ale verk*. The complete works have appeared in several different editions and locations under different editorship. See the edition edited by Dovid Pinski (New York: Farlag Yidish, 1920), in thirteen volumes, and the later Vilna edition (Vilna: Vilner Farlag fun B. A. Kletskin, 1925–29), in nineteen volumes.

———. *The I. L. Peretz Reader*, edited by Ruth Wisse. New Haven: Yale University Press, 2002. See especially Wisse's introduction to the volume.

———. *Selected Works of I. L. Peretz*, edited by Marvin Zuckerman and Marion Herbst. Malibu, CA: Joseph Simon/Pangloss, 1996. This volume includes a selection of both Peretz's literary and journalistic work.

Roskies, David G. *A Bridge of Longing: The Lost Art of Yiddish Storytelling*. Cambridge: Harvard University Press, 1995.

Wisse, Ruth R. *I. L. Peretz and the Making of Modern Jewish Culture*. Seattle: University of Washington Press, 1991.

———. "The Political Vision of I. L. Peretz." In *The Emergence of Modern Jewish Politics: Bundism and Zionism in Eastern Europe*, edited by Zvi Gitelman, 120–31. Pittsbugh: University of Pittsburgh Press, 2003.

See also, in the general section above: Fishman, *The Rise of Modern Yiddish Culture*; Goldsmith, *Architects of Yiddishism at the Beginning of the Twentieth Century*; Veidlinger, *Jewish Public Culture in the Late Russian Empire*.

PART II. SOCIALISM AND THE QUESTION OF JEWISH PEOPLEHOOD

Chaim Zhitlowsky

Cassedy, Steven. *To the Other Shore: The Russian Jewish Intellectuals Who Came to America*. Princeton: Princeton University Press, 1997.

Michels, Tony. *A Fire in Their Hearts: Yiddish Socialists in New York*. Cambridge: Harvard University Press, 2005.

Weinberg, David H. *Between Tradition and Modernity: Haim Zhitlowski, Simon Dubnow, Ahad Ha-Am, and the Shaping of Modern Jewish Identity*. New York: Holmes and Meier, 1996.

Zhitlowsky, Chaim. *Gezamelte shriften*. 11 vols. New York: Dr. Chaim Zhitlowsky Farlags-komitet, 1917–31. This multivolume Yiddish collection is the most complete edition of Zhitlowsky's published works. The Zhitlowsky Farlags-komitet ("Zhitlowsky publication committee") also published the thematic volume *Yidn un yidishkayt* in 1938, most of the articles in which had appeared in various volumes of *Gezamelte shriften*.

See also, in the general section above: Fishman, *The Rise of Modern Yiddish Culture*; Frankel, *Prophecy and Politics*; Goldsmith, *Architects of Yiddishism at the Beginning of the Twentieth Century*; Janowsky, *The Jews and Minority Rights*.

Vladimir Davidovich Medem

Gechtman, Roni. "Conceptualizing National-Cultural Autonomy: From the Austro-Marxists to the Jewish Labor Bund." *Jahrbuch des Simon-Dubnow-Instituts/Simon Dubnow Institute Yearbook* 4 (2005): 17–49.

Medem, Vladimir. *Sotsialdemokratiia i natsional'nyi vopros*. 2nd ed. St. Petersburg: Tribuna, 1906. This book-length essay, originally published in 1904, explains Medem's views on assimilation, the rights of nationalities, the role of socialists in national struggle, and the meaning of Jewish "cultural-national" autonomy.

————. *Vladimir Medem, the Life and Soul of a Legendary Jewish Socialist*. Translated by Samuel Portnoy. New York: Ktav, 1979. This is an English translation of Medem's Yiddish memoir, *Fun mayn leben*.

Tobias, Henry J. *The Jewish Bund in Russia from Its Origins to 1905*. Stanford: Stanford University Press, 1972.

Zimmerman, Joshua D. *Poles, Jews, and the Politics of Nationality: The Bund and the Polish Socialist Party in Late Tsarist Russia, 1892–1914*. Madison: University of Wisconsin Press, 2004.

See also, in the general section above: Fishman, *The Rise of Modern Yiddish Culture*; Frankel, *Prophecy and Politics*.

Jacob Lestschinsky

Alroey, Gur. "Demographers in the Service of the Nation: Liebmann Hersch, Jacob Lestschinsky, and the Early Study of Jewish Migration." *Jewish History* 20, nos. 3–4 (2006): 265–82.

Brenner, Michael. *The Renaissance of Jewish Culture in Weimar Germany*. New Haven: Yale University Press, 1996.

Estraikh, Gennady. "Jacob Lestschinsky: A Yiddishist Dreamer and Socialist Scientist." *Science in Context* 20, no. 2 (2007): 215–37.

Kuznitz, Cecile. *YIVO and the Making of Modern Jewish Scholarship*. New York: Cambridge University Press, forthcoming.

Trachtenberg, Barry. *The Revolutionary Roots of Modern Yiddish, 1903–1917*. Syracuse, NY: Syracuse University Press, 2008.

See also, in the general section above: Frankel, *Prophecy and Politics*; Moss, *Jewish Renaissance in the Russian Revolution*.

The Kultur-Lige

Abramson, Henry. *A Prayer for the Government: Ukrainians and Jews in Revolutionary Times, 1917–1920*. Cambridge: Distributed by Harvard University Press for the Ukrainian Research Institute and Center for Jewish Studies, Harvard University, 1999.

Gitelman, Zvi Y. *Jewish Nationality and Soviet Politics: The Jewish Sections of the CPSU, 1917–1930*. Princeton: Princeton University Press, 1972.

Kazovsky, Hillel. *Khudozhniki Kul'tur-Ligi/The Artists of the Kultur-Lige*. Moscow: Gesharim/ Mosty kul'tury, 2003. In Russian and English with color plates.

Vozrozhdenie: Organ evreiskoi revolionnoi mysli. Many of the key figures involved in the Kultur-Lige first published their ideas in this short-lived journal. Issues 1 and 2 were published in London, January–February 1904; issues 3 and 4 were published in Paris, November 1904.

See also, in the general section above: Fishman, *The Rise of Modern Yiddish Culture*. Of particular importance on the Kultur-Lige, see Moss, *Jewish Renaissance in the Russian Revolution*.

PART III. PRESERVATION AND RECONSTRUCTION IN THE REPUBLICS

Horace M. Kallen

Biale, David. "The Melting Pot and Beyond: Jews and the Politics of American Identity." In *Insider/Outsider: American Jews and Multiculturalism*, edited by David Biale, Michael Galchinsky, and Susannah Heschel, 17–33. Berkeley: University of California Press, 1998.

Cohen, Mitchell. "In Defense of Shaatnez: A Politics for Jews in a Multicultural America." In *Insider/Outsider: American Jews and Multiculturalism*, edited by David Biale, Michael Galchinsky, and Susannah Heschel, 34–54. Berkeley: University of California Press, 1998.

Greene, Daniel. *The Jewish Origins of Cultural Pluralism: The Menorah Association and American Diversity*. Bloomington: Indiana University Press, 2011.

Hollinger, David A. *Postethnic America: Beyond Multiculturalism*. 10th anniversary ed. New York: Basic, 2005.

Kallen, Horace M. "Nationality and the Hyphenated American." *Menorah Journal*, April 1915, 79–86.

Magnes, Judah L. "The Melting Pot." In *Dissenter in Zion: From the Writings of Judah L. Magnes*, edited by Arthur Goren, 101–6. Cambridge: Harvard University Press, 1982. This is Magnes's sermon at Temple Emanu-El in New York, on October 9, 1909.

Zangwill, Israel. *The Melting Pot: Drama in Four Acts*. New York: Macmillan, 1909. The play was first performed in 1909 and has been republished in many editions.

See also, in the general section above: Goren, *The Politics and Public Culture of American Jews*; Pianko, *Zionism and the Roads Not Taken*.

Mordecai M. Kaplan

Eisen, Arnold, and Noam Pianko, eds. "Mordecai Kaplan's *Judaism as a Civilization*: The Legacy of an American Idea." Special issue, *Jewish Social Studies* 12, no. 2 (2006). This special issue includes essays on a range of aspects of Kaplan's thought and its influence.

Goldsmith, Emanuel, Mel Scult, and Robert M. Seltzer, eds. *The American Judaism of Mordecai M. Kaplan*. New York: New York University Press, 1990.

Kaplan, Mordecai M. *Judaism as a Civilization: Toward a Reconstruction of American-Jewish Life*. New York: Macmillan, 1934. Kaplan's seminal work has been republished in paperback by the Jewish Publication Society.

Scult, Mel. *Judaism Faces the Twentieth Century: A Biography of Mordecai M. Kaplan*. Detroit, MI: Wayne State University Press, 1993.

See also, in the general section above: Goren, *The Politics and Public Culture of American Jews*. Of particular importance on Kaplan, see Pianko, *Zionism and the Roads Not Taken*.

René Hirschler

Hyman, Paula. *The Jews of Modern France*. Berkeley: University of California Press, 1998.

Lazare, Lucien. *Rescue as Resistance: How Jewish Organizations Fought the Holocaust in France*. New York: Columbia University Press, 1996.

Malinovich, Nadia. *French and Jewish: Culture and the Politics of Identity in Early Twentieth-Century France*. Oxford: Littman Library of Jewish Civilization, 2008.

Ryan, Donna F. *The Holocaust and the Jews of Marseille: The Enforcement of Anti-Semitic Policies in Vichy France*. Urbana: University of Illinois Press, 1996.

Avrom Golomb

Karlip, Joshua M. "At the Crossroads between War and Genocide: A Reassessment of Jewish Ideology in 1940." *Jewish Social Studies* 11, no. 2 (2005): 170–201.

———. "The Center That Could Not Hold: 'Afn sheydveg' and the Crisis of Diaspora Nationalism." Ph.D. diss., Jewish Theological Seminary of America, 2006.

See also, in the general section above: Fishman, *The Rise of Modern Yiddish Culture*.

Israel Knox

Balint, Benjamin. *Running Commentary: The Contentious Magazine That Transformed the Jewish Left into the Neoconservative Right*. New York: Public Affairs, 2010.

Biale, David, Michael Galchinsky, and Susannah Heschel, eds. *Insider/Outsider: American Jews and Multiculturalism*. Berkeley: University of California Press, 1998.

Halpern, Ben. "The Americanization of Zionism." *American Jewish History* 69, no. 1 (1979): 15–33.

Wenger, Beth S. *History Lessons: The Creation of American Jewish Heritage*. Princeton: Princeton University Press, 2010.

See also, in the general section above: Goren, *The Politics and Public Culture of American Jews*.

EPILOGUE

Simon Rawidowicz

Myers, David N. *Between Jew and Arab: The Lost Voice of Simon Rawidowicz*. Waltham, MA: Brandeis University Press, 2008. This study of Rawidowicz's thought also includes an English translation of Rawidowicz's essay "Between Jew and Arab."

Rawidowicz, Simon. *State of Israel, Diaspora, and Jewish Continuity: Essays on the "Ever-Dying People."* Edited by Benjamin Ravid. Foreword by Michael A. Meyer. Waltham, MA: Brandeis University Press, 1998. This anthology includes selected translations of some of Rawidowicz's key political writings. See, in particular, the informative "Introduction: The Life and Writings of Simon Rawidowicz," by Benjamin Ravid, Rawidowicz's son.

See also, in the general section above: Pianko, *Zionism and the Roads Not Taken*.

Translation Credits

Perets Smolenskin, "The Eternal People,"
    translated by Shalva Klement
Simon Dubnov, "Jews as a Spiritual (Cultural-Historical) Nation
among Political Nations,"
    translated by Polly Zavadivker
Nathan Birnbaum, "The Jewish Renaissance Movement,"
    translated by Alexander von Thun
Nathan Birnbaum, "Jewish Autonomy,"
    translated by Daniel Becker
I. L. Peretz, "Paths That Lead Away from *Yidishkayt*,"
    translated by Anna Fishman Gonshor
Chaim Zhitlowsky, "A Jew to Jews,"
    translated by Polly Zavadivker
Chaim Zhitlowsky, "Why Only Yiddish?"
    translated by Anna Fishman Gonshor
Vladimir Davidovich Medem, "The Worldwide Jewish Nation,"
    translated by Sarah Failla
Jacob Lestschinsky, "Jewish Autonomy Yesterday and Today,"
    translated by Anna Fishman Gonshor and Esther Frank
"The Founding Tasks of the Kultur-Lige" and "The Kultur-Lige,"
    translated by Anna Fishman Gonshor and Esther Frank
René Hirschler, "A Basis for Jewish Consciousness,"
    translated by Shaina Hammerman
Avrom Golomb, "What Is Jewish Tradition?"
    translated by Anna Fishman Gonshor
Simon Rawidowicz, "Jerusalem and Babylon,"
    translated by Frank Talmage and originally published as
    "Jerusalem and Babylon" in *Judaism* 18 (1969): 131–42

*All new translations were edited by Simon Rabinovitch, with assistance
from Debra Caplan, Jessica Fechtor, Shaina Hammerman, Daria Kabanova,
Joel Pinsker, and Michael Steinlauf.*

Index

Babylon: Babylonia as diaspora cultural center, xvii, 205, 226–27; Babylon/Jerusalem dichotomy, xxvi, xxxvi, 219–231; church-state separation and, 177n17; "household" image of, 229; messianic idea in, xix; as symbol for diaspora, 220

Bartal, Israel, xxiii–xxiv, xxxi–xxxii

Basle program, xxv, 180, 229n14

Beit Hatfutsot Museum (Tel Aviv), xx

Belgium, 96

Ben-Gurion, David, xxxi, 219n1

Ben Menachem, Moshe. *See* Mendelssohn, Moses

Bergelson, Dovid, 138, 138n45–46, 141

Biale, David, 156

Bialik, Haim Nahman, 141, 198n63

Birnbaum, Nathan, xxxi, 45–46

Biro-Bidjan (Birobidzhan), 212, 212n84

Bogrov, Grigorii Isaakovich, 99n14, 101, 101n20

Boraisha, Menachem, 208, 208n79

Borochov, Ber, 83

bourgeois nationalism, 105

Bourne, Randolph, xxxiii, xl (n39)

Brandeis University, xxxvi, 218

Buber, Martin, xxxix (n21), 46, 47n45

Buckle, Thomas Henry, 14, 14n15

Bukovina, 55, 55n54, 91–94, 117

Bundism, xxviii, 82, 105. *See also* socialism

Canada, 34

Chamberlain, Houston Stewart, 47, 47n46

chosenness, xvii–xviii, xviii–xix

Christianity: accommodation of civic law and, 163; Christian Enlightenment influence on Judaism, 8n7; church-state separation and, 176; European oppression of Jews and, 88; failure of global unity of, 165; forced Jewish conversion, xviii, 11; national culture and, 38, 158; post-emancipation Christian antisemitism, 95; Protestant

Reformation, 10, 173; in Roman settlements, 29–30. *See also* religious reform

cities (as diaspora settlements), 49, 95–96, 130

citizenship: assimilation and, 10–13; citizenship during Roman era, 28–29; "civism" (civic solidarity), 34–36; condescension/persecution and, 21; European Jewish land rights, 30–31; nations first granting citizenship, 19n21; U.S. Jewish naturalization initiatives, 162–64. *See also* emancipation; rights

civil rights. *See* rights

class: access to Jewish religious culture and, 142–43; autonomy movement and, 130–37; communal self-government and, 125–27; desire for assimilation and, 11, 16n1, 82, 157–58, 165; flow of cultural influence, 110; Jewish landowner social type, 92; Jewish merchant class emergence, 127–29; Jewish Question and class sympathies, 85; national cohesiveness and, 82; opposition to assimilation and, 6–9; post-emancipation poverty, 90–94; professional class mobility, 94; U.S. cultural pluralism and, 159–160, 163–64; U.S. Jewish assimilation and, 208–9; working-class literary contributions, 138

Cohen, Hermann, xxvi, 220

Cohen, Robin, xxxvii (n4)

collective consciousness: civic solidarity and, 33–34; common destiny as source of, xxiv–xxv, 112–15, 184; cultivation of group identity, 157–164; emigration/immigration and, 118, 122; folk character and, 192–93; global Jewish culture, 111–12, 117–122; Kallen's "natio" (national self-consciousness), 156–58; national difference in diaspora states, xxx; religious culture as source of, xxv, xxxii, 57, 112, 115, 175–79, 200; religious

Galicia, xxviii, 55, 55n54, 91–94, 117

galut, xix–xx, xxvi, xxxvi, 18n20, 211, 218

Germany: attempts at national/cultural unity, 165–66; civic solidarity in, 35–36; diaspora cultural center in, xxi, 34, 205; emancipation movement in, 37, 87; Germanification movement, 38; Jewish intellectuals in, 11–12, 12n13; Jewish patriotism in, 35–36, 35n36; Jewish religious reform in, xxxi, 4, 7–8, 10, 35–36; national character influence on Jews, 13–16; national liberalism in, 50; opposition to messianic Judaism, 18–19; Protestant Reformation in, 173; resistance to assimilation in, 18–19, 18n19; restrictions on Jewish professions, 11–12, 11n12; Roman-era settlements in, 28–31; U.S. ethnic Germans, 159, 159n3, 161

Golomb, Avrom, xviii, xxxii, 189–190

Gordis, Daniel, xxxviii (n16)

Gordon, A. D., 83

Gordon, Yehuda Leib, 103

Graetz, Heinrich, xix, 11n11

Greece, 174

Grégoire, Abbé Henri, 87, 87n5, 90

Gvirol, Solomon Ibn, 98, 98n14

Ha'am, Ahad, xix, 125, 211, 211n83

halakha, 6–8, 9–10, 21, 142–43, 197–202

Halevi, Judah, 98, 98n14, 228, 228n12

Halpern, Leivik, 196, 196n51

Hartglas, A., 108–10

Hasidism, xxxix (n21), 56, 138, 192n31

Haskala: overview, xxi–xxii, xxxviii (n18); Hebrew as literary language and, 4; as Jewish Renaissance manifestation, xxxix (n21); nationalist critique of, xxxiv; overview of Jewish literature, 98–100, 99n14; Smolenskin influence on, 3–5. *See also* Jewish Renaissance

Hebrew language: *galut* as depiction of exile, xix–xx, xxvi, xxxvi, 211; Hebrew cultural organizations, 147; as idiom of Haskala, xxi–xxii, 4; popular access to Hebrew culture, 142–43; sin-punishment paradigm and, xix–xxi; Yiddish-Hebrew cultural disputes, 147–48

Herder, Johann Gottfried von, 27–28

Herzl, Theodor, xxxix (n20), 21n23, 45

Hess, Moses, xxvi, xxxix (n23), 45–46, 225, 225n8

Hirschler, René, xxiv–xxv, xxxii, 182–83

history: ahistoricity of tradition, 195–96; historic wandering figures, 30n30, 194–96, 195n49; proximity of religious time and, xviii, 196–97; religious history as basis for solidarity, 3–4, 113–15; sin-punishment diaspora paradigm and, xviii–xix; Torah as historical memory, 4

Hobbes, Thomas, 171, 171n8

Holocaust: destruction of European Jewry, xxxv, 211–12, 217, 219–220; Haman as biblical precursor, 42, 42n43; security as eternal concern and, 230; U.S. as Jewish homeland and, 203–4

imperialism: assimilation of imperial culture, xxx; diaspora nationalism and, xxxiv; excessive patriotism distinguished from, 174–75; Jewish rights and, 28–29, 43, 52; submission to foreign religions, 177, 200–201

Inquisition, 88

intellectuals: assimilationist tendencies and, 44, 131–37; class mobility of educated Jews, 93–96; defensive isolation and, 40, 74–77; Enlightenment values and, 94; fruition under oppressive regimes, 11–12, 12n13; intellectual opposition to oppression, 88–90, 112–13; intellectual Zionism, 47; medieval European Jewish philosophy, 186; protection of national rights and, 39–40; U.S. Jews and, 214–15

Ireland, 28, 35, 162

Islam, 176

107–8, 157; diaspora national language, 54–55; English as Jewish language, 204; language of exile, xx–xxi. *See also* Hebrew language; Yiddish language

Latvia, 141

League of Nations, 185, 185n22

Lebensohn, Mikhah Yosef, 99n14

Lessing, Gotthold Ephraim, 10, 10n9, 90, 90n6

Lestschinsky, Jacob, xxix, 125–26, 206, 206n75

Levanda, Lev Osipovich, 99n14, 101–2, 101n21

Levinzon, Yitshak Ber, 99n14

liberalism: activist opposition importance for, 50; "granting" of civic rights and, 43; solidarity of conviction in, 89–90; universal freedom and, 87–88

Lieberman, Aharon, 103, 103n25

Lilienblum, Moshe Leib, xxxix (n25), 99n14

literature: I. L. Peretz contributions to, 56; overview of Jewish literature, 98–100; Romantic nationalist approach, 190; working-class literary contributions, 138

Lithuania: culture leagues in, 141, 144; early Jewish settlements in, 31–32; Holocaust destruction of Jews, 211; Jewish People's Party in, xxxi

Lurianic Kabbalah, xviii, xxxvii (n6)

Luther, Martin, 10

Macauley, Thomas Babington, 90, 90n6

Magnes, Judah L., 156–57

Maimonides, 98, 98n14

Marienstras, Richard, xxxv

Marx, Karl, xxxix (n23), 228, 228n13

Mazzini, Guiseppe, 45–46, 174

Medem, Vladimir Davidovich, xxviii, 105–7

melting pot, xv–xvi, 156, 161

Mendele Moykher-Sforim, 56, 128, 128n39, 138, 138n45, 147

Mendelssohn, Moses: biographical sketch, 10n9, 98n14; contributions to Jewish literature, 98; humanism of, 16–17; on Jerusalem, 225, 225n7; Lessing friendship with, 90n6

messianic idea in Judaism: overview, xix–xx; hope of redemption as unifying theme, xxii–xxiv, 18–19, 229; sin-punishment diaspora paradigm in, xviii–xix; socialist utopianism and, xxvi–xxvii; U.S. as a "promised land" and, xxxiii. *See also* sin-punishment diaspora paradigm

Mill, John Stuart, 172, 172n10

Mirabeau, Honoré-Gabriel, comte de, 87n5, 90, 90n6

Mitchell-Innes, Alfred, 176, 176n14

Montenegro, 19–20, 20n22

Montesquieu, Charles Louis de Secondat, 90, 90n6

Moss, Kenneth B., xxix, 141

multiculturalism: Americanization as liberated nationality, 164; Bourne "trans-nationalism," xl (n39); conditional citizenship and, 27; as condition for diaspora nationalism, xxix–xxx; cultivation of group identity, 157–164; cultural harmony national model, 166–68; divided national loyalty and, 156; equality in multicultural states, 96; equal rights movements and, xxxiv; "hyphenation" image of, 155–59; as Jewish idea, xxxiii; Kallen "cultural pluralism," 155; Kallen orchestra metaphor and, xv–xvi, 167–68; multinational states, 28

Musar literature, 6, 6n3

natio (national self consciousness), 156–58

nationalism: artificiality of boundaries and, 107, 117; common culture as basis for, 108–11; definition of nation, 108–10, 119–120; Dubnov theory of, 24; folk vs. national culture, 120–21; Jewish nationality, 26–27; language as basis

162–64; Jewish intellectuals in, 214–15; Jewish philanthropy in, 214; Jewish universalism and, xv, 213; religion of democracy in, 170, 172, 176–79; religious Judaism in, xxxii, 178–79; resistance to assimilation in, xvi–xvii, xxxiii–xxxiv, 208–11, 213–15; Synagogue role in, 169, 179–180; urban Jewish settlements, 130; Zionism in, xxv, xxxv, 203–4, 207, 209–11, 215

usury, 93, 95

Vital, David, xxxix (n20)

wandering Jew legend, 30, 30n30, 194–96, 195n49

Wells, H. G., 162–63, 162n5

Wertheimer, Jack, xv

Western Europe: assimilation in, xxvii, 44, 94–96, 116–17; Jewish national culture in, 110–11; Jewish Question in, 85–87; Western European Zionism, xxxii

White Russia, 141, 144

Wilson, Woodrow, xxxiii, 158–59

Wise, Stephen S., 206n76

Wisse, Ruth R., 56

Yerushalmi, Yosef Hayim, xviii

Yiddish language: Birnbaum Jewish Renaissance and, 46; Bund advocacy of, 105; development of, 48–49; Golomb publications in, 189–190; Hebrew-Yiddish cultural disputes, 147–48; holy

texts in, 98; Jewish diaspora culture and, 111; as Jewish national language, 121, 121n35; Kultur-Lige Yiddish renaissance, 141, 145–46; Peretz publications in, 57, 97; popular/folk access to, 143; Russian Jewish writings in, 99–103; socialist Zionist advocacy of, xxvii–xxviii, 82–83; working-class Yiddish literature, 138–39, 138n45; Zhitlowsky advocacy of, 82

Zangwill, Israel, 156

Zeitlin, Hillel, 58, 62–63

Zhitlowsky, Chaim, xxvi–xxvii, 81–82, 108–10

Zilberfarb, Moyshe, 146, 146n49

Zionism: coining of term, 45, 47; diaspora nationalism and, xv–xvi, xxiv, xxxi, xxxiv–xxxv, 3; equal rights movements and, xxxiv; eternality and, xxv, 170, 180–81; intellectual Zionism, 47; Jewish Renaissance and, 45–47; messianic Zionism, 170; negation of diaspora in, xix, 226, 228–29, 228n13; opposition to Yiddish culture promotion, 147–48; socialist political Zionism, xxvi–xxix, 81–83; statehood as key issue, 206, 206n74; U.S. Jewish nationalism and, 203, 207, 209–11, 215; Western European accommodationism and, xxxii; worldwide Jewish unification and, 123; Yishuv as autonomist idea, xxxi–xxxii. *See also* sovereignty

Zionismus, xxxi

CPSIA information can be obtained
at www.ICGtesting.com
Printed in the USA
BVOW09s1433130318
510114BV00001B/2/P